WILLIAM WELLS BROWN
AND
CLOTELLE

WILLIAM WELLS BROWN
AND
CLOTELLE

A PORTRAIT OF THE ARTIST
IN THE
FIRST NEGRO NOVEL

BY

J. Noel Heermance

ARCHON BOOKS
1969

SBN: 208 00693 1

Library of Congress Catalog Card Number: 75–75450

Printed in the United States of America

Contents

Introduction

At first blush it may seem a waste of effort to trace, as Mr. Heermance has done below, the literary development of a writer as limited and pedestrian as William Wells Brown. Moreover, it runs counter to the usual practice, which is to find how a great author achieves his excellence. If the subject is admittedly not an outstanding writer, why bother?

The answer, of course, is: there are significant extenuating circumstances in this case. First, William Wells Brown was not just an American writer; he was a *Negro* American author, the first black man to write a novel, the first to write a play, the first to write a book of travels. Historically, then, he is a very important author in an area of American literature which is being recognized for the first time. Second, the major portion of Brown's life was spent with one of the finest movements in our national history—the Abolition Movement. An important agent of the Massachusetts Abolition Society, Brown's publications and activities give us a unique insight into the workings of that famous group. And, third, as this is a reprint of a novel that will be strange in several ways to present-day readers, the literary development of Brown, as presented in Mr. Heermance's full and scholarly essay, will give added meaning to the reading of this pioneer work.

In addition, it is always fascinating to watch the struggles of a fellow human to attain perfection in any field. And when this struggle is beset with the overwhelming handicaps that William Wells Brown encountered, its recital becomes an absorbing saga. Considering Brown's background as slave and fugitive, his ambition to become a literary artist impresses us as sheer effrontery. Before he could even consider his ultimate objective, this man had to learn the basic essentials we now take for granted, like reading and writing, and this after he was twenty years old! And yet he never faltered. Brown was not a five-talent man like Frederick Douglass; he was a one-talent, at best a two-talent man. But he invested and re-invested his limited capital in every way possible, and it paid off remarkably well. There is something appealing in his typically American ingenuity, optimism, and doggedness. When we think of these circumstances, we tend to forget some of the artistic shortcomings of Mr. Brown. The surprising thing is that he wrote at all.

In his introduction to this reprint of *Clotelle*, Mr. Heermance has emphasized the "slave narrative"—a little known but important segment of American biography. Neglected by most scholars as all things pertaining to Negro writing have been neglected, the slave narrative is that rare bird: a literary form native to American letters. Although many students of American life and literature have never heard of the slave narrative, there are literally hundreds of them in our libraries. They constitute a rich and almost virgin field, particularly for scholars who have just "discovered" the Negro. In addition to being an excellent and significant contribution to this field, Mr. Heermance's detailed analysis of the narratives of William Wells Brown and Frederick Douglass should help to spur other scholars to research in these autobiographies of ex-slaves. It will be rewarding.

A reprint of *Clotelle* has long been needed, and the new and burgeoning interest in Negro American literature makes this issue doubly valuable. For one thing, *Clotelle* will give most of its readers an entirely new view of slavery. For those who know the institution only through the sentimental and idyllic misrepresentation of it found in Southern apologists like Thomas Nelson Page, this novel will come as a shock. Here one finds all of the sordid aspects of the peculiar institution— slave pens, nigger drivers, broken families, illegitimate off- spring of lustful masters—all of them delineated by a writer who experienced them at first hand. Harriet Beecher Stowe *learned* about some of these atrocities; Brown *knew* them through personal experience. And he has given us a full picture. There is enough material—interesting material—in this book to till ten novels its size. This, of course, is one of its weaknesses. But in spite of the literary shortcomings the work obviously has, William Wells Brown's *Clotelle* is truly a fascinating novel. To read it, along with Mr. Heermance's scholarly and illuminating introduction, is a delightful and rewarding experience.

Arthur P. Davis
Howard University

WILLIAM WELLS BROWN
AND
CLOTELLE

CHAPTER ONE

William Wells Brown: The Man

Flight to Freedom

In March of 1815, William Wells Brown was born on the farm of Dr. John Young near Lexington, Kentucky. His slave mother, Elizabeth, was a strong, intelligent woman, and his father was Young's half-brother. Accordingly, Brown officially "belonged" to Young, and was early separated from his mother, though they both lived on Young's farm. Not long afterwards, both Brown and his mother went with the Young family when it moved to Missouri and settled on another farm, sixty miles above St. Louis and a mile from the Mississippi River.

Though his mother worked at hard labor in the fields, William, because of his father's relation to Young, did not have to undergo the long fourteen hour backbreaking toil which was the fieldhand's lot. Instead, he was employed as a house servant and sometimes assisted in his master's medical department, two tremendous advantages for a slave, especially one who planned to flee to freedom one day.

Nevertheless, Brown's life was not an easy one, largely because he was always being punished by Mrs. Young, the doctor's wife, for some supposed offence or other. The reason for this is significant and shows the incredible intertwining of guilt, resentment and cruelty which slavery developed in the South.

Essentially Mrs. Young felt angry and humiliated at the idea
of having the "Negro relations" of her husband's half-brother
constantly in her sight. As Brown's daughter has noted in her
1856 biography of him, this was a constant problem for all
mulatto house servants under slavery. "The nearer a slave approaches an Anglo-Saxon in complexion," she tells us, "the
more he is abused by both owner and fellow-slaves. The owner
flogs him to keep him 'in his place,' and the slaves hate him
on account of his being whiter than themselves."

When Brown was thirteen years old, Young moved from
rural Missouri to the vicinity of St. Louis, at which point,
though he bought a farm of three thousand acres, he decided
that he financially needed to "rent" Brown out to a local inn-
keeper in the city. It was here that Brown first felt the need—
and the capacity—to escape his bondage. While on the earlier
farm, even with occasional beatings and humiliations from
the overseer and Young's wife, Brown had not really felt des-
perate enough to flee his situation, especially since he had no
other place to flee towards. Now, however, removed from his
mother and having attained an older age, he found himself
subjected to the orders and whims of a Major Freeland. Freeland was an inn-keeper ostensibly, but was actually more
famous as a gambler and drinker. Even worse for a youngster
in Brown's position, Freeland's frequent drunken sprees often
turned him into a source of physical danger for any servant
unlucky enough to cross his liquored path. Brown had been
with Freeland less than a month, therefore, when he found
himself subjected to a punishment which Freeland especially
enjoyed administering, drunk or sober. As Brown himself describes it in his *Narrative*, he was tied up in the smoke-house
and whipped, after which Freeland built a fire made of tobacco stems and proceeded to "smoke" him. "Virginia Play"
was Freeland's term for this little interlude.

By this time Brown had become somewhat used to the occasional drunken beatings which he received, but this sort of
warped "cuteness" was too much for him simply to accept as

a matter of course. Immediately after he was freed from this "Play," then, he took off and ran away, heading back to his master's farm in order to tell Young of the mistreatment which he had suffered at Freeland's hands. Instead of receiving the sympathy which he expected, however, Brown found himself flogged further by Young and callously sent back to Freeland as if nothing out of the ordinary had happened. Disillusioned and feeling somehow betrayed, the thirteen-year-old boy now found himself contemplating still another flogging when he returned to Freeland's, and promptly ran away again: this time into the woods, where he remained until hunted and tracked down by Negro-hunters and their dogs. He still received Freeland's whipping, of course, but now his own self-integrity and determination to fight slavery's arbitrary cruelty was developing inside him. From this moment on Brown began to plan his escape north.

After serving with Freeland for several months, Brown was hired out as a servant on one of the steamers running between St. Louis and Galena. Here his desire for freedom and strong sense of personal identity received new stimulation. For on these trips Brown saw other people going freely from place to place, moving casually and easily in the world around them as if this were the most natural thing to do. And suddenly it became clear to him—in whatever way things like this become clear to thirteen-year-old boys—that this sort of freedom to travel and visit was an inherent part of human existence. His determination to escape was now unshakeable.

In addition to his general observations and the "expanded" feeling which he derived from this association with people freely traveling, Brown was also influenced by several specific experiences during his steamboat work. The major one of these was his witness of, and vicarious participation in, a Fourth of July celebration in St. Louis. The spirit of the celebration was free and exuberant, and it made a sharp contrast to the normally repressed air which dominated a slave servant's daily life. Equally important were the thoughts expressed during the celebration by Thomas Hart Benton, United States Senator from Missouri and a noted orator of the period. His text was the Declaration of Independence, and the concepts which he fervently enunciated were hardly calculated to keep a boy like Brown content with his life in slavery. Instead, they stirred his imagination to the possibilities of a free life, as he heard for the first time the declarative statement of all men's inherent independence.

"We hold these truths to be self-evident," the voice intoned, "that all men are created equal; that they are endowed by their Creator with certain inalienable rights; that among these are life, liberty, and the pursuit of happiness; that to secure these rights, governments are instituted among men, deriving their just powers from the consent of the governed." Suddenly Brown's deepest feelings were no longer merely personal, nebulous ideas in a young boy's head. They were now crystallized and sanctioned by men of authority and official importance. This was the final clarification and sanction which Brown's mind needed, so that freedom and escape now became his constant goal.

At the end of that summer, Brown's position on the steamboat was terminated, and he was again hired out, this time to a Mr. John Colburn, keeper of the Missouri Hotel in St. Louis. His period under Colburn was an especially unhappy one for several reasons. On the one hand, Colburn was, in Brown's own terms, an abusive and cruel "hater of the Negro," despite the fact that he came from a free Northern state. Yet even more tragically, while Brown was in the city working under Colburn, Young sold away the rest of Brown's family, with only his mother remaining near enough for him to visit.

Following his difficult time under Colburn, however, Brown was hired out to Elijah P. Lovejoy, the famous abolitionist publisher and editor in St. Louis, who ultimately lost his life at the hands of a mob for defending his anti-slavery editorials. This period was the most favorable one which Brown spent in slavery, and he notes in his *Narrative* how Lovejoy was a good man and the best master that Brown had ever worked for. Furthermore, Brown's work in the publisher's printing office provided him with an education as well as a humane home atmosphere. As Brown himself assessed this period, "I am chiefly indebted to him, and to my employment in the printing office, for what little learning I obtained in slavery."

Soon, however, Brown's apprenticeship with Lovejoy was ended when Brown himself was seriously beaten by the father of a St. Louis youth who had attacked Brown earlier and had been repulsed. The result of this "vengeance" by the father was a concussion and five weeks of complete inactivity, during which time he lost the job at Lovejoy's. He subsequently was hired out as an "assistant" to a slave trader named Walker, and accompanied him from St. Louis to New Orleans as Walker herded his cargo of slaves into the Deep South. There the slaves were sold on degrading auction blocks, and so disgusted was Brown with the whole atmosphere and purpose of Walker's "profession" that he refused to work with him any longer when the slave caravan came back to St. Louis and Brown was able to go back to Young's. Nevertheless, the searing memory of the pain and degradation involved for the slaves stayed with him, and he subsequently included his memory of these experiences in several of his major writings.

About this time Young found himself in even greater need of cash and therefore decided to sell Brown. Unlike the fate which befell the rest of his family, especially his brothers and sister, Brown was not simply sold at random to the highest bidder. In fact, because of his proven ability to successfully hire out, Young gave Brown a general pass permitting him to move about on his own in the area in order to find a purchaser who would pay five hundred dollars for him. Such proceedings were not unheard of under slavery, but they were considerably rare, and thus Brown presumably had much to be thankful for since he was now in a position to choose the sort of man he wanted to be owned by. At the same time, when we remember that Brown was actually Young's nephew and that

Brown's new freedom was simply the freedom to sell himself
into continued bondage, we realize just how limited this so-
called "leniency" actually was.

Far from brooding over the ironies beneath the offer, however, Brown characteristically saw this pass as a major opportunity—the opportunity to escape. He immediately went to his
mother, who was now owned by a gentleman in St. Louis itself, and persuaded her to flee with him to Canada. That night
they crossed the Mississippi River and set out North; and for
ten days they kept moving, traveling at night and sleeping
in the day. On the eleventh day, however, they began to relax
their vigilance and sense of urgency; they thereupon decided,
for greater comfort, to travel during the day and travel on
open roads instead of through the dense woods through which
they had been stumbling in the dark for over a week. Unfortunately this was a period of extensively circulated runaway
slave notices, which slaveholders put in Northern newspapers
and sent to local postmasters of towns through which they
thought their fugitive slaves might pass. Within hours of that
eleventh day morning, then, Brown and his mother were captured on the open road. That night they were on their way
back to St. Louis.

The results of this attempt were twofold. On the one hand,
the spark of freedom in Brown had been completely kindled
now and would never be extinguished. He had been near the
promised land, and he realized even more clearly now the
way in which it could be reached. On the other hand, definite
punishments were meted out to slaves who attempted to escape, and this time was no exception. Hence Brown's mother
was immediately sold South to slave drivers, never to be heard
from again; and only because of Young's promise to Brown's
father was Brown not sold down the river himself.

Instead, he was sold to a merchant tailor named Willi, in
St. Louis, and then to a Captain Enoch Price, a steamboat
owner and commission merchant in the same city. Suddenly
opportunity had presented itself again, and this time would

probably be Brown's last. No slaveowner could afford to keep around a slave who showed himself determined to escape, because such a slave was bad for the whole farm's morale. Deep South slavery was the only practical punishment for such a slave, brother's promise or no brother's promise, and very few slaves ever made it to freedom from the isolated and brutal plantations of lower Mississippi, Alabama, and Louisiana. This time, then, Brown had to be careful.

His position with the Prices was not especially harsh. He was well cared for and assigned to be their coachman, almost as if to grace their household in St. Louis as a kind of nouveaux riche status symbol. Because of Price's constant involvement with steamboats and their operation, however, Brown soon found himself working once more on a riverboat, as Price deemed this more valuable to him than having Brown ceremoniously drive the family carriage through the St. Louis byways. This was Brown's opportunity. At the same time, the Prices were aware of the "opportunity" involved, and, valuing Brown highly, they hoped to dissuade him from any such attempt. Thus Mrs. Price purchased a pretty slave from a nearby farm whom she thought Brown might become romantically interested in, and things even got to the point of a proposed marriage between the two. The purpose of this match from Mrs. Price's point of view was partially altruistic, because she did like Brown, but was even more a practical gambit: an attempt to emotionally tie Brown to St. Louis so that he would not be tempted to escape North if he were allowed to accompany Price on the riverboat.

Brown's reaction to all this shows just how careful he knew he had to be. On the surface he proclaimed his interest in the girl, his satisfaction with the Prices' as a home, and his complete lack of interest in anything else. Beneath the necessary facade, however, he was far more honest with himself. "But the more I thought of the trap laid by Mrs. Price to make me satisfied with my new home, by getting me a wife," he tells us, "the more I determined never to marry any woman on earth until I should get my liberty. But this secret I was compelled to keep to myself."

With this marriage seemingly set and Brown seemingly contented by it, it wasn't long before Price allowed him to accompany the family on a steamboat trip to Ohio, a free state. This was his ultimate chance, and Brown was prepared for it. When the boat docked in Cincinnati and several of the other passengers disembarked, Brown quietly made himself useful, took up and carried some person's trunk onto shore, and immediately headed for the woods. With the advent of nightfall, he was on his way North in "the sight of my friend—truly the slave's friend—the North Star," which accounts, of course, for the prominence of the North Star as a symbol in so many slave narratives and even in the title of Frederick Douglass' first independent anti-slavery newspaper, "The Northern Star."

For the next several days Brown traveled at night and slept in the day, though it was December and Ohio and he had nothing warmer on him than the thin clothes which he had been used to wearing in St. Louis. Nevertheless, as he had learned while trying to escape with his mother, it was vitally necessary to avoid all daytime travel, so he had no choice but to expose himself to the winter nights and make as much distance as he could with the warmth of only a small tinder-box. Nor was warmth the only physical problem he faced. Because he had needed to seem casual and uninterested in escape when the boat docked at Cincinnati, Brown had deliberately not packed any significant food supply for his escape. On the fourth day, therefore, his meager provisions gave out, and only an open barn with twelve ears of corn kept him alive.

When, on the sixth day, Brown was caught in a freezing rain storm, still without warmth and still low on food, he realized the need to take shelter in another barn. Simultaneously it became clear to him that he would need to discover himself to someone and ask for the aid he so desperately needed now. The day after the storm was over, then, he lay in the woods near the main road and awaited a face that he thought he could trust. After he let two men pass by, Brown observed the face and dress of a passing Quaker and suddenly felt the courage to approach him. The man, Wells Brown, took Brown home with him, where he stayed for almost two weeks, recovering his strength from the fever and cold which had ravaged his body the last two days. Then, after receiving the hospitality of his adopted father's name and adding it to the "William" which, though he was grateful to his host, he was determined to keep because "it was taken from me once against my will" so that now he was "not willing to part with it again on any terms," he set off for Cleveland and his ultimate freedom. The year was 1834.

Freedom Itself

After discussing the boyhood of the man, and the character and personality in him that led him to escape the harshness of that boyhood, we come now to examine the kind of man William Wells Brown was in the world of freedom which he so dedicatedly sought and sacrificed for. It is important to us, first of all, to note how he spent his early years in the North. After arriving in Cleveland and securing temporary employment as a waiter, Brown then found a much better job on a steamboat covering the Great Lakes. More important than the personal comfort and security which this position offered him, however, is the way he used it to actively aid his fellow fugitive slaves escape to Canada.

Having come into contact with Benjamin Lundy's anti-slavery newspaper, *Genius of Universal Emancipation*, Brown immediately saw a means of taking his strong determination for freedom and harnessing it "for the emancipation of my brethren yet in chains." Accordingly, he quickly became an active member of the "Underground Railroad" in Cleveland, helping slaves get to Canada by making arrangements "to carry them on the boat to Buffalo or Detroit, and thus effect their escape to the 'promised land.' " In fact, so successful and well known among the slaves did he become for this that he often had four or five slaves on board at one time; and, by his own count, in the single year of 1842, "I conveyed, from the first of May to the first of December, sixty-nine fugitives over Lake Erie to Canada."

Equally early in his freedom, Brown embraced the temperance cause; and, in company with a few friends, he began a "temperance reformation among the colored people of the city of Buffalo." Such was his determination that he managed to build an especially strong membership in the city, so that, according to his own calculations, within three years a society of "upwards of 500 members was raised out of a colored population of 700." Nor was this merely a passing interest of his. Rather, his concern for temperance was very deep, especially since he saw it within the framework of his life in slavery. Liquor's effect on the slaveholders and overseers, he realized, was to make even more brutal and cruel, men who were already dehumanized by their participation in the sordid power which the institution of slavery offered them. Indeed, Brown could still remember the drunken sprees and "Virginia Play" of his first "renter," Freeland.

Yet far more than his concern for the effect of liquor on slaveholders was his concern with its effect on his fellow fugitive slaves. He saw drinking as one of the more pernicious legacies which slavery left its victims: conditioning them to have a need for liquor even after they had successfully escaped slavery's more obvious physical tyrannies. Brown knew, as we know in even greater historical detail today, how slaveholders deliberately gave their slaves liquor on Sundays and holidays; how they deliberately offered prizes to the slave who could drink the most; and, once the slaves had all begun drinking, how the slaveholders offered further bets and prizes to contestants in violent wrestling matches, head butting contests, and the like. All of this was consciously instituted by the slaveholders in order to debase the slave as a man, return him to an animal level of enjoyment, and thereby "enslave" him even more deeply by causing him to lose his dignity and self-respect. The result of this "brainwashing" was what Brown found in Buffalo, and he was strongly determined to resist it and restore his fellow fugitives to their inherent level of human dignity. This was the basis of his temperance work—a work which lasted throughout his life.

Within a few years after he was settled in Cleveland, Brown suddenly combined his "Underground Railroad" interest with his Temperance Society activities, and the result was the beginning of his literary career as we know it today. In the autumn of 1843, then, "impressed with the importance of spreading anti-slavery truth as a means to bring about the abolition of slavery," and feeling more secure in this verbal approach because of his oratorical and organizational work with the Temperance Society, Brown officially joined the Western New York Anti-Slavery Society and began lecturing as an agent. Having three months of leisure time that winter, when the ice curtailed steamboat passage on Lake Erie, he began to speak on the subject of American Slavery throughout the Buffalo and western New York area. As his daughter has noted, Brown was the kind of man who was not satisfied with merely gaining his own freedom; rather, "he felt it his duty to work for others." This is how he began his life-long dedication to that commitment, therefore, and where he first began his serious literary work.

As we assess the dedication of the man here, let us note that this sort of work was not easy; nor was there any remuneration involved. Far from the ease and security of modern television debates and panel discussions, the anti-slavery orator's difficult traveling, his uncertain sleeping accommodations, and the cold auditoriums all made this a physically arduous undertaking. Furthermore, since the early audiences of the anti-slavery movement were so emotionally unpredictable and the speaker had to step very sensitively until he knew where his audiences' beliefs and feelings lay, these speaking engagements were an emotional drain as well—especially for a fugitive slave who was so emotionally involved and committed to his subject matter that his personal feelings and past experiences were constantly exposed to whatever harshness might develop from the audience.

In addition to all of these general problems which the early Abolitionist speaker faced, Brown's specific conditions in 1843 Buffalo were especially severe. As his daughter has noted, "Buffalo and its vicinity was at that time one of the worst places in the State, with the exception of New York City, for colored persons." In fact she further describes the emotional tenor of the area in terms of its "hatred to the black," which she sees as the basic reason why all the public schools in the area were closed to Negro children and why "the Negro-pew was the only place in the church where the despised race were permitted to have a seat." When Brown visited the town of Attica, for example, and gave his lecture on slavery, "so great was the hatred to the Negro, that after the meeting was over, he looked in vain for a place to lodge the night." Even after visiting every tavern and public house in the town, he was unable to find a place to sleep and was finally forced to spend the bitter cold night in the church vestry, pacing the aisle from eleven at night until six in the morning simply in order to keep warm. In short, it was a difficult calling in a difficult place; yet Brown willingly and dedicatedly undertook it.

We have an interesting testimonial to Brown's dedication here from the Massachusetts Anti-Slavery Society, in the preface to Brown's *Three Years in Europe*. Praising the "general respect and approbation" which he won for himself as agent and speaker, this same testimonial, moreover, makes an interesting assessment of Brown's basic personality and character. "He combines true self-respect with true humility, and rare judiciousness with great moral courage," the testimonial tells us, and this is relevant to us since it will control Brown's life for the next five years.

In 1848, there was a suggestion by a number of Brown's

abolitionist friends to purchase his freedom from his Southern master, so that Brown would not have to fear capture and re-enslavement. For even before the Fugitive Slave Law of 1850, it was nationally legal for an escaped slave to be seized and sent back into slavery, no matter what Northern state he had fled to. Two years earlier, in fact, it had been deemed expedient by British friends of Frederick Douglass to secure his personal security and services for the anti-slavery cause by the purchase of his freedom from his master in Maryland.

This same course was therefore suggested for the protection of Brown, especially since his work as agent and lecturer was like Douglass' and constantly took him into places and situations from which capture could arise. Nevertheless, when Price wrote to Edmund Quincy of Boston in January, 1848, offering to sell Brown to Quincy or his friends for three hundred and twenty-five dollars, Brown's reaction was immediate scorn and an outraged sense of his personal—almost cosmic —integrity. "I cannot accept of Mr. Price's offer to become a purchaser of my body and soul," Brown wrote. "God made me as free as he did Enoch Price, and Mr. Price shall never receive a dollar from me or my friends with my consent." Brown's strong sense of dignity carried the day, and the purchase was not made.

The direct result of this decision, however, was Brown's voluntary "exile" to Europe for the next five years. In 1849, despite his determination to be a free man in a free country without subsidizing the "peculiar institution" by buying his freedom, it was becoming clear to him that America was no safe place for an escaped slave. For this reason he began to seriously consider flight to England. Simultaneously, a trip abroad for him was also suggested by professional, anti-slavery considerations. Ever since Frederick Douglass had emotionally and intellectually captured England by his visit there in 1845–46, it was deemed very valuable to send talented Negroes to England and the Continent to prominently destroy the myths and stereotypes of Negro inferiority which had been spread to those areas by Southern spokesmen and their apologists. Even more specifically, there was a Peace Congress being held in Paris, and the Committee of the American Peace Society wished Brown to represent them there. For all these reasons, then, he made ready to flee America for Europe.

On July 20th, 1849, he sailed for Europe and arrived in Liverpool on the 28th. After a brief stop in Dublin, he proceeded to Paris where, in company with the elite of Europe, he admirably maintained his reputation as a public speaker. His brief address produced a deep effect, and at its conclusion he was greeted and warmly received by such eminent figures as Victor Hugo and Richard Cobden. Such warm attention was even further continued at the various social affairs after the Congress, given by such men as M. De Tocqueville for the enjoyment of the members of that Congress. In short, the meeting was a great personal success for Brown.

Likewise, Brown's work and efforts continued on this scale even after the Congress. In August, 1851, for example, he was chosen chairman of the first major meeting of those fugitive slaves who now were residing in England—a significant honor, reflecting his anti-slavery stature. As such, he organized the proceedings and delivered the opening, keynote address. At the same time, perhaps even more important than his address was the fact that he went beyond mere oratory and began to devote himself concretely to the problems of American fugitive slaves. Although residence in Canada was not really favored by most of the fugitive slaves for reasons of geography and climate, it was clearly preferable to slavery. Brown therefore addressed himself to overcoming the economic problems which a slave faced in trying to support himself in Canada and suggested the establishment of a Manual Labour School there.

Unfortunately, however, while Brown's studied and structured program was unanimously passed and approved at a later meeting in Glasgow, Scotland, it never received the amount of support which was needed to bring it into physical existence. Yet it is significant to us because it again shows Brown's determined interest in creatively and concretely working on the social problems confronting those fellow fugitives who had escaped slavery physically only to find that they carried many of its shackles within themselves.

In 1850 the Fugitive Slave Law was passed in America, and this sealed Brown's immediate fate, for it greatly increased the danger which he would face if he were to return to America. As Brown summarized the law one year later in a London speech, it was "in every respect an unconstitutional measure" which "set aside the right formerly enjoyed by the fugitive of trial by jury" and thereby "afforded to him no protection, no opportunity of proving his right to be free." In effect, Brown concluded, "it placed every free coloured person at the mercy of any unprincipled individual who might wish to lay claim to him." Needless to say, Brown saw no prospects of returning to his native land at this point. One major problem now presented itself, however: how to support himself, his wife and their two young daughters. The answer was literature, and perhaps we should be ironically grateful to this period of enforced exile for definitely crystallizing Brown's writing skill as he now found himself necessarily a professional writer.

Even before he had come to Europe, he had begun to show himself as a skilled and prolific writer. In 1848, while he was enlarging and bringing out new editions of his *Narrative*, he published a collection of songs intended to be sung at abolition meetings. Though he did not write any of the songs himself, he functioned here as professional compiler and editor of the volume, and it had such success that it went into a second edition in 1849.

Thus, when Brown got to Europe in the summer of 1848 and found that he couldn't return after 1850, he was faced with two alternatives as to how he would stay in England. He could remain there either as a charity ward of the abolitionist groups which philanthropically supported most of the fugitive slaves overseas, or he could remain as a self-supporting writer and lecturer. Being the sort of man who prized his independ-ence and personal dignity highly, he chose the latter course. Nor was this an easy role to uphold. Indeed, we have clear accounts in Brown's *Three Years in Europe* of how uncertain and arduous a period this was for him as he sometimes found himself alone and often low on funds in large, fog-shrouded London.

In addition to his traveling and public speaking, Brown also did a significant amount of pure writing. Besides working on follow-up editions of his *Narrative* and the *Anti-Slavery Harp*, he also published a polemical pamphlet entitled *A Description of William Wells Brown's Original Panoramic Views of the Scenes in the Life of an American Slave, from His Birth in Slavery to his Death, or His Escape to His First Home of Free-dom on British Soil*. And, as his reputation grew and came to the favorable attention of the English press, he now became a regular contributor to several London newspapers, devoting himself primarily to American subjects in short articles for *The Daily News, The Morning Chronicle,* and *The Leader*.

Yet the final tribute here was worth it. As we learn from "The Memoir" in the front of Brown's *Sketches of Places and People Abroad* (1854), Brown clearly distinguished himself by the independent strength of his character.

Most of the fugitive slaves, and, in fact, nearly all the colored men who had visited Great Britain from the United States, have come upon begging missions, either for some society or for themselves. Mr. Brown has been almost the only exception. With that independence of feeling which those who are acquainted with him know to be one of his chief characteristics, he determined to maintain himself and family by his own exertions,—by his literary labors, and the honorable profession of a pub-lic lecturer.

As the culmination of his traveling and writing career in Europe, Brown wrote *Three Years in Europe: or, Places I Have Seen and People I Have Met*, the first strictly travel book ever written by an American Negro. Written as a series of letters, and having a diary feeling about it, the book covered most of Brown's travels and experiences in England and Europe since his arrival in 1848 up to the date of the book's publication in 1852. Not only did he discuss all of the standard museums and monuments, but he also showed his great interest in important and interesting literary celebrities, many of whom he visited on his travels. Indeed, a full list of the important men whom he met is, by itself, a significant testament to his importance on the English and European scene at the time.

Then he came home. After he had been abroad for four years, friends of his finally convinced him that it was better to purchase his freedom and return to America to fight slavery than it was to lie fallow in England while America's great moral decision was being made. This time Brown acquiesced, and his reason was characteristic of his dedication to his work. "I might have remained in a country where my manhood was never denied," he recalls for us in his later *Sketches of Places and People*; "I might have remained in ease in other climes; but what was ease and comfort abroad, while more than three millions of my countrymen were groaning in the prison-house of slavery in the Southern states? Yes, I came back to the land of my nativity, not to be a spectator, but a soldier—a soldier in the moral warfare against the most cruel system of oppression that ever blackened the character or hardened the heart of man." And a crusading soldier is exactly what he became.

Back in this country, he now devoted the rest of his life to lecturing and writing. He had always been a strong social reformer, both on the platform and in print, and this is where his efforts continued to go. Part of his efforts were spent on temperance and its organizational work, but by far his greatest efforts went into the civil rights work of the period. Subsequently, with the end of the Civil War and the corresponding end of the Abolition movement per se, Brown shifted his focus somewhat and began to write about the need for the country to change its attitudes and preconceptions about Negroes. This meant the clear need to see them in historically positive terms. So many myths, so much slander had been written about the race as a whole, that he now realized how important to a man was his individual self-respect and the general respect which his race commanded in the eyes of the country as a whole.

For these two reasons Brown dedicated his writing after *Clotelle* in 1864 to historically destroying all the myths of "inherent" Negro inferiority. In their place he proposed to show Negroes in a more human and more heroic light. It was to be "propaganda," to be sure, but it was "propaganda" dedicated to expressing some major truths which the country had long overlooked or distorted. His first historical book of this period, then, was *The Black Man, His Antecedents, His Genius, and His Achievements* in 1863. Written in two separate parts, its purpose was nevertheless unified. The initial essay of twenty pages was a direct statement by Brown attacking the myths of the Negro's "natural inferiority." The second and far larger part provided the biographical sketches of over fifty Negroes who had risen successfully in American society on the basis of the same hard work and diligence which characteristically marked the rise of the country as a whole. More important than the opening essay, these sketches nevertheless shared the same purpose as the essay: to concretely show Negroes in the human and successful light which the stereotypes had deliberately suppressed.

Brown's second major effort in this vein came after the war was completely over, and this, in contrast to the "human success" interests of the first volume, sought to show the heroic, patriotic aspects of various Negro men. *The Negro in the American Rebellion, His Heroism and His Fidelity* was a book which covered exactly what its title indicated, and covered it in a glorifying rather than historically objective manner. At the same time, even as we note the patriotic fervor in the writing and the deliberate selection within the material itself, we need to remember that histories throughout that period, and successive periods as well, tended to stress this sort of fervent presentation of the American revolution. Furthermore, one needs only look at a bibliography of histories covering slavery and the Civil War, even to this day, to see how almost unanimously they are either apologetic or crusading, choosing their position and interpretive viewpoint on moral and emotional grounds. In short, not only is scientific historiography a recent emphasis generally, but it is still a relative infant in the specific sphere of racial and regional relationships in this country. Brown's patriotic histories need no apology, then, since they were merely reflecting the accepted approach of those around and even after him.

His last major work with this aim was *The Rising Son* in 1874, which was essentially an enlargement of *The Black Man* of 1863. This later book contains over sixty sketches of "Representative Men and Women," and its purpose is the same as the early version's. Indeed the purpose of that book was essentially Brown's purpose throughout all these histories. "If this work shall aid in vindicating the Negro's character," he wrote in the conclusion of *The Black Man*'s "Preface," "and show that he is endowed with those intellectual and amiable qualities which adorn and dignify human nature, it will meet the most sanguine hopes of the writer." This was Brown's purpose in these three historical books, and he was clearly conscious of his goal throughout these works.

Brown's final book, coming four years before his death, was *My Southern Home: or, The South and Its People.* Published in 1880, it is a series of reminiscent essay-sketches; and this book, coupled with his continuing temperance work, occupied his efforts after his publication of *The Rising Son.* He died in 1884, having dedicated his life to fighting for and fulfilling "those intellectual and amiable qualities which adorn and dignify human nature."

When we approach Brown as a writer, now, we need to see him within the social and literary context in which he developed. Born in 1815, he was sixteen years old when William Lloyd Garrison founded the *Liberator* and brought the existing abolitionist sentiment to the forefront of American social and political thought. This national Abolitionism was well on its way, therefore, when Brown escaped slavery in 1834, ready to begin a new life at age nineteen. Indeed his personal interests fit in perfectly with the growing social interest of the North, and this helped influence the course to which he soon dedicated his life.

At the same time, in addition to its moral and social influence on Brown, the Abolition movement also had a strong literary influence on him. There were, basically, two major modes of expressing anti-slavery sentiment within the movement: oral public speeches and fugitive slave narratives. Each in its own way was intended to attack slavery and its evils, and thus the two worked closely and effectively together. Needless to say, Brown was deeply influenced by both these forms, and they strongly affected most of his early literary output.

When Brown finally blossomed into a creative artist and wrote the first Negro novel and the first Negro play, therefore, it is our understanding of how constricting those two Abolition genres were which makes his creative jump to art so significant and deeply impressive. On a lesser note we are further impressed when we note his pioneering efforts with his travel book and histories, as once more he showed his ability to transcend the oration and slave narrative and work within a literary medium which he, himself, had chosen. Brown's social and literary context, then, will not only show us the influences on his work, but will form for us as well the rock mountain base from which he finally soared as a creative artist. This understanding of both background and foreground will mark our complete portrait of the artist.

CHAPTER TWO

Negro Abolitionism: Its Physical and Literary Expression

Because so many of our American histories have overlooked the many contributions of Negroes to this country's physical and cultural growth, it is not surprising that their discussions of the Abolitionist movement reflect the same bias. The standard historical text approaches the Abolitionist period with white in its eye and assigns the vast bulk of its interest and coverage to white Northerners like William Lloyd Garrison, Gerrit Smith, John Greenleaf Whittier, and, later, John Brown. It matters not whether they are treated as dedicated Christians concerned with effecting a new society through moral suasion, third party politics, or public poetry; or whether they are branded as fiery-eyed fanatics, raging through the mid-West countryside on their way to Harper's Ferry. The point is not so much how these white Abolitionists are portrayed, but rather that they are the only ones who are portrayed. In fact it is almost as if the definition of "abolitionist" immediately calls to mind a strong, white, New England face—and this is the major problem here.

The facts are, of course, considerably to the contrary. To be sure, the various white abolitionists do deserve the veneration and moral accolades which we tend to give them today.

At the same time, in contrast to such greatly one-sided coverage, we very much need to note the tremendous and often pioneering accomplishments of those Negro abolitionists who gave the movement so much of its vigor, eloquence, and primary sense of need.

In terms of vigor, obviously the most direct form of abolition was not composed of editorials in the *Liberator* or mass meetings in Boston's Faneuil Hall. Rather, the most outspoken expressions were those provided by the many slaves in the South who threw off the degradation and cruelty of their position and initiated direct revolts against the slaveholding system. Gabriel, Denmark Vesey and Nat Turner are, of course, the most famous leaders of these revolts, but it is also clear to us today that a great many other insurrections and uprisings took place in the South of the early 1800's. Indeed, it has only been our reluctance to search out and acknowledge proofs of this that has kept us from crediting this strong will for freedom which lay buried beneath the stereotyped "contented slave"—a concept which exists in our minds almost solely because it is the picture which Southern apologists, from the 1830's until today, have wanted us to see.

Of perhaps greater numerical importance than those slaves who attempted to revolt and physically "abolish" slavery's cruel dominance over them were those slaves who sought to escape the brutal system through flight to the North. Related and equally significant were those individuals and groups of Negroes who formed the so-called "Underground Railroad" to help these fugitive slaves reach Canada and its freedom. With the combined diligence and concern of both Negroes and whites, this loosely knit yet highly effective "Railroad" provided the escaping slaves with a wide range of aids. Included was everything from the basic food, clothing and sleep to such larger aids as the forged traveling papers which helped Frederick Douglass escape Maryland and the protective sense of community which gave Henry Bibb the feeling of assurance

that, without going to Canada, he could work safely in Perry-
burgh, Ohio, while saving money to go back South and rescue
his wife and child.

In all these aspects of the "Railroad" it was the various
Negro communities and individuals along the way North which
formed the significant quantity of people actively helping the
fugitive slaves escape from the South. In fact, as we noted
above, men like Brown who held sensitive positions on steamboats, railroads and other conveyances going North found
themselves in a perfect position to aid vast numbers of escaping slaves. This was where grassroots "Abolitionism" in the
North essentially began.

Soon, of course, more fully organized Negro organizations
developed. These focused their attention on freeing the Southern Negro from slavery and the Northern Negro from the
prejudice which approximated slavery in the nominally "free"
states. In 1787, for example, Philadelphia Negroes under
Richard Allen, Absalom Jones and others formed a Free African Society—an organization which began for merely social-
izing purposes but which soon devoted itself to anti-slavery
agitation and protection of escaping slaves. Within eleven years
there were outgrowth African Society groups in Newport
(Rhode Island), New York City, and Boston.

Anti-slavery organizations such as these continued to spring
up, so that by the 1830's—when those national anti-slavery
groups of Garrison and Gerrit Smith began, and when our
history books therefore tend to suggest that "Abolitionism"
itself began—there already existed about fifty Negro anti-
slavery organizations spread throughout the country, ready to
join with and make successful those later, but larger groups.
Indeed, only two months after the launching of Garrison's
Liberator in 1831, Philadelphia Negroes under William Whipper, Robert Purvis, and James Forten supported and contributed to its maintenance. In fact, in the earliest and most trying
years of the *Liberator*, the number of Negro subscribers far
outweighed the number of white supporters, so that in 1831,
400 of that newspaper's 450 subscribers were Negro; and,

even as late as 1834, seventy-five per cent of its more than 2,300 subscribers were Negro. Clearly, concerned Negroes were the crucial cornerstone of the early Abolitionist movement.

Of greater importance to us, of course, is the more verbal and literary level of this early Negro abolitionism. As far back as the 1760's, a concerted attempt to throw off slavery was made by a Massachusetts group of Negroes who attempted to challenge the entire legal concept of slavery by bringing an action of trespass against their masters. One decade later similar groups of Negroes initiated a petition campaign in which local and state governing bodies were urged to destroy slavery on grounds that clearly echoed the "inalienable rights" and "consent of the governed" concepts which were the basis of the Declaration of Independence written during the same decade. Indeed, so strong was the movement among organized New England Negro groups that there are records of at least eight such petitions submitted to legislatures in Massachusetts and New Hampshire between 1773 and 1779.

Nor did this movement stop here. It lasted throughout the century, and it led to our first really tangible examples of anti-slavery prose written by Negroes in this country—a kind of public, didactic rhetoric that was essentially the first major type of formal Negro literature in America. It was, in fact, one of the two major kinds of literary expression which Negroes were writing when William Wells Brown came onto the scene, both of them naturally influencing most of his early writing. But more about that later.

The first of these individual petitions was written and signed by Prince Hall, a Massachusetts Masonic official and veteran of the Revolutionary War. Presented to the Massachusetts legislature in 1788, it advocated outlawing the slave trade. So powerful was it that it was soon followed by petitions of various whites in Massachusetts, and the eventual result of this publicity and pressure was the passage that year of a state ban on the slave trade. A similar petition was written in Philadelphia in 1799 by religious leader Absalom Jones and other free men of color, calling for the end of the slave trade and eventually slavery itself, and calling for the immediate repeal of the Fugitive Slave Act of 1793. Unfortunately, however, Philadelphia did not have Boston's moral concern; nor were the people ready for such complete abolition. The petition, therefore, died a complete and overwhelming death at the legislature's hands.

More specifically literary and more outspokenly didactic were the anti-slavery orations and pamphlets which were being written by Negroes from 1788 on. One of the leading magazines in the nation, Matthew Carey's *American Museum* in Philadelphia, ran two pieces denouncing slavery and calling for a greater practice of what the Declaration of Independence had proscribed. Both of these articles—"Negro Slavery" by a writer who signed himself "Othello" but whose racial origin is highly uncertain, and "Slavery," whose authorship is noted as being "By a Free Negro"—seem to have been speeches made by concerned Negroes who sought a larger audience by publishing them as essays in Carey's magazine. As such, we will look at them in greater detail later.

Paralleling these articles were a number of pamphlets in the 1790's by men like Richard Allen, Absalom Jones, Prince Hall, and Benjamin Banneker. For the most part these pamphlets devoted their attention to combating stereotypes about the Negro's so-called inherent inferiority and to attacking as well the various myths about how happy and carefree he was as a slave in the South. In both of these aspects they laid the foundation for the future abolition literature—both that before the Civil War and that which then sprang up at the end of the century to combat the re-emergence of these myths in the hands of Southern novelists and historians like Thomas Nelson Page and Ulrich Phillips. Indeed these pamphlets laid the foundation for even our "abolition" of prejudice literature today, since the same Negro "inferiority," "debased nature" myths seem to fester still in various dark crevices of our national psyche.

By 1827, with the growth of those numerous Negro abolition groups and the social and economic power which they
represented, came the first Negro newspaper in America, *Freedom's Journal*. It was a weekly, published in New York by
Samuel E. Cornish and John B. Russwurm, and its basic purpose was to discuss and advocate freedom for Southern Negroes and civil rights for those Negroes in the North. Significantly enough, the name which the paper took in 1829 showed
even more clearly its social interest in *Rights for All*.

Following this first venture into Negro journalism and Negro sponsored direct editorialization, there soon came several
other socially concerned Negro newspapers: the *African Sen-
tinel and Journal of Freedom* in Albany, N. Y. in 1831; the
Weekly Advocate in 1837; and eventually the first large scale
crusading Negro newspaper, Frederick Douglass' *North Star*
in Rochester in 1847. Beginning in the same period were several equally polemical and dedicated magazines: David Ruggles'
Mirror of Liberty in New York in 1838 and William Whipper's
National Reformer, published in Philadelphia that same year
by the American Moral Reform Society.

Thus, up to and through the 1830's we can see just what
sort of Negro literature was being written and read. It was
social cause material, strongly polemical and dedicatedly attacking slavery and discrimination throughout the country.
And, as such, it laid the directly didactic groundwork for all
the early Negro prose, even as it inculcated in subsequent Negro generations its didactic tone towards the reader, its anti-
slavery material, and its generally direct and argumentative
approach to its material.

With the establishment and spread of the national American
Anti-Slavery Society in 1833, two new genres were developed
for the Negro writer. The first to develop was the presentation
of direct platform orations by fugitive slaves to Northern audiences, orations which stressed the evils and cruelties of slavery
through the narration of painful experiences and hardships
which the ex-slave had personally undergone in the South.

The second and more literary of these was the development of written narratives by the same sort of fugitive slaves who set down on paper in great chronological detail what slavery had done to them and to Southern Negroes in general.

The birth of these two genres, more than anything else, marked the real birth of Negro literature as a significant literary expression, and for this reason these were the two major modes of expression which William Wells Brown found on the scene when he fled slavery in 1834 and became an anti-slavery agent in 1843. Their importance to us, then, is that they were the first two forms of writing which Brown practiced as a writer, and, being the only Negro literature predominant at the time, they were his stepping stones to his pioneering efforts with the first novel and first play in Negro literature. In order to see how Brown transcended his literary environment, we need to look more closely at that environment and understand, as well, how Brown worked within it in his early apprentice years.

CHAPTER THREE

Negro Oratory Prior To Brown

When we come now to discuss Negro anti-slavery oratory and the essential "genre" which it developed before and around William Wells Brown, we usually begin with the printed speech by "Othello" which we alluded to above. Because of its 1788 date, this speech tends to represent several important trends for modern historians. To begin with, it is seen as proof of how early Negroes were capable of sustained speaking talent and how early they felt the need to express their resentment of the slavery system. Furthermore, with its prestigious inclusion in the leading American magazine of the period, Carey's *American Museum*, historians today like to use the speech to point out how liberally Negro writers could be regarded in the North of the late 1700's and how prominent the topic of slavery was during the period.

The latter point seems basically justifiable, since the topic of this speech and the later one "By a Free Negro" are indeed "Negro Slavery" and "Slavery," but the first three seem more fiction than fact since the case for claiming "Othello" to be a Negro is far from proven. Indeed, the only "evidence" we have about the author behind the pseudonym is the fact that Abbé Grégoire, in his *De la Litterature des Nègres*, saw fit to categorize "Othello" as a Negro, for reason or reasons of which we have no record today.

This obviously is pretty flimsy evidence, especially when we realize that "Othello" as a pseudonym would be a very effective way for a white writer to seek authenticity through "word magic" and when we realize also that most Shakespearean Othellos throughout history up to that time had been played almost exclusively by white actors. More important than the mere doubt created by this conjecture is the fact that there is absolutely no internal evidence in the speech that the writer is Negro. In fact, the full weight of such evidence seems all to the contrary. On the one hand, the diction and sentence structure are highly stylized and polished, as the writer frequently expresses himself on a level which seems to feel at home with such entities as "the mild effulgence of approving Providence and the angry countenance of incensed divinity!" Of course, this is not conclusive evidence of anything, since we know that an ex-slave named Frederick Douglass quickly became an equally eloquent orator after his escape from Maryland bondage in 1838, but it does give us some pause. In addition to this initial doubt about "Othello's" Negro identity is the fact there is no real, tangible acquaintance with slavery shown in the speech, nor even the kind of second-hand knowledge of details which we might expect a Northern free Negro to have pictured to himself when contemplating his less fortunate brothers in the South.

More important than either of these points, however, is the kind of self-identification through pronouns which "Othello" exhibits, for it seems rather obvious throughout the speech that he aligns himself with white America and somehow feels "towards" the Negro from an outside vantage point. As he opens his discussion of the slave trade, for example, "Othello" immediately comes to terms with the moral problem involved, and his pronouns here are significant.

Yet when *we* take *them* from Africa *we* deprive *them* of a country which God hath given *them* for *their* own, as free as *we* are, and as capable of enjoying that blessing.

> Like pirates *we* go to commit devastation on the coast
> of an innocent country, and among *a people* who never
> did *us* wrong.

The italics here and below are mine, but the sense of racial
separateness is clearly "Othello's."

On a more personal, almost biological level, he notes further
the kinds of problems which slavery has created, and here
again he aligns himself with the white portion of society.

> Being once accustomed to subsist without labor, *we* be-
> come soft and voluptuous; and rather than afterwards
> forego the gratification of *our* habitual indolence and
> ease, *we* countenance the infamous violation, and sacri-
> fice at the shrine of cruelty, all the finer feelings of ele-
> vated humanity.

Examples of this pronoun identification are literally legion
throughout the speech, so perhaps we might skip to the closing
sentence and note how they control even the final voice in
the speech. After citing how slave families are torn asunder
and how such fear exists among them that "these unfortunate
wretches dare not even interpose in each other's behalf,"
"Othello" makes his final appeal to his white audience: "Let
us reverse the case," he tells them, "and *suppose* it *ours*—all
is silent horror!"

For these reasons, therefore, "Othello's" speech in the
American Museum of 1788 will be irrelevant to our discussion
of Negro thought and oratorical expression. So too will be
the speech on "Slavery," authored "By a Free Negro," which
also appeared in the *American Museum* one year later and
which is generally credited with being the second extant
speech of "Negro Orators." The problem here is that the
"Free Negro" in question is generally agreed to have been
a native of the West Indies; and this shift in culture and geography essentially takes this speech outside the realm of the

American Negro expression which is our principal concern here. Our major discussion of Negro oratory, therefore, begins in 1808 with Peter Williams.

The Early Orators

With the abolition of the Slave Trade in 1808 and the consequently growing optimism about abolishing slavery altogether, Negro oratory assumed its first discernible identity as a unique genre. It borrowed, of course, from contemporary writing around it, as all social and literary expressions do. But the point is not so much to conjecture about its origins, as it is to note the genre's basic elements and how those elements influenced Brown's own writing.

The occasions which called forth speeches during the first thirty years of this oratory varied, but the general themes, tones, and points of interest tended to remain the same. The abolition of the Slave Trade in 1808; growing discrimination against free Negroes in Northern states like Pennsylvania in 1813; the formation of the American Colonization Society in 1816 and its growing desire to remove Negroes from this country as their economic value as slaves seemed to be on the wane: issues as diverse as these formed the initial "occasions" for these various speeches. The speeches themselves, however, showed a much greater uniformity.

As the genre began with Peter Williams' "Oration on the Abolition of the Slave Trade," its tone was generally quiet and, in a sense, almost tame. Basically, Williams was content to historically "Review, for a moment, my brethren, the history of the Slave Trade," and this orderly, chronological development was infused with a tone marked by "suitable demonstrations of joy, thanksgiving, and gratitude" to "our heavenly Father, and to our earthly benefactors." The only expression of strong emotion came in Williams' discussion of America's basic motives for institutionalizing slavery and the

slave trade. In a note of profound social criticism that was
to surface throughout these discussions of slavery and haunt
us even through today, Williams saw the fundamental problem
in this country as "the desire of gain" which, "surpassing the
bounds of reasonable acquisition, violated the sacred injunctions of the gospel, frustrated the designs of the pious and
humane," and enslaved "the harmless aborigines."

With James Forten's 1813 address on "A Late Bill Before
the Senate of Pennsylvania," attacking a bill before that legislature which was designed to prevent free Negroes from settling in that state, the Negro's anti-slavery and anti-prejudice
oratory of the early 1800's began to take definite shape. The
"shape" which Forten gave them was the use of irony for attacking the fundamental inconsistencies of having slavery in a
nominally Christian and democratic country.

Couched in a style that dramatized the irony, Forten's address is significant for the almost classical way in which it
handles the basic inconsistencies involved. Indeed, he begins
his attack on the proposed exclusion bill by a pointed reference to the Declaration of Independence. "We hold this truth
to be self-evident, that God created all men equal," he tells
us, "is one of the most prominent features in the Declaration
of Independence, and in that glorious fabric of collected wis-
dom, our noble Constitution." Hence, "whatever measures are
adopted subversive of this inestimable privilege, are in direct
violation of the letter and spirit of our Constitution." Thus
Forten learned—as almost every Negro anti-slavery orator
after him would relearn—how to juxtapose ironically the basic
humanitarian concepts of the American "Credo" with both
slavery and prejudice, in order to show how profoundly "un-
democratic" these latter "institutions" were. Nor was Forten
content to let the irony merely work on its own; instead, he
found it valuable to point out directly the inconsistency involved and thereupon note how "It seems almost incredible
that the advocates of liberty should conceive the idea of selling
a fellow creature to slavery."

Supporting his general introduction of this "democratic" irony was Forten's more specific and dramatic juxtaposition of the sharply different meanings which July 4th had for the white and for the Negro American. Beyond the basic hypocrisy of celebrating "freedom" so religiously while surrounded by shackled slaves, Forten notes an even greater and almost symbolic irony: the fact that the greater the whites' "liberation," the more suffering in store for the slave. "It is a well known fact," he begins, "that black people, upon certain days of public jubilee, dare not be seen after twelve o'clock in the day, upon the field to enjoy the times; for no sooner do the fumes of that potent devil, Liquor, mount into the brain, than the poor black is assailed like the destroying Hyena or the avaricious Wolf! I allude particularly to the *Fourth of July*!— Is it not wonderful, that the day set apart for the festival of liberty, should be abused by the advocates of freedom, in endeavoring to sully what they profess to adore."

Of equal prominence with this "un-democratic" irony was Forten's introduction of the second great hypocrisy in American life. This was the irony of a clearly anti-Christian slavery flourishing, once more, in a strongly self-dedicated "Christian" land. Why "are we not to be considered as men?" he asks. "Are we not sustained by the same power, supported by the same food, hurt by the same wounds, wounded by the same wrongs, pleased by the same delights, and propagated by the same means?" In short, on its basically cosmic, Christian level, "Has the God who made the white man and the black left any record declaring us a different species?"

The answer to this was profoundly clear for sincerely Christian America even before it was asked by Forten; and, as subsequent Negro orators developed and sharpened its essential truth, this irony would underscore slavery's moral evil more and more effectively as the early nineteenth century unfolded. Indeed, when the Abolitionist poets wrote of the impending struggle and the Union soldiers marched off to civil war, they both saw themselves as moral forces in a political world. *HIS* truth was marching on.

With the birth of the American Colonization Society in 1816 and its growing determination to remove free and slave Negroes back to Africa, a new motif was introduced. Still prevalent, of course, was the emphasis on Christianity and the moral hold which it had on the American character; so that addresses like that by James Forten and Russell Perrott to the "Humane and Benevolent Inhabitants of . . . Philadelphia" could lament that, if colonization was enacted, "Soon will the light of Christianity, which dawns among that section of our species, be shut out by the clouds of ignorance, and their day of life be closed, without the illuminations of the Gospel."

Yet more important than this increasingly "traditional" approach was a new element of anti-slavery appeal. This was a harsh, dramatically punctuated description of the cruel family fragmentation which such a policy would entail—a brutal replay of the inhuman violence that had marked the slave auctions and middle passage which initially had wrenched the slave from Africa and traumatically dragged him to the New World.

> Parents will be torn from their children—husbands from their wives—brothers from brothers—and all the heart-rending agonies which were endured by our forefathers when they were dragged into bondage from Africa will be again renewed, and with increased anguish.

The strong, almost graphic voice of Forten and Perrott here was new in 1817. Nevertheless, it would soon become the basic voice of a whole generation of anti-slavery orators: the fugitive slaves like Frederick Douglass and our own interest, William Wells Brown.

Perhaps the culmination of this first thirty year period of Negro oratory is to be found in the July 5, 1827 "Address Delivered on the Abolition of Slavery in the State of New York" by Nathaniel Paul, Pastor of the African Baptist Society in Albany, N.Y. To begin with, slavery's origin is seen by Paul in the same economic terms which Williams had introduced.

"Influenced by the love of money," slavery is "a hateful monster, the very demon of avarice and oppression." As such it is clearly anti-Christian and "so contrary to the laws which the God of nature has laid down as the rule of action by which the conduct of man is to be regulated towards his fellow man, which binds him to love his neighbor as himself, that it even has, and ever will meet the decided disapprobation of heaven." Likewise, a second familiar feature of the address is the manner in which Paul finds himself graphically enumerating the physical evils of slavery and, like so many orators to follow, centering his discussion of this on the "more than savage barbarity" in which "husbands and wives, parents and children are parted to meet no more."

Of greatest importance, perhaps, is the growing power and incisive scorn which accompanies the recognition of the anti-Christian and anti-democratic ironies inherent in American slavery. No longer is the irony merely pirouetted across the page with soft mincing steps; now it is forcibly and outspokenly hurled directly at us. "Strange, indeed, is the idea that such a system, fraught with such consummate wickedness, should ever have found a place in this the otherwise happiest of all countries—a country, the very soil of which is said to be consecrated to liberty, and its fruits the equal rights of man," Paul begins. "But strange as the idea may seem, or paradoxical as it may appear to those acquainted with the constitution of the government, or who have read the bold declaration of this nation's independence; yet it is a fact that can neither be denied or controverted. . . ." Indeed, Paul concludes bluntly, "America is first in the profession of the love of liberty, and loudest in proclaiming liberal sentiments towards all other nations, and feels herself insulted, to be branded with anything bearing the appearance of tyranny or oppression. Such are the palpable inconsistencies that abound among us and such is the medley of contradictions which stain the national character, and renders the American republic a byword, even among despotic nations."

Remond and Douglass: Direct Prelude to Brown

Towards the end of the 1830's, with the rapid spread of the American Anti-Slavery Society across the North and the concurrent "reign of terror" in the South, in which no dissent against slavery was tolerated from Negro or white, Negro oratory developed its most serious—and most important for us— level of attack on the "peculiar institution." The lines of sentiment and policy now were drawn more clearly between North and South, making anti-slavery polemic and debate more pointed and practicable, since a ready, unified abolitionist audience could be counted upon. Also, more importantly, the growth of the anti-slavery societies as an organized network of social concern offered many Negroes a platform and audience to which they could consistently address themselves.

Making up these important new voices were two types of speakers: those who were free Northern Negroes like Charles Lenox Remond and those who were fugitive slaves, newly escaped from the South, like Henry Highland Garnet, Frederick Douglass, and William Wells Brown. Remond, the earliest and essentially most pioneering of these orators, was both free and economically comfortable in his Salem, Massachusetts home. Yet he early committed himself to the anti-slavery movement and was, in fact, one of the seventeen members of the first anti-slavery society formed in America. In 1838 he became a lecturer of the American Anti-Slavery Society, touring Massachusetts, Rhode Island and Maine. So popular did he become in these circles that throughout the early forties he was constantly sought after wherever a Negro's opinion of slavery was needed on an abolitionist platform.

As we briefly look at Remond now, we are struck by just how influential and prototypic he was for this new generation of Negro orators. For, almost singlehandedly he seems to have initiated and developed this major phase of the genre which so clearly influenced and became part of Brown. There were, to be sure, some elements in his speeches which were carry-

overs from the earlier addresses of Williams and Forten, the
most notable one being his deep faith in Christian principle
and his profound belief that "He who has promulgated to us
all truth—who is Himself the fountain of justice—the source
of truth—the perfection of loveliness—has announced from
the hill of Sinai, that man cannot attempt the bondage of his
fellow-man without being guilty of a deadly crime."

More important than the few continuances, however, was
the whole host of new feelings and approaches which Remond
introduced. We find in him, first of all, a much stronger sense
of outrage and concern, resulting in new tones that become
sarcastic and even sharply bitter. Hence it is not unusual to
hear him sarcastically refer to slavery as that "domestic institution which has come down unbroken from the 'world's
grey fathers,' the holy patriarchs, with whom angels walked
and talked." Nor are we surprised to find that the traditional
anti-democratic and anti-Christian ironies now become sharper,
almost caustic, even as the cruelties of slavery are becoming
more graphically portrayed. "When I see a woman condemned
to wear such a collar as it were cruelty to bind around the
neck of a dog," Remond declares, "working in that collar, eat-
ing in it, aye, even sleeping in it, for no other crime than
merely that of having asked permission to visit her child in an
adjoining plantation—when, I repeat, I look on sights like
these, my frame shudders with disgust—my blood freezes, and
my heart bursts with indignation as I exclaim, 'If these things
be the result of Christianity or of patriotism, may heaven deliver me from the influence of either!' "

Related to this more caustic tone was a greater awareness
and graphic portrayal of just what barbarities slavery did entail. We have just seen an example of how Remond concretely
enumerated inhuman aspects of the institution, and it is equally
significant to note how this detailed recital of evil fit in with the
new perspective of the new anti-slavery orator: that of first
hand, eye witness knowledge. Remond was not an escaped
slave, it is true, yet somehow he identified more closely with

the slaves in the South than had any of his predecessors, and thus he essentially introduced the "first hand experience" approach which was to be the initial power of later orators like Brown. In an 1841 address in Ireland, for example, Remond's approach to his audience was one stressing his personal, American Negro awareness of contemporary slavery in this country. "I have testified only to that which I have seen," he told them; "—I have borne evidence solely to that which I have witnessed."

Nor was this eye-witness concreteness an isolated aspect in Remond. In fact coupled with its enumeration and personal observation was a more didactic technique which sought a similar kind of "realistic" authenticity. This was the use of direct "documentation" by citing actual newspaper articles and advertisements from the South in order to condemn the South's own slavery, a technique which Brown was later to rely on heavily. Addressing a British audience in 1841, therefore, Remond ushered in this soon-to-be traditional technique. "I hope the meeting will bear with me while I read one or two extracts confirmatory of the remarks I have made," he prepared his audience, and then continued with his new approach to the obvious, recorded satisfaction of his ardent listeners. "I will refer to a source which has had a powerful action on a great and influential part of the District of Columbia. If a colored man goes to Columbia to attend the funeral of a deceased relative, he is liable to be seized, bound and detained, till he proves his freedom. [Hear! hear!] He must prove it while immured with the bolts and bars of a dungeon, otherwise he is sold as a slave. [Hear! hear!] There are two young men being flogged as slaves whose father receives a pension for his services in the Revolutionary War. [Hear! hear!]"

The final technique which Remond introduced into Negro anti-slavery oratory was destined to become just as extensively used as this "documentation" approach. In fact, it shared some of its attributes. This was the orator's borrowing of romantic, sentimental, or dramatic verse by which to intensify the emo-

tional climate and mood that his speech sought to develop.
Thus Remond concludes his 1841 address to the Irish by
noting that, despite America's various shortcomings and faults,
"I adopt with pleasure, as wholly consonant with my own
sentiments, the beautiful lines of an American poet, once resi-
dent in England:

> I love thee—witness Heaven above
> That I, that land—that people love;
> And, rail thy slanders as they will,
> Columbia, I will love thee still.
>
> Repent thee, then, and quickly bring
> Forth from the camp the accursed thing;
> Consign it to remorseless fire,
> Watch till the latest sparks expire—"

and so on, until the patriotic emotion is sentimentally established as the address' final tone. This was very effective as a
technique throughout the period following Remond, especially
since oral poetry was still very much in vogue then. And, indeed, it was soon to become even more extensively used in
later orations and writings of our own William Wells Brown.

The final stage of this anti-slavery oratory was marked by
the emergence and impact of fugitive slave speakers like Frederick Douglass and William Wells Brown. Because Douglass
did begin speaking on the Abolitionist circuit a few years before Brown and since he was essentially the dominant anti-
slavery figure throughout the twenty years before the war, it
is relevant for us to examine some of the nuances which he
added to the developing oratorical tradition. Furthermore,
when we remember that Douglass and Brown were contemporaries in the same movement and that Brown was actually
brought into the Massachusetts Anti-Slavery Society group
in 1847 primarily to fill the gap left there when Douglass officially broke away from the Garrisonian camp in Boston and

moved to Rochester in order to start a paper of his own, we
realize just how closely related Brown and Douglass were as
orators.

By and large, of course, the sentiments and general themes
of all these anti-slavery speakers, from Peter Williams to William Wells Brown, were dedicated to the same purpose: the
exposure and abolition of a cruel, anti-democratic and anti-
Christian evil. Despite this general similarity, however, it has
been clear so far that the tactics and approaches tended to
change as different speakers arrived on the scene, and this is
equally the case with Frederick Douglass. A brief look at his
famous Moorfields, England speech of May 12, 1846—chosen
because it ante-dates Brown's first extant speech by a full year
and a half—is interesting because of the mixture of innovation
and tradition which Douglass brings to it.

On the one hand, it is clear that Douglass, like Brown, did
owe a major debt to his predecessor Remond. This was
Remond's use of printed material from the South by which to
authoritatively "document" his personal descriptions of the
evils in that region. "Can it be possible that such things as
these exist in the United States?" asks Douglass rhetorically,
referring to his prior enumeration of slavery's many cruelties.
"Are not such deeds condemned by the law and denounced
by public opinion? Let me read to you a few of the laws of
the slaveholding states of America. I think no better exposure
of slavery can be made than is made by the laws of the states
in which slavery exists. I prefer reading the laws to making
any statement in confirmation of what I have said myself; for
the slaveholders cannot object to this testimony, since it is the
calm, the cool, the deliberate enactment of their wisest heads,
of their most clear-sighted, their own constituted representa-
tives."

On the other hand Douglass did introduce here much that
was new. There was, first of all, the "pseudo-apology" for his
inability to speak eloquently, a technique which every fugitive
slave orator used as a preface to his speeches. A mock apology

at best, this was a very effective ploy both for establishing the speaker as a genuine escaped slave and for reaffirming the kind of debased institution which slavery was. "I have nothing to commend me to your consideration in the way of learning, nothing in the way of education, to entitle me to your attention," Douglass begins. "But I will take it for granted that you know something about the degrading influences of slavery, and that you will not expect great things from me this evening, but simply such facts as I may be able to advance immediately in connection with my own experience of slavery."

As important as the "apology" here was the key concept involved in "my own experience." For what made the fugitive slave orator so significant and so unique for the anti-slavery scene was his ability to indict slavery on the basis of his own graphically moving sufferings in the South, and no fugitive orator failed to utilize this dramatic perspective. In fact, it was the initial *raison d'être* for most of them as speakers. Discussing the "barbarous inhumanity on the part of the slaveholders toward their slaves" therefore, Douglass early in his speech repaired to his own experiences in Maryland to support his contention that slavery, necessarily, depended upon this cruelty. "My experience," he notes, "confirms the truth of this proposition. When I was treated exceedingly ill, when my back was being scourged daily; when I was whipped within an inch of my life—life was all I cared for. 'Spare my life,' was my continual prayer. When I was looking for the blow about to be inflicted upon my head, I was not thinking of my liberty; it was my life." It is only this tremendous, physical fear that keeps a slave submissive, Douglass shows, and thus slavery can exist only if this brutalizing continues. The logic of the graphic appeal is now brought home to the apathetic or semi-committed abolitionist audience: this is why slavery must be abolished, because to condone slavery is to directly and necessarily condone the violent cruelty which slavery is based upon.

With this premise of "necessary" brutalizing, it is easy to understand the basic purpose of such fugitive slave orators.

They existed in order to bring, in eye witness fashion, all of slavery's grotesque evils to the ears of both sympathetic and apathetic Northern listeners. This is why we find, in addition to the more detached "documentation" of slavery's evils, a tremendous first-hand emphasis on the physical instruments of slavery's harshness: "The whip, the chain, the gag, the thumb-screw, the blood-hound, the stocks, and all the other bloody paraphernalia of the slave system" which "are indispensably necessary to the relation of master and slave."

Likewise, this is why we have moments of torture grotesquely described in great detail. "I am afraid you do not understand the awful character of these lashes," Douglass suggests to us. "You must bring it to your mind. A human being in a perfect state of nudity, tied hand and foot to a stake, and a strong man standing behind with a heavy whip, knotted at the end, each blow cutting into the flesh, and leaving the warm blood dripping to the feet."

And it is why human moments of emotional pain are made especially moving through direct dramatization. "If you would see the cruelties of this system, hear the following narrative," Douglass begins, and then goes on to relate essentially the same "auction tragedy" which Brown related far more effectively in his speech on "The Slave Trade" in *The Liberty Bell* two years later.

It is fitting, perhaps, that Brown and Douglass should intersect here, for this is what essentially happened in the 1840's as well. Thus, with Williams, Forten, Remond, and Douglass as essential background, we are now in a position to look directly at William Wells Brown as an orator. Developing as an untutored, fugitive slave polemecist initially, it will be obvious just what debts he owes to the oratorical tradition which preceded and surrounded him. At the same time, since he was an individualist at heart, our awareness of this background tradition will help us see also just where Brown the artist asserted himself and just what abilities he showed in this, his first, craft.

CHAPTER FOUR

William Wells Brown as Orator

When we come to discuss William Wells Brown as orator, we find certain limitations placed upon us from the very beginning. For despite the fact that Brown delivered numerous addresses throughout his life, over one thousand in just his five years in England, we have very few of them available to us today, including those articles which were intended to approximate speeches in written form. Nevertheless, they show an interesting variety and breadth in themselves and an equally interesting sense of mature development as a group.

Salem Lecture

Brown's first published speech was made under the auspices of the Massachusetts Anti-Slavery Society, which published a "phonograph" report of it from its No. 21 Cornhill address in Boston. It was *A Lecture Delivered before the Female Anti-Slavery Society of Salem* and was given November 14, 1847 at that town's Lyceum Hall. Significantly, the lecture begins —and also ends—with the standard, purposeful "apology" of every fugitive slave who spoke before educated abolitionist audiences. "In coming before you this evening," Brown begins, "I do not appear without considerable embarrassment; nor am I embarrassed without a cause." The cause, he suggests, is the obvious cultivation and learning of his listeners, who have had extensive educations from common schools, high schools, and colleges. Brown, on the other hand, has been a slave most of his life, and "When I recollect that but a few years since, I was upon a Southern plantation, that I was a Slave, a chattel, a thing, a piece of property,—when I recollect that at the age of twenty-one years I was entirely without education, this, every one will agree, is enough to embarrass me."

The "apology" is deftly made and it has its desired effects. On the one hand, it does relieve the ex-slave orator of any grammatical or formal clumsiness which his language may be heir to and does, as well, emphasize the authenticity of his speech as "a fugitive slave." On the most important other hand, it is a damning indictment of the South and its treatment of Negroes, and is, simultaneously, a testament to the Negro's inherent abilities as a man—specifically his ability to learn and cultivate himself to the level of public speaking despite the many obstacles which slavery had put in his way.

As we move into the lecture, we are not surprised to find that its dominant purpose is to enumerate the evils of slavery as a system that "tears the husband from the wife, and the wife from the husband; that tears the child from the mother, and the sister from the brother; that tears asunder the tenderest ties of nature." Likewise, we are not surprised to learn that it is a system devoted to subjecting the slave to pain and cruelty, a system that is clearly symbolized by "its bloodhounds, its chains, its Negro-whips, its dungeons, and almost every instrument of cruelty that the human eye can look at."

However, the greatest evil of slavery lies in its depriving the slave of his inherent religious and political nature, of those "inalienable rights" with which every man has been endowed "by his Creator;" and with this new material we can see that a major part of Brown's appeal to his female anti-slavery audience is going to stress anew the traditional anti-Christian and anti-democratic aspects of the South's "peculiar institution." The major evil of slavery, then, is that it is "a system that strikes at the foundation of society, that strikes at the foundation of civil and political institutions. It is a system that takes man down from the lofty position which his God designed that he should occupy, that drags him down, places him upon a level with the beasts of the field, and there keeps him, that it may rob him of his liberty."

Pursuing this indictment of American Christianity even more directly, Brown launches into a discussion of the American Bible Society. There is no finesse here, no real wit; the hypocrisy and irony are simply placed declaratively before his hearers when he notes how the Society "is sending bibles all over the world for the purpose of converting the heathen," yet "three millions of Slaves have never received a single bible from the American Bible Society." In fact, Brown tells us, just a few years earlier, the American Anti-Slavery Society offered the American Bible Society a donation of $5,000 if they would send bibles to the Slaves, or even "make an effort to do it;" but the American Bible Society "refused even to *attempt* to send the Bible to the Slaves." This is an interesting anecdote for us, not only in its indictment of the Bible Society but also in its implicit statement about just how much the whole Abolitionist movement was concerned with the ironic contradiction of American Christianity's disregard of the slave in the South.

On the same subject of unmasking this ironic immorality, Brown's tone soon becomes more incisive. Thus, in discussing the American Tract Society and noting that he has nothing to say "against any association that is formed for a benevolent purpose, if it will only carry out the purpose for which it was formed," Brown notes how only a short time prior to this address the Tract Society offered a reward of $500 for the best treatise against the sin of dancing, but "not a single syllable" has ever been published "against the sin of Slaveholding." "Go into a nice room, with fine music, and good company," he continues sardonically, "and they will publish a tract against your dancing; while three millions are dancing

every day at the end of the master's cowhide, and they cannot notice it! Oh, no; it is too small fry for them!"

Growing out of his attack on the hypocrisy of the Christian
church's position, Brown soon puts his finger on the economic
genesis of the problem: American greed, the same "avaricious
disposition" which Peter Williams denounced thirty-nine years
earlier. He tells the true story of a friend of his, Ellis Clisby
of Amsterdam, N.Y., who was accustomed to donate yearly
to the American Tract and Bible Societies. Two years prior to
Brown's speech, when approached once more, Clisby declined
to contribute, but told the agent that he would give $50 if
the Board of New York would publish a tract against the sin
of Slaveholding. One year later, when the agent was again
making his rounds, he told Clisby that the Committee had
said that they dare not publish such a tract. "If they published
it their Southern contributions would be cut off." The point to
all this is painfully clear to Brown:

> So they were willing to sacrifice the right, the interest,
> and the welfare of the Slave for the "almighty dollar."
> They were ready to sacrifice humanity for the sake of
> receiving funds from the South.

The *coup de grâce* is administered to this hypocritical Christianity nine pages later in a very poignant, yet bitter, vignette.
Attacking the ironic way in which Southern Christianity not
only tacitly condoned slavery but actually was used by slaveholders to psychologically brainwash and subdue slaves who
were already physically manacled and enchained, Brown is
"carried back to the time when" he saw a young Negress auc-
tioned off in the South. The highest bid for her was $400 and
the auctioneer was about to sell her at that price, when the
owner made his way through the crowd and whispered something to the auctioneer. As soon as the owner left, the auctioneer announced to the waiting buyers that he had unfortunately "failed to tell you all the good qualities of this Slave. I

have told you that she was strong, healthy, and hearty, and now I have the pleasure to announce to you that she is very pious. She has got religion." At that information the bidding immediately quickened its tempo, and the girl was finally sold for $700. The point, laments Brown didactically, in case we have failed to grasp it, is obvious: "her body and mind were sold for $400, and her religion was sold for $300." Hypocritical Christianity and American greed have triumphed again.

As we have seen above, the fundamental ironies which anti-slavery orators generally attacked were always two in number: those dealing with Christianity and those dealing with democracy. Brown here is no exception, even using documentation to emphasize his point. "I have before me" he begins, "an advertisement where some Slaves are advertised to be sold at the South for the benefit of merchants in the city of New York, and I will read it to you." He does so, and especially stresses that the Negro mother and three small children are to be sold "on Saturday, the 22nd day of December." This leads Brown to pointedly ruminate a bit.

Now if I know anything about the history of this country, the 22nd day of December is the anniversary of the landing of the Pilgrims; the anniversary of the day when those ambassadors, those leaders in religion, came to the American shore . . . fleeing political and religious tyranny, seeking political and religious freedom in the New World.

The harsh irony is clear here and is made even clearer when Brown climactically points out that "The anniversary of that day is selected for selling an American mother and her four [sic] children for the benefit of New York merchants."

Indeed, this historical irony now receives Brown's direct, expository assault as he elaborates upon the advertisement he has just read. After a fairly pointed but unemotional juxtaposition of the principles of freedom and liberty which moved the colonists to revolt in 1776 with the concept of Slavery which now exists in the South; and after a parallel comparison of a minor tax on tea and paper with the brutal conditions in the South where the Slave "has no tea; he has no paper; he has not even himself; he has nothing at all;" Brown launches a wry and increasingly bitter attack on the irony of the characteristic 4th of July oratory in this country where, as a South Carolina governor has correctly noted, "Slavery is the cornerstone of our Republic."

> I know that upon the 4th of July, our 4th of July orators talk of Liberty, Democracy, and Republicanism. They talk of liberty, while three millions of their own countrymen are groaning in abject Slavery. This is called the "land of the free, and the home of the brave," it is called the "Asylum of the oppressed;" and some have been foolish enough to call it the "Cradle of Liberty." If it is the "cradle of liberty," they have rocked the child to death. It is dead long since, and yet we talk about democracy and republicanism, while one-sixth of our countrymen are clanking their chains upon the very soil which our fathers moistened with their blood. They have such scenes even upon the Sabbath, and the American people are perfectly dead upon the subject. The cries, and shrieks, and groans of the Slave do not wake them.

Brown's extensive use of "documentation" here and elsewhere we will discuss later, in the context of his growing art, so perhaps it is enough at this point to simply note how directly concerned he is with supporting his general and personal statements with authoritative "documents" as proof, in the standard manner which we noted in Remond and Douglass above. "I have before me a few advertisements," he begins, "taken from public journals and papers, published in the Slaveholding States of this Union. I have one or two that I will read to the audience, for I am satisfied that no evidence is so effectual for the purpose of convincing the people of the

North of the great evils of Slavery as is the evidence of Slaveholders themselves."

Leaving his document-stocked preserve, Brown branches
out to attack still another irony on the political-racial scene
of his—and our—day. He notes, then, how America goes out
of its way to aid oppressed peoples of other lands in living
up to its rhetorically derived "Asylum of the oppressed" concept, even as its own land is filled with people brutalized and
suffering under an obviously bleak and sordid oppression.
While mentioning America's concern for the Greeks struggling
for liberty and "the poor, down-trodden serfs in Ireland,"
Brown pointedly notes and prologues for us much of our own
feelings in the 1960's.

> The American people are a sympathizing people. They
> not only profess, but appear to be a sympathizing people
> to the inhabitants of the whole world. They sympathize
> with everything else but the American Slave.

Nor does Brown allow the point of this irony to slip away
from us. Having risen to an international perspective, he pur-
sues the paradox of America's world professions with its own
backyard practices, and labels the contradiction as the blatant
"hypocrisy" which it is. At the same time, he is very sophisticated in proceeding with this point. Thus he puts this ex-
plosive, but true, epithet in the mouths of unfriendly foreign
observers, a technique which both frees Brown from its onus
and also intensifies the amount of squirming which it causes
his audience. Yet the point is still clearly and starkly made.
"But what will the people of the Old World think?" he asks
rhetorically.

> Will they not look upon the American people as hypo-
> crites? Do they not look upon your professed sympathy
> as nothing more than hypocrisy? You may hold your
> meetings and send your words across the ocean; you may
> ask Nicholas of Russia to take the chains from his down-

trodden serfs, but they look upon it all as nothing but hypocrisy.

Indeed, this is a significant moment in Brown's speech. Not only has he found a deft use of "personae" through which to make his harsh point, while displacing his audience's ire from himself to the ventriloquist's dummy; and not only has this given him the distance and perspective to somehow discuss this hypocrisy in terms of "your meetings," "your words," and "your professed sympathy," where his whole perspective earlier had stressed his closeness to his audience in terms of "our countrymen" and the blood of "our fathers." But through this approach he has also staked out new ground from which to attack American slavery—that of reaching the American people less through conscience than through their touchy sense of newly-national, anti-Old World pride. The succeeding several paragraphs then constitute a psychologically brilliant and deftly handled appeal which Brown makes to his fellow Americans' desire to be first in everything and to feel superior to England and the Continent (a very real issue in 1847).

In showing how the various countries of Europe are questioning and acting against slavery, therefore, he asks

Shall the American people be behind the people of the Old World? Shall they be behind those who are represented as almost living in the dark ages?

It is an interesting and subtly handled piece of external pressure brought to bear on the American ego, and it shows just how early Negro thinkers learned to couch their local political needs in the lap of American foreign policy. For having no political power at home, and seeing that little public sentiment would be morally forthcoming unless stirred, they began to see a chance for a certain emotional leverage to be gained from Americans' concern over their foreign image and their need to be liked and respected throughout the world.

Despite all of the ironies and increasingly bitter indictments

in the lecture, Brown very skillfully ends on a positive and
exhortative note, buttressed quite solidly by the same "borrowed verse" which we saw Charles Lenox Remond utilize
six years earlier. Though American Christian and democratic
character is so bad in the eyes of observers both at home and
abroad, there is still a strong future hope: the Abolitionist
movement. "I believe it is the Anti-Slavery movement that is
calculated to redeem the character of the American people,"
he tells his audience. "Much as I have said against the character of the American people this evening, I believe that it is
the Anti-Slavery movement of this country that is to redeem
its character."

It is true that will stand. Yes, it was planted of the very
best plant that could be found among the great plants in
the world.

> "Our plant is of the cedar,
> That knoweth not decay;
> Its growth shall bless the mountains,
> Till mountains pass away;
> Its top shall greet the sunshine,
> Its leaves shall drink the rain,
> While on its lower branches
> The Slave shall hang his chain."

The ultimate expression of this optimism is the *Lecture's*
final appeal to the audience. "This is a subject in which I ask
your cooperation," Brown announces. "We are not those who
would ask the men to help us and leave the women at home.
We want all to help us." Indeed, "I hope that every individual
here will take hold and help carry on the Anti-Slavery movement." On that note the curtain descended and William Wells
Brown's first speech was history.

While this is where Brown essentially ended his speech, we
should note one major facet of its overall structure: it has none

. . . except for the general progression from overwhelming problem to optimistic "solution." Instead, it moves sporadically from personal narratives to philosophic pronouncements to general anecdotes to sharp, "too small fry for them" ironics.

Interspersed among these various subject matters and kinds of speaking voices are a variety of techniques like the "apology," "documentation," and "borrowed verse," which we know Brown shared with other orators in the field. Thus a "lecture" such as this is more a dramatic compendium than a neatly laid-out, logical argument. Nor is this bad. In fact, this is what the fugitive slave address was meant to be—a large, realistic, rambling-yet-concrete indictment of all of slavery's many cruelties and ironies in as many approaches to the audience as practicable.

In stressing the large, loping formlessness here, however, we shouldn't let ourselves believe that there was no planning to such a speech or that there was no structured approach at all. Just the fact that so many of the standard anti-slavery techniques and ironies make their presence known here shows how much this address has been "planned" for variety. The only point is that with this emphasis on variety and the substances which make up that variety, the individual beads of the didactic necklace become far more important than the string which holds them together or the necklace's overall form and beauty. Variety, juxtaposition, and concrete action—these were the important aspects of the fugitive slave oration.

At the same time, the art of providing this variety with some sense of personal, concrete realism was quite important, and Brown shows himself very much in control of this structural need. The essential purpose of the fugitive slave orator, of course, was to embody and personally symbolize slavery's inhumanity, so that a good orator like Brown, even amidst his flowing rhetoric and sharp ironies, never let the audience forget his past origin and its present importance to those assembled. Indeed, Brown makes this transition very deftly in his *Lecture*. "When I get to talking about Slavery as it is," he suddenly reminisces, "when I think of the three millions that are in chains at the present time, I am carried back to the days when I was a Slave upon a Southern plantation; I am carried back to the time when I saw dear relatives, with whom I am identified by the tenderest ties of nature, abused and ill-treated. I am carried back to the time when I saw hundreds of Slaves driven from the Slave-growing to the Slave-consuming states."

Indeed, so effective and so consciously used is this structural technique that Brown utilizes it again at the end of his lecture where he is strongly determined to inject a final concrete, immediate sense of slavery's cruelty into the minds of his departing audience. "I would that every one here could go into the Slave-States," he announces, "could go where I have been, and see the workings of Slavery upon the Slave." Once more he ruminates, and once more the power of a fugitive slave's perspective becomes graphically clear.

> When I get to talking upon this subject I am carried back to the day when I saw a dear mother chained and carried off in a Southern steamboat to supply the cotton, sugar, or rice plantations of the South. I am carried back to the day when a dear sister was sold and carried off in my presence. I stood and looked at her. I could not protect her. I could not offer to protect her. I was a Slave, and the only testimony that I could give her that I sympathised with her, was to allow the tears to flow freely down my cheeks . . . I am carried back to the day when I saw three dear brothers sold, and carried off.

There is a good deal of repetition of ideas and feelings which he had introduced earlier, just as there is repetition within the passage itself and within so many passages throughout the address; and this is what was intended. For the blatant evils of slavery could not be over-emphasized in the eyes of the Abolitionists, and thus this constant citation and re-citation of those evils was deemed a necessary part of the orator's delivery. Furthermore, as every good orator has always been aware, public delivery of events and ideas constantly needs repetition to account for the loss of attention and lapse of meaning which always accompanies oral communication between a speaker and a sizable, scattered, "large-hall" audience. No matter how good the lyceum acoustics; no matter how attentive the sympathetic listeners; much was lost across the chasm between podium and floor, and it was to overcome this attrition that Brown felt free to repeat phrases and allusions, returning to the same points several times from several different directions.

In fact, in its ultimate sense, this use of repetition was the only "structure" which the anti-slavery orator was required to perfect. With each individual anecdote and concept, as we have seen, he needed repetition to drive the point home. And, on a far more significant level, he indulged this same didactic repetition throughout the whole address: for "variety" was simply "repetition" in a veiled and multi-colored dress.

The American Slave-Trade

Brown's second "speech" was a piece on "The American Slave-Trade," which appeared in *The Liberty Bell* in 1848. The article was quite short, presumably because it had been placed in this little anti-slavery collection as merely one of thirty-nine short pieces. The whole book itself seems to be almost a polemical anthology of first-class anti-slavery sentiment, including, along with the piece by Brown and an article by the equally fledgling Frederick Douglass, the work of such noted abolitionist and literary figures as Elizabeth Barrett Browning, Thomas Wentworth Higginson, Theodore Parker, James Russell Lowell, Edmund Quincy, and William Lloyd Garrison. Among this company, it is easy to see the great importance which both Brown and Douglass had on the Abolitionist scene. As for Brown's piece itself, its setting tells us a great deal about its own content. Indeed the purpose and general atmosphere of this compilation as a whole is perhaps best seen in its title page's announcement that it is written "By Friends of Freedom" and that it is published by the National Anti-Slavery Bazaar in Boston.

In its large type, wide margin, seven page briefness, therefore, Brown's piece essentially has space to develop only one dramatized anecdote showing the basic cruelty of the slave trade, and he shows some interesting dramatic artistry in the process. He precedes his narrative anecdote, predictably enough, with the standard enumeration of slavery's cruel paraphernalia: the "Slave-prisons, Slave-auctions, hand-cuffs, whips, chains, blood-hounds, and other instruments of cruelty" which "are part of the furniture which belongs to the American Slave-Trade," and he repeats the kind of "invitation to reality" which he gave his audience in the *Salem Lecture* when he states, as if addressing a real audience and representing a whole platform of abolitionist speakers, that "We" wish "no human being to experience emotions of needless pain, but we do wish that every man, woman, and child, in New England, could visit a Southern Slave-prison and auction-stand."

With the rhetorical preliminaries out of the way, Brown then launches into the heart of his address: his first-person anecdote of how the auction block rips husband and wife apart, never to be reunited. "I shall never forget a scene," he begins, "which took place in the city of St. Louis, while I was in Slavery." Having gotten us onto the scene and having established his credentials as authoritative narrator, Brown now reaches into the story itself. He relates how a man and his wife, both slaves, were brought from the country into the city to be sold at auction. "Austin & Savage, Auctioneers," he enumerates, reaffirming again that "I was present."

As the actual bidding unfolds, Brown's perspective is both empathetic and sensitive, achieving a strong sense of immediate intimacy. "My eyes were intensely fixed on the face of the woman," he tells us, while she was being sold, and this vantage point enables him to see the tears and anguish in her eyes. Then, shifting perspectives, he draws near the man and his new master "to listen" as the man attempts to convince his master to buy Fanny. The man's plea is plaintive and moving, but all to no avail as Fanny is sold to a different master and thus wrenched away from him forever.

The final dialogue between the pair is delicately stoical (in marked contrast to the artificial melodrama which Douglass injected into his version of a similar anecdote, in his 1846 speech which we examined above) as the separated slave couple promise to meet in heaven. At this point Brown shifts his perspective a third and final time and focuses closely on the faces of the observers of this tragic moment—observers who not only corroborate Brown's feelings of empathetic pain but who also evoke from his reading audience a greater sense of physical, and thereby emotional, identification than did the two slaves. "I saw the countenances of a number of whites who were present," he tells us, "and whose eyes were dim with tears, at hearing the man bid his wife farewell." With this, the story is over, and, essentially, so is the article as a whole. It has been short and limited; but it has also shown Brown's growing reputation as one of the only two Negro writers included. It has shown, as well, his budding sense of dramatic artistry.

The Appendix

Brown's next "address" also came in 1848 and took the form of an "Appendix" to his "Second Edition, Enlarged" *Narrative*. For us it is a fascinating document.

In some ways it has many elements of what we have come to see as typical anti-slavery material and tone. There is, of course, enumeration of slavery's cruelty, made especially effective here by Brown's creation of harsh, forceful words—

through hyphens and active, slashing participles—in order to
emphasize his point and his linkage of all this cruelty to the
irony that the slaveholders profess themselves to be religious.
Despite the fact that slaveholders "hide themselves behind the
church," so that a "more praying, preaching, psalm-singing
people cannot be found than the slaveholders at the South,"
Brown tells us, this pretense cannot obscure the awful truth
beneath the facade, and the falseness of the slaveholders will
soon become clearly and nationally understood. Indeed, their
child-robbing, man-stealing, woman-whipping, chain-forging,
marriage-destroying, slave-manufacturing, man-slaying religion,
will not be received as genuine" in forthcoming years.

Coupled with this anti-Christian irony and enumeration of
cruelty is also the usual anti-democratic irony; and they actually are fused together in the early part of the "Appendix."
Attacking democracy's ironic performance as a whole and the
unmistakable fact that "Slavery is a national institution,"
Brown notes how the national government itself licenses men
to traffic as slave-traders, and he even dramatically pictures
how the "American slave-trader, with the constitution in his
hat and his license in his pocket, marches his gang of chained
men and women under the very eaves of the nation's capitol."
The physical irony of this picture now launches Brown into
a direct attack on this inconsistency "in a country professing
to be the freest nation in the world." The rhetoric of the moment follows the usual anti-slavery pattern.

> They profess to be democrats, republicans, and to be-
> lieve in the national equality of men; that they are "all
> created with certain inalienable rights, among which are
> life, liberty, and the pursuit of happiness." They call
> themselves a Christian nation; they rob three millions of
> their countrymen of their liberties, and then talk of their
> piety, their democracy, and their love of liberty. . . .

A further typical aspect of the article is its use of borrowed verse: both for the usual, sentimental, "heart-rending" effect and for the exhortative, dramatic effect to be gained by the dramatic surge which poetry can provide. Hence, not only do we have the plaintive soul of the freedom-seeking slave enumerate his pathetic problems and exclaim with a tinge of strength

> "From life without freedom, oh, who would not fly
> For one day of freedom, oh! who would not die"

but we also have the more powerful, prophetically "certain" verse which follows Brown's strong statement that "slavery must and will be banished from the United States soil.

> 'Let tyrants scorn, while tyrants dare,
> The shrieks and writings of despair;
> The end will come, it will not wait,
> Bonds, yokes, and scourges have their date;
> Slavery itself must pass away,
> And be a tale of yesterday.' "

However, it is the new material and new tone which intrigues us here. Even the early paragraphs, in fact, introduce a more forceful interest and perspective of the crusading orator in Brown. And, coupled with this growing determination for the slave to attain freedom is an equally growing strength to attack the Northern, national government when it is aiding the South's evil.

"The rising of the slaves in Southampton, Virginia, in 1831," Brown tells us, "has not been forgotten by the American people. Nat Turner, a slave for life,—a Baptist minister . . . commenced the struggle for liberty; he knew his cause was just, and he loved liberty more than he feared death." Consequently, even though the federal government was appealed to by the Virginia authorities; and even though a company of United States troops ("Yes! Northern men, men born and brought up in the free states, at the demand of slavery, marched to its rescue. . . .") was sent into Virginia to put down the rebelling slaves ("men whose only offense was, that they wanted to be free"), the soldiers only succeeded in physically rechaining the poor slave and "did not succeed in crushing his spirit." In fact, exhorts Brown in conclusion,

> Not the combined powers of the American Union, not the slaveholders, with all their northern allies, can extinguish that burning desire of freedom in the slave's soul!

Clearly there is a fiercer fire in Brown now, and its righteous sense of self-integrity is becoming more intense.

To some extent, the best of the new Brown was saved for last, because it is the second portion of his article which strikes us most forcefully and dominates our impressions of the growing vigor and strength of his new perspective. "But I will now stop," he tells us after the first five of his twenty-nine pages, "and let the slaveholders speak for themselves. I shall here present some evidences of the treatment which slaves receive from their masters; after which I will present a few of the slave-laws. And it has been said, and I believe truly, that no people were ever found to be better than their laws."

The dominant portion of the "Appendix," therefore, will be turned over to "documenting," in the slaveholders' own words, the depth and scope and graphic harshness of the evil which they practice, and this documentation now becomes especially incisive and almost savage in its effectiveness. Nor does Brown let his readers miss the power of these documents through their obliviousness or unconcern. Rather, he directly addresses us and impresses the documents' importance on us. "I beg of the reader not to lay this book down until he or she has read every page it contains," he requests. "I ask it not for my own sake, but for the sake of three millions who cannot speak for themselves."

The documents themselves are compelling—both for the power which they derive from their graphic realism and for the fact that all their sordid harshness is in the mouths of the very Southerners whom they are describing. The savage inhumanity and violence, therefore, are delivered to us directly: their grotesque sadism glaring out at us with no further discussion added—or needed—by Brown. The starkness of the direct truth is more than sufficient as we are taken on a daylight journey through nightmarish terrain.

The "religious" Southern clergy receives its ironic due:

> One of my neighbors sold to a speculator a Negro boy, about 14 years old. It was more than his poor mother could bear. Her reason fled, and she became a perfect *maniac*, and had to be kept in close confinement. She would occasionally get out and run off to the neighbors. On one of these occasions she came to my house. With tears rolling down her cheeks, and her frame shaking with agony, she would cry out, 'Don't you hear him—they are whipping him now, and he is calling for me!' This neighbor of mine, who tore the boy away from his poor mother, and thus broke her heart, was a *member of the Presbyterian church.*
>
> —Rev. Francis Hawley, Baptist
> Minister, Colebrook, Ct.

as does the Southern "democratic" government, as we shall see it exemplified by an "officer of justice" in a moment.

Yet it is the general Southern world of violence which receives the dominant share of documented notice here. The common man, who makes a living from it:

> Negro Dogs.—The undersigned having bought the entire pack of Negro Dogs, (of the Hays & Allen stock,) he now proposes to catch runaway Negroes. His charge

will be three dollars per day for hunting, and fifteen dollars for catching a runaway. He resides three and a half miles north of Livingston, near the lower Jones' Bluff road.

> William Gambrel
> —Livingston County (Alabama) *Whig*
> of November 16, 1845;

the ordinary slaveholder, whose spite and hatred even overcome his love of property:

About the first of March last, the Negro man Ransom left me, without the least provocation whatever. I will give a reward of 20 dollars for said Negro, if taken DEAD OR ALIVE,—and if killed in any attempt an advance of $5 will be paid.

> Bryant Johnson
> Crawford Co., Ga.
> —*Macon* (Georgia) *Telegraph*;

the well-to-do slaveowner:

A wealthy man here had a boy named Reuben, almost white, whom he caused to be branded in the face with the words 'A slave for life.'

> —*St. Louis Gazette.*

Together, they are capable of making barbarity into a grotesque social occasion:

ANOTHER NEGRO BURNED.—We learn from the clerk of the Highlander, that, while wooding a short distance below the mouth of Red river, they were *invited to stop a short time and see another Negro burned.*

> —*New Orleans Bulletin*

Together, their warped sadism knows no bounds. "A colored man in the city of St. Louis," Brown tells us, "was taken by a mob, and burnt alive at the stake. A bystander gives the following account of the scene:—

> After the flames had surrounded their prey, and when his clothes were in a blaze all over him, his eyes burnt out of his head, and his mouth seemingly parched to a cinder, someone in the *crowd*, more compassionate than the rest, proposed to put an end to his misery by shooting him, when it was replied, that it would be of no use, since he was already out of his pain. 'No,' said the wretch, 'I am not, I am suffering as much as ever,—shoot me, shoot me.'
>
> 'No, No,' said one of the fiends, who was standing about the sacrifice they were roasting, 'he shall not be shot; I would sooner slacken the fire, if that would increase his misery;' and the man who said this was, we understand, an *officer of Justice*.
>
> —*Alton Telegraph*

Nor is this violence meant for slaves alone. The bell tolls for thee as well, Brown suggests to his readers. "The cry of the whole South should be death, instant death, to the abolitionist, wherever he is caught," shouts the *Augusta* (Ga.) *Chronicle*, and the *New Orleans True American* goes into greater detail:

> We can assure the Bostonians, one and all, who have embarked in the nefarious scheme of abolishing slavery at the South, that lashes will hereafter be spared the backs of their emissaries. Let them send out their men to Louisiana; they will never return to tell their sufferings, but they shall expiate the crime of interfering in our domes-

tic institutions by being BURNED AT THE STAKE.
                            —*New Orleans True American*

The savage trip is over. The South's "domestic institutions" have all been encountered in their natural habitats, and we have piercingly seen the *True American's* "truth." The "Appendix" will finally conclude with a compilation of the various slave codes of the Southern states, once more "documenting" the harshness of the system. Then the spell is broken, and we are allowed to come out into the fresh sanity of our own sunlit world. "Reader in Wonderland" has been the purpose of our journey through this surrealistic horror chamber, and its effect eludes mere surface description. It is as fine a "lecture" as Brown will make.

St. Domingo

We pass over now Brown's informal, brief and essentially plain speech before the Paris Peace Convention in 1849. The speech and the conference are important to us largely because Brown was chosen to address this august group of world figures and because he was so well received while in Paris. Both of these points indicate the stature which he had come to possess by that year. At the same time, the speech itself does not have any major significance for us directly, and is valuable only for the social and professional recognition which it conferred upon this young polemicist and morally concerned ex-slave.

The last speech which we have is a different story and is of great interest to us for the differences it shows from his earlier work. Delivered in May, 1854, to an English audience at the Metropolitan Atheneum in London, it was then repeated seven months later to an American audience in Philadelphia. *St. Domingo: its Revolutions and its Patriots* is the title and subject of the address, and it shows a strong, new sense of abolitionist forcefulness which far transcends Garrison's "moral suasion" and Gerrit Smith's political interest with the Liberty Party. The oppression of Slavery throughout the world is a physical one, Brown sees, and the way to freedom is correspondingly physical. What was true for the slaves in St. Domingo (Haiti) in 1806 is true for America in 1854.

The first item which we notice in the address is the way it begins with an inflammatory invocation of violent rebellion, embodied, gracefully enough, in two lines of borrowed verse from "Childe Harold." The sentiments themselves are strong and harsh as concepts, but they are deliberately tempered by Brown with their deliverance in verse, especially the controlled, balanced verse of an acknowledged, respected poet like Lord Byron.

> Hereditary bondsmen! Know ye not
> Who would be free, themselves must strike the blow?

Our initial interest here then is in Brown as a technician, as we note his new use of direct quotation and borrowed verse. Whereas usually it was used for poetic effect and emotional pull, evoking sentimental emotion from an already sympathetic audience, here it is used for authority of thought and political policy. More importantly, here it is deftly used to soften the blow of the revolutionary message, as the romantic, yet controlled verse of Byron does not at all shock an audience in the way that direct, forceful prose would. Thus the fist is couched in a generic glove called verse, and the glove itself conveys tradition and respectability. The use of literary quotation by Brown, then, has become quite sophisticated.

Along with this new sophistication we find that Brown's moralizing voice is also more mature and sophisticated. Discussing the French part of St. Domingo, he notes how in a society consisting of whites, mulattoes, and slaves, the slaves were the most numerous and thus had a certain physical strength on the island, even if their political and social power

was non-existent. But more significant than this physical
strength, says Brown, is the fact that the slaves were unjustly
oppressed. "Right is the most dangerous of weapons," he tells
us, "—woe to him who leaves it to his enemies."

At the same time we find some "traditional" elements of
Negro oratory here as well. We recognize immediately Brown's
standard reference to the irony of slavery in an American
democracy, and we note how he develops this with a strong,
powerful voice which first emphasizes the irony and then nails
it in. Discussing the appearance of one of the mulatto deputies
who appeared before the Constituent Assembly in Paris to
seek equal rights for the mulattoes on St. Domingo, Brown
relates the deputy's approach and then Brown's own feelings
about it.

> In urging his claims, he said, if equality was withheld
> from the mulattoes, they would appeal to force. This was
> ably seconded in an eloquent speech by the noble-hearted
> and philanthropic Barnave, who exclaimed at the top of
> his voice, so as to be heard at the remotest part of the
> Assembly. "Perish the colonies, rather than a principle!"
> Noble language this! Would that the fathers of the Amer-
> ican Revolution had been as consistent.

And, on a more personal, slave narrative basis, we notice his
concern in describing the mulattoes in Haitian society. Significantly enough, the status and problems of the mulattoes in St.
Domingo paralleled very closely their status in the South, and
this, of course, was of interest to Brown, as both his narrative
and his daughter's biography of him attest. Thus he spends
a great deal of time in discussing them. "As in all countries
where involuntary servitude exists," he begins, "morality was
at a low stand." Owing to the amalgamation of whites and
blacks, therefore, "there arose a class known as mulattoes and
quadroons. This class, though allied to the whites by the tenderest ties of nature, were their most bitter enemies" because,

like their American counterparts, they "had no rights" and "felt their degradation even more keenly than the bond slaves."

Added to this frustration of high expectations with no tangible successes in the white world, was the fact that the mulattoes in St. Domingo, like those in the South, had no roots or friends in the darker, slave world either. Their isolated middle ground was one of freedom, which of course made them better off than their Southern counterparts. But, at the same time, there was a tremendous turbulence and isolation that went with this position. "They were haughty and disdainful to the blacks, whom they scorned, and jealous and turbulent to the whites, whom they hated and feared," and this of course struck home to Brown on a direct level, if only as a reminder of the world which he had once inhabited.

The overall point of the speech, however, was far larger than any of these individual elements. It was, in fact, Brown's determination to describe historically and somewhat heroically the freeing of the slaves in St. Domingo and the essentially forceful approach which they took to secure these rights. The major importance of this 1854 speech, then, is Brown's growing forcefulness and dedication to self determination for the whole race of slaves in the South, by any means necessary.

Basically the lecture itself is a bit of history, told fervently and clearly about St. Domingo's slaves, their problems, and eventual success in obtaining freedom in the late eighteenth and early nineteenth centuries. At the same time, it is obvious that Brown was not asked to give an address simply to record historical events in purely objective terms. Rather, there is a point to be made here, and it is the realization of this point which is our concern.

As we have seen above, there are some typical Abolitionist ironies and techniques used here by Brown, which indicate that he is still predominately interested in attacking American slavery; and perhaps this is the only clue we really need. For it seems fair to assume that in describing and detailing how the Negro slaves of St. Domingo managed to rise and gain their freedom in the Caribbean, Brown would be making an implicit statement about the parallel role which history also offers the American slave in the South.

His early discussion of the island, then, sets the scene sociologically for the drama which is to follow. Especially concerned with the French part of the island, he notes how there were 20,000 whites, who held the political, social and economic reins of that part of the island; 30,000 free mulattoes, whose freedom was more a source of frustration than anything else, because they had no social or political rights and thus had no open areas into which they could channel their free energies; and 500,000 slaves, who held no rights or freedom at all. With the beginning of the 1789 democratic Revolution in France and its dramatic episodes in the Tennis Court and at the Bastile, the mulattoes on St. Domingo saw this as their chance to attain authorized freedom from the new French government. Accordingly, they sent a deputized group to France to plead their case before the Constituent Assembly and ask for equal rights with the whites. When the Assembly passed a decree granting these claims, however, the struggle had only begun.

When Oge, the leader of the mulattoes, returned with the news, the whites on the island determined that the new decree should not be enforced. A number of the mulattoes were equally determined that it should be and took up arms to support the righteousness of their claims. The ensuing battle found the mulattoes defeated and Oge put to death.

Having been a detached historian up to this point, Brown now begins vicariously to take part in the events and bring them to emotional life, infusing them with his own feelings. The strong abolitionist in him begins to assert itself; and the mulattoes, who had been as abusive to the slaves as had the whites, now became "free blacks" in Brown's eyes, as the heroic nature of their fight for liberty raised them in his sight.

The free blacks were defeated, and their brave leader, being taken prisoner, was, with a barbarity equalled only by its folly, broken alive on the wheel. The revolt was suppressed for the moment, but the blood of Oge and his companions bubbled silently in the hearts of the Negro race; they swore to avenge them.

The next major step in the struggle came when the mulattoes saw that they could not physically free themselves alone. They therefore pragmatically aligned themselves with the slaves, whom they formerly had scorned, and pressed for the general emancipation of the slaves, which thereupon harnessed the slaves' numbers and strength to the mulattoes' cause. The "alliance" was made, and, under the courageous leadership of Toussaint, the fifty-year-old slave grandson of a powerful West African King, the violent, chaotic struggle was finally won, to the extent that the Colonial Assembly granted the mulattoes equal rights and asked, in return, their aid in restoring order to the island. Having gained their own objectives, the mulattoes now treacherously joined with the whites and broke the back of the slaves' freedom movement. This left the rest of the struggle for freedom to Toussaint and the slaves as a group, and this is what Brown's history—and empathetic feelings—now pursue.

It is an extremely complicated affair, with Spain, France and England all adding to the fragmentation and uncertainty which were the result of the conflicting loyalties among various whites, mulattoes and slaves; and Brown demonstrates remarkable historical clarity in presenting this tumultuous period. But the importance of this speech is not his clarity as a historian; rather, its significance lies in his feelings toward the slaves' struggle and his identification with it as a phenomenon which ought to be paralleled in America's South.

The result of this is not only the heroic descriptions of the slaves' leaders, men generally described, like Christophe, in terms of "imposing appearance," "majestic carriage," with eyes "full of fire"; or described, like Dessalines, as men of "bold, turbulent, and ferocious spirit," whose furrows and incisions on the face, neck and arms "pointed out the coast of

Africa as his birthplace." Nor is it merely the kind of empathetic exultation with which Brown marks the final moment of slave victory, as the French sail from the island for the last time and the slaves now celebrate their freedom. "Every heart beat for liberty," Brown relates in almost lyrical rapture, "and every voice shouted for joy. From the oceans to the mountains, and from town to town, the cry was Freedom! Freedom! and the women formed themselves into bands, and went from house to house, serenading those who had been most conspicuous in expelling the invaders."

Rather, more important than this subtle alignment of mood between Brown and historical events is his direct linkage of the St. Domingo slave fight for freedom with the American slaves' fight for the same freedom. "Like Nat Turner, the Spartacus of the Southampton revolt, who fled with his brave band to the Virginia swamps," Brown tells us, "Toussaint and his generals took to the mountains." Nor .does Brown leave it at this. His final clarion call to the American slaves to arm and free themselves is much more direct and forceful than his mood alignment above or his softened verse exhortation from "Childe Harold" in the beginning of the speech. Indeed, it is a real call to arms.

> Who knows but that a Toussaint, a Christophe, a Rigaud, a Clervoux, and a Dessalines, may some day appear in the Southern States of this Union? That they are there, no one will doubt. That their souls are thirsting for liberty, all will admit. The spirit that caused the blacks to take up arms, and to shed their blood in the American revolutionary war, is still amongst the slaves of the South; and, if we are not mistaken, the day is not far distant when the revolution of St. Domingo will be reënacted in South Carolina and Louisiana.

In fact, Brown pronounces benediction over this possibility when he invokes Thomas Jefferson officially to sanction it on religious and practical grounds. Thus Brown concludes the whole speech by quoting Jefferson's fears that just such a righteous revolt would take place in the South. "Indeed," Jefferson is quoted as saying, "I tremble for my country when I reflect that God is just; that his justice cannot sleep forever; that, considering numbers, nature, and natural means only, a revolution of the wheel of fortune, an exchange of situation, is among possible events; that it may become probable by supernatural interference!"

Nor does Brown let the moment of self-righteous strength and determination pass into Jefferson's hands alone; for it is William Wells Brown, the fugitive slave determined to be free, who passes final judgment on the thoughts of revolution and the hope they offer for the future. Immediately following Jefferson, then, in the final voice of the address, Brown rises to full height and dramatically repeats his call to arms. "And, should such a contest take place," he tells us,

the God of Justice will be on the side of the oppressed blacks. The exasperated genius of Africa would rise from the depths of the ocean, and show its threatening form; and war against the tyrants would be the rallying cry. The indignation of the slaves of the South would kindle a fire so hot that it would melt their chains, drop by drop, until not a single link would remain; and the revolution that was commenced in 1776 would then be finished, and the glorious sentiments of the Declaration of Independence, "That all men are created equal, and endowed by their Creator with certain inalienable rights, among which are life, liberty, and the pursuit of happiness," would be realized, and our government would no longer be the scorn and contempt of the friends of freedom in other lands, but would really be LAND OF THE FREE AND HOME OF THE BRAVE.

Brown's climactic power and determination here are unmistakeable.

With this strong note of protest our discussion of Brown

as orator concludes, since this is the last extant address we have of his. So striking is its power and tone, however, that it does deserve some further discussion, if only to understand where this new Brown had come from. To begin with, the time was 1854, only six years before the Civil War was to break out; and already people were beginning to realize the military possibilities at hand. Hinton Helper's *Impending Crisis* would be published within three years, and the country as a whole had felt itself on edge since 1850 and the emotionally charged atmosphere which led to the famous Compromise of that year.

Furthermore, Brown himself was on edge and felt from afar the probability that the South would never voluntarily give up slavery as an institution or even attempt a gradual emancipation. This truth was borne even more directly to him by the passage of the Fugitive Slave Act as part of that 1850 Compromise, which all but meant that Brown could not safely return and remain in the United States which he had left in 1848, for fear of being hunted down and returned to Southern bondage.

More important than any tension in him, however, was the fact that the young fugitive slave of 1848 was now a much more assured and self-possessed man in 1854. He had been in Europe and England sporadically for five years now, and the free air there had given him a greater sense of himself and his powers as an individual human being. Indeed it is significant that the first presentation of this speech was given in London before a sympathetic and enthusiastic British audience. Furthermore, while overseas, he had spoken to and before many imporant international figures, so that his horizons were now larger because the environment outside and the creative man within were increasingly larger.

The most profound change in Brown's life over these five years, however, came not from the people and places he had met or the geographical and sociological air he had breathed. Rather, it had come from the new Brown whom he had found inside himself. For, during this period, Brown as speaker and writer had stopped being a chattel of Enoch Price and had stopped becoming, as well, a "cared for" ward of Garrison and the Anti-Slavery Societies. Instead, unlike every other fugitive slave in Europe, he refused to accept sympathetic contributions and well meant charity to support himself and his family. Thus, with his determination not to return to America in 1850, he set out to support himself as a writer and public speaker—earning his own way on the basis of his own talents and abilities. And the culmination of this resolve, occurring just one year before *St. Domingo*, was most important. This was his publication in 1853 of *Clotel*, the first novel by an American Negro. The novel was, of course, recognized by him as the tremendous achievement which it was, and it marked his successful attainment of new heights and a powerful new sense of worth. All of this, therefore, is what had made Brown the man he was in 1854, and this is very much of the tone and feeling that lies at the heart of *St. Domingo*.

CHAPTER FIVE

Slave Narratives As A Genre: Frederick Douglass As Prototype

The second major genre on the anti-slavery scene before Brown was that of the slave narrative: a literary form which had had a long tradition before the 1840's. While the form and substance it assumed in the '40's are most significant to us because of the influence they directly exerted on the young Brown, the development of the genre as a whole is also important as a perspective for understanding the later versions. A brief survey will suffice.

The two earliest slave narratives were not really "protest" writings at all, nor did they basically emphasize or depict slavery. Coming in the latter half of the eighteenth century, they were actually closer to religious tracts and Defoe-like novels than they were to the protest autobiographies which later formed the anti-slavery "slave narratives" which we tend to refer to today. The first of these narratives, published in Boston in 1760, was *A Narrative of the Uncommon Sufferings and Surprising Deliverance of Briton Hammon, A Negro Man.* Written by Hammon himself, the book shows a certain rudimentary approach to narration of the story and description of the background setting, which in themselves tend to support the book's claim that the author and his story are genuine. As for the narrative itself, it is the account of the experiences of a slave who left Plymouth, Massachusetts with his master's permission in 1747, bound for Jamaica. The ensuing events include shipwreck, captivity by Indians, imprisonment by Spaniards, and a final, coincidental meeting with his master on a ship from England to Massachusetts. The dramatic interest of the "uncommon sufferings" is strongly interwoven with the religious perception and assumption of his "surprising deliverance," and the book tends to owe greater debts to various religious and fictional literatures of the eighteenth century than it does to anything that we would see today as uniquely slave writing of slave experiences.

The other narrative of this period was in some ways even more sensationally fictional and religious in the account of *A Narrative of the Lord's Wonderful Dealings with J. Marrant, a Black . . . Taken Down from His Own Relation.* Published in London in 1785, it was written by John Marrant, with an undetermined amount of aid by "the Rev. Mr. Aldridge," and it is most remarkable for its folk lore and its sense of the miraculous and adventurous, all within a religious framework. The best example of this perhaps is his capture by Cherokee Indians, who immediately sentence him to death. Instead of fear and lamentation, Marrant displays a blissful Christian acceptance in the face of his "martyrdom," and this unnerves the savages to the point that they delay the execution and bring Marrant before their king to face trial. In short order the king demands his death, a Pocahontas-like princess pleads for his life, Marrant miraculously prays to his God in the Indians' own language, and the whole tribe is converted. Action, pathos, miraculous adventure: Marrant's *Narrative* has all of these, and consequently is an extremely unique book, having little relation to the later slave narratives which we are ultimately concerned with.

In the next sixty years, several other narratives and memoirs were published by authors who identified themselves as "a Native of Africa," a "Man of Colour," "an African Prince,"

etc.; but most of these have little relevance to our interest in
Brown. Some, like *The Slave; or, Memoirs of Archy Moore*
in 1836, are clearly not the work of an ex-slave at all, often
being imposter autobiographies of a fictional "slave"; others,
like the *Anecdotes and Memoirs of William Boen* in 1834,
are so concerned with the writer's theological beliefs and debts
to Quakerism, Methodism, etc. that they lose all personal individuality in the welter of their religious rhetoric.

With the birth of William Lloyd Garrison's *Liberator* and
the development of the American Anti-Slavery Society in New
England in the 1830's, however, slave narratives began to take
on a new importance and a new purpose. They were now
vehicles of abolitionist propaganda, and this is where our basic
interest lies. For these slave narratives were one of the two
dominant forms of prose literary expression which Brown
found on stage when he made his escape from slavery in the
South and finally found himself working directly in the anti-
slavery cause.

As a group, these narratives had one central purpose, and
that was to realistically describe and portray slavery and its
evils from a concrete, first person, eye-witness point of view—
a process very much linked to those orations which we noted
above. In fact, to some extent we might almost be justified
in seeing the slave narratives as essentially anti-slavery orations in print.

On the other hand, of course, there were considerable differences despite this congruency of purpose. For one thing,
the slave narrative was longer: was a book of more than one
hundred pages usually, which offered the writer far more room
to attack and document slavery's cruelties in far greater detail.
Furthermore, as a detailed account of the slave narrator's own
experiences in the South, the narrative was usually more personal than the general oration, and it characteristically stuck
closer to tangible facts and events without as much of the general rhetoric and abstract philosophizing which the oration
was often given over to. Thus, quite frequently the extra detail

which the narrative went into would be of a specifically personal, and therefore unique and exotic, nature which made each narrative intriguingly different from its brethren. Likewise, and perhaps most importantly, this combination of detail and personal voice led to a book which frequently had a characteristic tone and personality all of its own—a far cry from the more "standardized" tone of the many slave orations.

We might best begin our discussion now by looking at the similarities involved.

In keeping with their joint polemical purpose, the narratives had certain approaches and materials in common. To begin with, they were out to enumerate slavery's cruelty, and therefore dedicated both direct description and supporting explanation to accomplish this purpose. Furthermore, given the extensive space, the more personal involvement, and the narrative structure itself, these books also featured forceful dramatization of some of slavery's evils which were too important to be merely enumerated.

Most often enumerated and dramatized here were aspects of the slave's early life and the sort of cruel dehumanization which was inflicted on all slaves generally under slavery; and our best example of this is Frederick Douglass' *Narrative of the Life of Frederick Douglass: An American Slave, Written by Himself,* which was published in 1845 by the Anti-Slavery Press in Boston. Written expressly in order to prove to the anti-slavery lecture circuit that Douglass was, indeed, a fugitive slave, even though his rapid growth as a sophisticated and talented orator seemed to imply otherwise, its importance to us is that it represents so well the kind of general material which these fugitive slave narratives had in common.

Essentially because it was a birth-to-maturity narrative, a kind of realistic "Bildungsroman", the question of self-identity and the lack of a complete family played a large role in this sort of book. Indeed, allusions to this were often the opening note to be found in the narrative, as the fugitive slave essentially "began at the beginning" and simply told his story from there. "I have no accurate knowledge of my age," Douglass begins, "never having seen any authentic record containing it. By far the larger part of the slaves know as little of their ages as horses know of theirs, and it is the wish of most masters within my knowledge to keep their slaves thus ignorant." In fact, "I do not remember to have ever met a slave who could tell of his birthday."

Generally there was no lamentation over the absence of a father's love, since the slave had never had such love at all and therefore felt no immediate sense of loss. When the father was infrequently mentioned, he was generally seen as some amorphic, distant figure who served as a peripheral target of moral reproach. "Father he might be, and not be husband," Douglass tells us in his later, 1892 version of his *Narrative*, "and could sell his own child without incurring reproach, if in its veins coursed one drop of African blood." But generally there was little mention of the father, except implicitly in the basic discussion of the slaves major lack of identity, birthright, and even birthday.

Of greater interest to these narrators was their early and brutal separation from their mothers. "My mother and I were separated when I was but an infant—before I knew her as my mother," Douglass tells us. "It is a common custom, in the part of Maryland from which I ran away, to part children from their mothers at a very early age. Frequently, before the child has reached its twelfth month, its mother is taken from it, and hired out on some farm a considerable distance off, and the child is placed under the care of an old woman, too old for field labor." Behind this forced separation of mother and child was a very definite, premeditated goal: the complete dissolution of any sense of a family unit. "For what this separation is done, I do not know," Douglass observes, "unless it be to hinder the development of the child's affection toward its mother, and to blunt and destroy the natural affection of the mother for the child. This is the inevitable result."

Needless to say, such a calculated dehumanization process

was a crucial pillar holding up slavery's magnolia-stained mansion. On the one hand, it meant that the slave was now more easily sold and managed as simply a single cog in the vast and brutal machinery of the "peculiar institution." On the other hand, and perhaps most importantly, it meant that the slaveowners could salve their church-going consciences by blandly claiming that the Christian stricture to love one's neighbor did not apply if one could prove to oneself that that neighbor which one was flogging was not really a fellow man at all, but actually only a member of some sub-species or other to which Christianity did not apply. The "inevitable results" here, then, formed the cornerstone of the slave system.

Interestingly enough, in several of the narratives the most poignant allusion to this lack of identity came later in the slave's life, when the question of name faced him and he suddenly realized how dear the mere letters of his name were to him and to his desire to get some tangible order in his life. Brown's discussion of this is perhaps the most sensitive, yet Douglass responds most explicitly to this point. When he first arrived in New Bedford, Massachusetts, therefore, Douglass found it necessary to change part of his present name for a number of practical reasons. He then gave his initial host, Mr. Nathan Johnson, "the privilege of choosing me a name, but told him he must not take from me the name of 'Frederick,'" for, as Douglass continues, "I must hold on to that, to preserve a sense of my identity."

One further common problem for the fugitive slave narrators is important here, and it is basically unique for these narratives as a whole. This was the question of how mulatto slaves fared under slavery's system, and it is relevant here because so many of the fugitive slaves were mulattoes and this condition was relevant to both their lives in the South and their ability to escape North and then write about their experiences. "I know of such cases," Douglass tells us about mulattoes whose masters are also their unproclaimed fathers, "and it is worthy of remark that such slaves invariably suffer greater hardships, and have more to contend with, than others," largely because their very presence is "a constant offence to their mistress," who is consequently "ever disposed to find fault with them" and who is "never better pleased than when she sees them under the lash."

As interesting as Douglass' comment is, it is significant as well. Many of these narratives, as a matter of fact, make specific and sometimes extensive comments on this subject, and the reason for this is the fact that the majority of these fugitive slaves were, themselves, mulattoes. Being the unproclaimed offspring of the plantation's master or his family, such a slave had both unique tribulations and equally unique advantages.

While the disadvantages of this "relationship" were sometimes painful, the advantages far outweighed them. First of all, it meant that the mulatto slaves were generally made house servants and personal valets, and thus were not, as were so many field hands, physically beaten and overworked so much that they became resigned to their lot. Instead, they had just enough freedom to recognize its existence and consequently to desire more. Thus, even though all these narrators agree, like Lewis Clarke, that such house slaves were "constantly exposed to the whims and passions of every member of the family," these pains and lesser attacks were not physically or emotionally debilitating; they were, instead, constant spurs to escape and achieve the security and peace which freedom would bring.

Another advantage for the mulatto house slave was the fact that his association around the house, its activities, and its occupants meant that he became better educated, could speak better, and thus was in a better position to make a successful escape. Relatedly, it also meant that he could then write about that escape later in a literary mode which was more rapidly mastered because of the quasi-education which his slave experiences had given him.

Finally, there was one other major advantage. This came from the fact that they had, obviously, lighter skin, which made flight and escape North so much easier and less conspicuous. This was especially important since the runaway was forced to travel through regions in which slave catchers were constantly on the alert for runaways who, if captured and returned, could net the catcher a sizeable reward. All of this is why these narratives were so frequently concerned with pertinent side discussions of the life of the mulatto slave in the South.

After this kind of personal discussion of childhood and a slave's early problems, the narratives next devoted their time to enumerating the various aspects of general cruelty which the slave faced as he grew up. Cited, of course, were the various "paraphernalia" like whips, chains, etc., which we noted above in the orations. Yet the focal point for most of these discussions was the description and enumeration of the kind of masters and overseers which the slave so often had to live and work under.

"The overseer's name was Plummer," Douglass tells us as early as page four, "A miserable drunkard, a profane swearer, and a savage monster. He always went armed with a cowskin and a heavy cudgel. I have known him to cut and slash the women's heads so horribly, that even master would be enraged at his cruelty." Master, however, was not exactly a "humane slaveholder" himself. "Instead he would at times seem to take great pleasure in whipping a slave," so that Douglass often was "awakened at the dawn of day by the most heart-rending shrieks of an own aunt of mine, whom he used to tie up to a hoist, and whip upon her naked back till she was literally covered with blood."

Nor did Douglass and the typical narrative content itself with mere enumeration like this. Often it let itself go into concrete detail in order to forcefully emphasize the cruelty involved. Thus we note the graphic descriptiveness and semi-

frenzied rhythm which Douglass employs in a passage immediately following the mention of his master's whipping of his
aunt.

> No words, no tears, no prayers, from his gory victim,
> seemed to move his iron heart from its bloody purpose.
> The louder she screamed, the harder he whipped; and
> where the blood ran fastest, there he whipped longest. He
> would whip her to make her scream, and whip her to
> make her hush; and not until overcome by fatigue, would
> he cease to swing the blood-clotted cowskin.

The ultimate form of this emphasis was direct dramatization of a moment of slavery's cruelty. Instead of mere discussion and enumeration, narration and description were forcefully used to make the moment come vibratingly alive before
the eyes and feelings of the reader. After discussing the severe
cruelty of the overseer Gore, then, Douglass recalls an incident
to support his declaration of Gore's "savage barbarity" which
"was equalled only by his consummate coolness." The incident
deals with a slave named Demby who, in order to escape the
pain of an undeserved whipping, bolted from Gore and
plunged into a creek up to his shoulders, refusing to come out.
Gore's reaction is then dramatized for us.

> Mr. Gore told him that he would give him three calls,
> and that, if he did not come out at the third call, he
> would shoot him. The first call was given. Demby made
> no response, but stood his ground. The second and third
> calls were given with the same result. Mr. Gore then,
> without consultation or deliberation with anyone, not even
> giving Demby an additional call, raised his musket to his
> face, taking deadly aim at his standing victim, and in an
> instant poor Demby was no more. His mangled body sank
> out of sight, and blood and brain marked the water where
> he had stood.

Lest we think that Douglass merely stumbled onto this dramatization approach as a mere extension of his personal interests, his statement following this section on Gore convinces us otherwise. "Whilst I am detailing bloody deeds which took place during my stay on Colonel Lloyd's plantation," he tells us, "I will briefly narrate another," at which point he relates the graphic details of another "fiendish transaction." Clearly Douglass is very conscious of his purpose and his technique here—as was the whole genre of fugitive slave narratives.

Discussion, enumeration, and dramatization—these were the basic approaches of the typical slave narrative. At the same time, since the purpose of these narratives was so clearly shared by the anti-slavery oration as well, and since a large number of the slave narrators were also anti-slavery orators, the narratives did contain certain elements which were "traditionally" used in the abolitionist speeches which we examined above. Once again, Douglass' *Narrative* is as prototypic as any.

There was, first of all, frequent use of the same anti-democratic and anti-Christian ironies which the orations so heavily depended upon. These were far less frequent or crucial for the narratives, yet, when they did appear, they were both incisive and emphatic. Discussing how his final masters, the Thomas Aulds, often starved their slaves and deliberately gave them less food than was necessary for them to live on, Douglass notes ironically how

A great many times have we poor creatures been nearly perishing with hunger, when food in abundance lay mouldering in the safe and smoke-house, and our pious mistress was aware of the fact; and yet that mistress and her husband would kneel every morning, and pray that God would bless them in basket and store!

On a related subject Douglass becomes even more discursive. Noting how in August of 1832 Captain Auld attended a Methodist camp-meeting and there "experienced religion," Douglass records how he, Douglass, initially indulged the faint hope that Auld's conversion would lead him to emancipate his slaves or at least become kinder and more humane. Instead, Auld became worse, and his new sense of religion only cemented and entrenched his basic cruelty. It is as if it served somehow as an authority to rationalize and justify the evil inside him. "Prior to his conversion," Douglass notes, Auld "relied upon his own depravity to shield and sustain him in savage brutality." However, "after his conversion, he found religious sanction and support for his slaveholding cruelty."

Nor does Douglass allow the irony here to mutely affect us on its own. He almost immediately proceeds to provide a more dramatized example of this abuse of Christian theology. "I have seen him tie up a lame young woman," he tells us,

> and whip her with a heavy cowskin upon her naked shoulders, causing the warm red blood to drip; and, in justification of the bloody deed, he would quote this passage of Scripture—"He that knoweth his master's will, and doeth it not, shall be beaten with many stripes.

The other major approach which these narratives seemed to inherit from the orations was the use of "borrowed verse" which formed so much of the emotional core in the anti-slavery address. Discussing his grandmother, who, at the death of her old masters, found herself left alone, since all her children had been sold from her, Douglass recalls how her new masters "put up a little mud-chimney" and forced her to support herself despite her great age. Far worse than that was the complete loneliness which they forced upon her as they were "virtually turning her out to die!"

> If my old grandmother now lives, she lives to suffer in utter loneliness; she lives to remember and mourn over

the loss of children, the loss of grandchildren, and the loss
of great grandchildren. They are, in the language of the
slave's poet, Whittier,—

> "Gone, gone, sold and gone
> To the rice swamp dank and lone,
> From Virginia hills and waters—
> Woe is me, my stolen daughters!"

One final aspect of the narratives which was frequently included was a discussion of how the narrator received his education: what opened his eyes to the possibility of escape; what
aided him in that escape; how he learned to read and write
well enough to be able to record his own narrative of those
various experiences. We will discuss in greater detail later the
polemical importance of this sort of discussion, and the importance which was placed on each narrative being actually
"written by himself;" but perhaps all we need do here is note
the general approach which the material took.

In accounting for his eager interest in education and the
ability to read and write, Douglass relates a very significant
anecdote about his early mistress, "Miss Sophie" Auld. A
"woman of the kindest heart and finest feelings" before slavery's "fatal poison" of "irresponsible power" distorted and
warped her basic goodness, she warmly began teaching Douglass his ABC's when he came to live with the Aulds in Baltimore at age twelve. At the point of progress at which Douglass could spell three and four letter words, however, Mr. Auld
discovered his wife's efforts and immediately forbade her to
continue. His words to his wife sank deeply into the youngster
as they revealed to him the crucial importance of reading.

"A nigger should know nothing," Douglass remembers Auld
as saying, "but to obey his master—to do as he is told. Learning would *spoil* the best nigger in the world." As Auld continued, the importance of education became even clearer to
young Douglass. "Now if you teach that nigger how to read,

there would be no keeping him. It would forever unfit him to
be a slave." As these words sunk into Douglass, they awoke
in him a determined desire to learn reading and writing. "It
was a new and special revelation," he notes, "explaining dark
and mysterious things, with which my youthful understanding
had struggled, but struggled in vain."

> I now understood what had been to me a most perplexing
> difficulty—to wit, the white man's power to enslave the
> black man. It was a grand achievement, and I prized it
> highly. From that moment, I understood the pathway
> from slavery to freedom.

From this moment on, Douglass's mistress was harshly careful to keep Douglass from reading anything, and this essentially began the twisting inside herself which finally turned
her into a crueler person than her husband. By now, however,
the desire for knowledge was burning strongly in Douglass,
and he simply sought out other "teachers" from whom to learn.
"The plan which I adopted, and the one by which I was most
successful," he tells us, "was that of making friends of all the
little white boys whom I met in the street. As many of these
as I could, I converted into teachers." Whenever he ran an
errand, therefore, he would take his book with him; and by
doing his errand quickly, "I found time to get a lesson before
my return." He would play and read with the poor white children in the Baltimore streets, sharing some of the Auld's sur-
plus bread with them while they, in return, "would give me
that more valuable bread of knowledge." In this manner Douglass finally learned to read.

Once he had this ability, a whole new world opened up for
him, and much of this new world was responsible for renewing
his realization of slavery's evil and his determination to escape
it. Most influential was a book called *The Columbian Orator*,
which he stumbled upon at this time. Such items in it as Sher-

idan's speech on Catholic emancipation led Douglass to acquire a new level of hatred for slavery, as Sheridan's powerful vindication of human rights on a philosophic level confirmed Douglass' own deep feelings on the subject. "The more I read," he recalls, "the more I was led to abhor and detest my enslavers. I could regard them in no other light than a band of successful robbers, who had left their homes, and gone to Africa, and stolen us from our homes, and in a strange land reduced us to slavery." The ferment inside Douglass was now intense.

At times, however, the ferment was more pain than satisfaction. For while Douglass' reading and thoughts had opened his eyes to "the horrible pit," it had offered no "ladder upon which to get out." The ladder soon came with the word "abolition" in his reading and with his growing realization that to escape North was the path to freedom.

One ability now remained for him to master, and that was the ability to write. Using as models the marked timbers for ships that he came across in the ship-yards to which he was hired, he soon began copying them in chalk on board fences, brick walls, and pavements. He would also challenge to contests, boys whom he knew could write; and, even as he lost, he learned those new letters which the other boy had to offer. Finally, when he had progressed to a higher level, he found a number of his master's son's old copy-books, stored as prized possessions in the attic. Thereafter he spent every free hour he had copying the books' words over and over again, until, even before his escape North, he was a good writer. In fact, it is significant to note that the climax of this development might very well have been Douglass' escape North *because* of his ability to forge traveling slips for himself and other slaves to make their attempt North. This initial flight was aborted through certain lack of secrecy among the participating slaves themselves, but the point is that Douglass' ability to write was so important and so well developed by this period in his life, that less than a year before his real escape through other means, he was almost able to *write* himself and others into freedom.

With this mention of Douglass' ultimate means of escaping, we come to the final trait of the general slave narrative which Douglass offers us. This is the practical and sensitive reluctance to disclose definite details. Such reluctance is especially significant with Douglass, especially when we remember that he originally undertook the *Narrative* in direct answer to those abolitionist audiences who, because of the sophistication and smoothness of Douglass' orations in front of them, soon came to doubt that he had ever really been a slave. For this reason Douglass wrote his *Narrative* to prove his past status.

Even so, at the point in the *Narrative* when he came to discuss his escape, Douglass' concern for the safety of his fellow slaves still in the South and his concern for their chances of escape kept him from revealing any details about the various people and devices which aided his escape. As he notes in his discussion, "I have never approved of the very public manner in which some of our western friends [in the Ohio, Pennsylvania, and western New York areas which aided William Wells Brown] have conducted what they call the *underground railroad*, but which, I think, by their open declarations, has been made most emphatically the *upperground railroad*." As he notes, they "do nothing towards enlightening the slave, whilst they do much towards enlightening the master. They stimulate him to greater watchfulness, and enhance his power to capture his slave." In short, Douglass concludes, there is more at stake here than the writing of a book to satisfy a general reader's curiosity. There is, as he felt all his life, a much higher priority: that of the suffering human beings involved.

CHAPTER SIX

Slave Narratives Continued:
Unique Personalities And Purposes

Narrative of the Sufferings of Lewis Clarke

A second representative narrative was that written by Lewis Clarke in the same year as Douglass' work. Containing much of the same material as its counterpart, Clarke's *Narrative of the Sufferings of Lewis Clarke, during a Captivity of More than Twenty-Five Years among the Algerines of Kentucky* is of greater interest to us, however, for its striking and incisive personal tone. Discussing his grandfather in the opening paragraph, Clarke observes that "He was considered a very respectable man among his fellow robbers—the slave holders," and he follows this opening broadside with what is almost the keynote passage of the book.

The night in which I was born, I have been told, was dark and terrible, black as the night for which Job prayed, when he besought the clouds to pitch their tent round about the place of his birth; and my life of slavery was but too exactly prefigured by the stormy elements that hovered over the first hour of my being.

In much the same vein, Clarke immediately continues and

describes his first harsh mistress, in flashing metaphors that are simultaneously bitter and somehow sharply comic.

> At the age of six or seven I fell into the hands of . . . Mrs. Belsey Benton, whose character will be best known when I have told the horrid wrongs which she heaped upon me for ten years. If there are any *she* spirits that come up from hell, and take possession of one part of mankind, I am sure she is one of that sort.

He then discusses the circumstances surrounding his acquisition by "this monster woman," and in the process discusses how she set the whole Benton family to fighting "a regular war of four years." As he observes,

> These wars are very common among the Algerines of Kentucky; indeed, slave-holders have not arrived at that degree of civilization that enables them to live in tolerable peace, though united by the nearest family ties . . . Some of the slave-holders may have a *wide* house, but one of the *cat-handed*, snake-eyed, brawling women, which slavery produces, can fill it from cellar to garret.

And later, on his first ride home with Mrs. Benton and her children, Clarke recalls how she made him sit on the bottom of the carriage and how she simultaneously set her "imps" to pinching him and pulling his ears and hair. These children, according to Clarke, "were stirred up by their mother like a litter of young wolves to torment me in every way possible. In the meantime I was compelled by the old she wolf, to call them "Master," "Mistress," and bow to them and obey them at first call."

Significantly enough, not only did Clarke let the fire and strength of his metaphors speak for him, but he was concerned enough with his polemical purpose to occasionally break in and didactically commit himself directly. Again referring to his termagant mistress, Clarke describes the punishment he received for merely drinking out of the same vessel which Mrs. Benton's children were using. "She expressed her utter abhorrence of such an act," he tells us, "by throwing my head violently back, and dashing into my face two dippers of water."

The shower of water was followed by a heavier shower of *kicks*—yes, delicate reader, this *lady* did not hesitate to *kick*, as well as cuff in a very plentiful manner—

Just as Clarke enumerated and commented on the torments he faced at Mrs. Benton's hands, so was he even more graphic about other horrors that occurred in the slavery system at large. One day, after committing some minor offense, Clarke was sent by his mistress to Mr. Benton's blacksmith shop. He refused to go, and graphically relates to us "the shop mode of punishment" which Mr. Benton normally administered there. He gives us a past example where a slave whom Mr. Benton owned but hired out had kept fifty cents of his weekly wages, instead of turning it all over to Benton as the "peculiar institution" demanded. When this "came to the knowledge of the Master," Clarke tells us,

He called for the money and it was not spent—it was handed to him; but there was the horrid *intention* of keeping it. The enraged Master put a handful of nail rods into the fire, and when they were *red hot* took them out, and *cooled* one after another of them in the blood and flesh of the poor slave's back.

Clarke concludes the narration of his time under Mrs. Benton by deliberately diverting attention from his experiences and consequently devoting some paragraphs to "giving a few more incidents" of Mrs. Benton's character. He further addresses the reader directly concerning the "portrait" of the woman, and discusses with us his reason for having "taken great pains" in compiling and presenting this "true to nature" picture. "I have given it from no malice, no feeling of resentment toward her," he tells us, "but that the world may know what is done by *slavery*, and that slave holders may know, that their crimes will come to light." The polemical purpose of this narrative—as all the narratives—is thereby made clear. It is basically an indictment drawn up, graphically pictured, and, in Clarke's case, forcefully and sardonically put forth.

As a partial afterthought we find another aspect of Clarke's approach which was standard slave narrative approach, and this was the invocation of Christian concern and reprieve on the head of the slaveholder who had just been so graphically and dramatically damned. "I hope and pray," he tells us, "that Mrs. B. will repent of her many aggravated sins before it is too late." The interest of such a statement, of course, was the position of moral superiority which it offered the former slave as he discussed the slaveholders who once had claimed a total superiority over him. Consequently, the general use of this approach was in keeping with the sense of Christian "moral suasion" by which Garrison and the early Abolitionists sought to undermine and destroy slavery in the consciences of those whites in the country who could be converted by an understanding of the moral evil which fundamentally lay at the heart of that "peculiar institution."

As a footnote it may be of interest to remember here that Clarke's overall tone is generally much stronger and more incisive than this "forgiving" Christian tone; and perhaps we should emphasize the power and denunciation he injects into this moment itself when he talks of Mrs. Benton's "many and aggravated sins." Thus we can almost see how this "benediction" and "plaintive Christian" approach is probably more a technique than a real statement by Clarke: for he was too directly involved—both physically and emotionally—in the warped cruelties of slavery to ever really achieve the detachment and serenity which such a "benediction" basically requires.

Intriguingly enough, while Clarke's *Narrative* is significant to us principally for the unique personality of its biting, incisive tone, the tone occasionally lightens and is capable of other, seemingly antithetical, qualities as well: sentimentality, detachment, and even a genially humorous wit.

Referring to his emotions that night after Mrs. Benton's kicking and verbal abuse of his seven-year-old's feelings, Clarke suddenly becomes very sentimental with us and raises directly the tragedy of broken families and uprooted slave children. In the process he even lapses into "borrowed" verse.

If there is any human being on earth, who has been so blessed as never to have *tasted* the cup of sorrow, and therefore is unable to conceive of *suffering*, if there be one so lost to all feeling as even to say that slaves do not suffer, when *families* are separated, let such an one go to the ragged quilt which was my couch and pillow and stand there night after night, for long weary hours, and see the bitter tears streaming down the face of that more than orphan boy, while with half suppressed sighs and sobs, he calls again and again upon his absent mother.

"Say, Mother, wast thou conscious of the
        tears I shed,—
Hovered thy spirit o'er thy sorrowing son?
Wretch even *then*! Life's journey just begun."

In a different vein, Clarke is occasionally quite witty in his use of dramatic structure and common sense tone. Describing an "offense" he committed in letting a turkey escape from its pen, he notes how Mrs. Benton was enraged. Feeling that no punishment which she could mete out would adequately cover such a heinous offense, she sent Clarke in to wake up Mr. Benton, who "had gone to bed drunk, and was now as fast asleep as drunkards ever are." Mrs. Benton's command was that Clarke should wake up the drunken warlord and "ask him to be *kind* enough to give me fifty good smart lashes." Clarke's reaction to this is direct and characteristically expressive: "To be *whipped* is bad enough—to *ask* for it is worse—to ask a drunken man to whip you is too bad."

Related to this semi-comic wit are the times when Clarke dips into the picaresque mold and writes with a dry wit about several "escapades" which slaves often found themselves involved in, when "we were cheated out of our two meals a day." At such times, Clarke continues dryly, "we always felt it a kind of special duty and privilege to make up in some way the deficiency." On such a human interest, comically heroic note, he launches into a number of incidents that occurred in this vein. Prefacing his first anecdote with the austere declaration of how a slave caught stealing a chicken or pig "had his back scored" most unmercifully. "Nevertheless," he notes dryly, "the pigs would die without being sick or squealing once, and the hens, chickens, and turkeys, sometimes disappeared and never stuck up a feather to tell where they were buried. The old goose would sometimes exchange her whole nest of eggs for round pebbles; and patient as that animal is, this quality was exhausted, and she was obliged to leave her nest with no train of offspring behind her."

Significantly enough, however, Clarke never allows the picaresque to be the sole note of such a section. Thus even as he records with heroic delight the forays of one old slave woman who "was altogether too keen and too shrewd for the best of them," he does not fail to root his delight in the fertile soil of righteous indignation and moral justice. Thus he tells us how she "would go out to the corn crib, with her basket, watch her opportunity, with one effective blow pop over a little pig, slip him into her basket and put the cobs on top, trudge off to her cabin, and look just as innocent *as though she had a right to eat the work of her own hands.*" (Italics mine) Indeed, he follows this tone of just indignation by noting in the very next sentence how it "was kind of first principle, too, in her code of morals, that they that *worked* had a right to eat."

Despite our interest in the unique narrative voice here and the interesting power and range which it attains, we need to remember constantly that Clarke's purpose in writing it was not so much the indulgence of his personal feelings or expressiveness as it was the same indictment of slavery which lay at the heart of all these narratives. Indeed, when we come to discuss the hard core polemic here, we must necessarily discuss the whole book which was published as the *Narrative of the Sufferings . . . of Lewis Clarke.*

The "Narrative" itself covers only half the book, and the sort of material which accompanies it is of equal interest. Preceding the "Narrative" is the standard biographical and polemical preface of these narratives, verifying the realisticness of Clarke and his story, while simultaneously telling us of the "most utter abhorrence of the Slave System" which the story has raised in others and should raise in us.

Following the central narration is an "Appendix" which contains a number of interesting items. There is, first of all, a four-page 'Sketch of the Clarke Family' by Lewis, listing and numbering the members in "1" through "10" order. While its purpose is indicatively biographical, numerous opportunities for direct polemic and dramatized cruelty are taken and elaborated upon, as when we learn in our discussion of Archy's death that "— the inheritance of the widow and poor orphans is, LABOR WITHOUT WAGES—WRONGS WITH NO REDRESS—SEPARATION FROM EACH OTHER FOR LIFE."

Immediately after this "Sketch" come nineteen pages devoted to a "Questions and Answers" section which is also written by Lewis and which also contains the same didactic human interest material which we found in the "Narrative" and the "Sketch" above. "How do slaves spend the Sabbath?"; "Are families often separated?"; "What makes them wash slaves in salt and water after they whip them?" These are the sorts of questions which "are often asked me, when I meet

the people in public," and Lewis then proceeds to answer them
graphically and pointedly in his characteristically strong and
vivid style. And should the reader not realize what moral to
draw from these answers, Clarke uses his concluding paragraph to tell us, in a voice that suddenly becomes more oratorical than narrative and one which might very well have been
the forerunner of Douglass' major point in his 1846 speech
which we examined above. "Now, in conclusion," he tells us,

> I just want to say, that all the abuses which I have re-
> lated, are *necessary*, if slavery must continue to exist. It
> is impossible to cut off these abuses and keep slavery
> alive. Now if you do not approve of these horrid suffer-
> ings, I entreat you to lift up your voice and your hand
> against the whole system, and, with one united effort,
> overturn the abominations of centuries, and restore scat-
> tered families to each other; pour light upon millions of
> dark minds, and make a thousand, yea, ten times ten
> thousand abodes of wretchedness and wo [sic], to hail
> and bless you as angels of mercy sent for their deliver-
> ance.

Having soared to such oratorical heights, Clarke's own
work in the book is completed. Still, the abolitionistic purpose
of the book is not deemed satisfied, and we find a final twenty-
one pages consisting of "a few pieces" of prose and poetry
which give "an accurate description of Slavery" and which
contain a certain sentimental verse value as well. John Greenleaf Whittier and Cassius M. Clay discuss and "denounce
slavery and the slave trade forever." Various excerpts from
Southern and Northern newspapers document the cruelties involved in the slave system. And finally, a bevy of abolitionist
poems concludes the section: some directly didactic ("And
shall we scoff at Europe's kings,/ When Freedom's fire is dim
with us,/ And round our country's altar clings/ The damning
shade of Slavery's curse?") and some in vivid parody form

("Come, saints and sinners, hear me tell,/ How pious priests whip Jack and Nell,/ And women buy, and children sell,/ And preach all sinners down to Hell,/ And *sing* of heavenly union.")

This section concludes the book, and it shows us just how closely intertwined the direct polemic of abolitionist oratory and verse was with indirect, narrative enumeration and dramatization. They were, essentially, two sides of the same Anti-Slavery Society coin, and we only need look at their harmonious fusion in Lewis Clarke's "anthologistic" *Narrative* and its printing "At the Stone Steps, 37 Cornhill," Boston, to realize how unified were these two prose forms of abolitionist literature.

Narrative of the Life and Adventures of Henry Bibb

A second narrative which is of interest to us for its unique features is Henry Bibb's *Narrative of the Life and Adventures of Henry Bibb*. Unlike many of the narrators, Bibb begins a direct, expository denunciation of slavery very early in the book and actually devotes much of his first chapter to a general discussion of its evils. Interestingly enough, however, despite this early emergence into direct polemic, Bibb is actually not as strong and vitriolic as either Brown or Clarke. The reason for this is his narrative perspective and the unique tone of voice which brings it to us.

The opening sentence seems a somewhat tame echo of Brown's savage natal allusion to his master as "the man who stole me;" likewise, it refrains from reaching for the power and dramaticness of Clarke's description of his birth night as one "dark and terrible." Instead, Bibb merely notes how "I was born May, 1815, of a slave mother, in Shelby County, Kentucky, and was claimed as the property of David White Esq." Nor does he attempt to put dramatic teeth into the waiting jaws of "property" here.

Discussing the slave's general lack of a father in the next

paragraph, he again follows the usual format and notes how "It is almost impossible for slaves to give a correct account of their male parentage" and how "All that I know about it is, that my mother informed me that my father's name was JAMES BIBB." There is a certain absence of fire and emotion here as the discussion is considerably detached and structured.

His discussion of his separation from his mother also is stated without emotion, and actually seems to recall in Bibb no real bitterness or pangs of remorse. Indeed he recalls the period not in terms of his mother at all, but in terms of the daughter of his new master. The terms of this allusion are of even greater softness here, as he sees this girl as "my play-mate when we were children." At the same time he does show some biting emotion in his discussion of his own early life, when he notes how "I was brought up in the Counties of Shelby, Henry, Oldham, and Trimble," and immediately amends that in a sharper voice to read: "Or, more correctly speaking, in the above counties, I may safely say, I was *flogged up*; for where I should have received moral, mental and religious instructions, I received stripes without number, the object of which was to degrade and keep me in subordination."

Related to this general tone of moderation and philosophic detachment is Bibb's evaluation of the uprootedness of his early years as a house slave and his overall feeling that it was good for him, both because it taught him about freedom and how to attain it and because it gave him an education. As he discusses this, he notes that "although I have suffered much from the lash, and for want of food and raiment; I confess that it was no disadvantage to be passed through the hands of so many families, as the only source of information that I had to enlighten my mind, consisted in what I could see and hear from others." "Enlightenment," then, like the "moral, mental and religious instruction" which he mentioned above, seems very important to Bibb, and perhaps this basic nature and interest of his accounts for the general softness in his narrative tone. Perhaps also his personalized and emotional closeness to these families (to the point that the daughter of one of his masters could be seen as a "playmate") also accounts for his balanced, philosophic voice.

Eventually we see the ultimate fusion at work here: Bibb's personal desire for selfhood and freedom is linked with his profound sense of religious order in the universe. The former point comes early. One of Bibb's first major "trades" which "I learned to perfection," he tells us, was "the art of running away." In fact, he "made a regular business of it" because it reflected his basic refusal to be whipped or degraded as a human being. "It is useless for a poor helpless slave, to resist a white man in a slaveholding State," he tells us, so that "the only weapon of self-defence I could use successfully, was that of deception." The result was that he often spent "almost half my time in the woods, running from under the bloody lash," and he continued to exercise this basic sense of integrity and self-assertion "until I had broken the bands of slavery, and landed myself safely in Canada, where I was regarded as a man, and not as a thing."

The reason for this strong sense of self-worth is both personal and religious, and we see Bibb's profound consciousness of this as he discusses his constant "longing desire to be free."

It kindled a fire of liberty within my breast which has never yet been quenched. This seemed to be a part of my nature; it was first revealed to me by the inevitable laws of Nature's God. I could see that the All-wise Creator, had made man a free, moral, intelligent and accountable being; capable of knowing good and evil. And I believed then, as I believe now, that every man has a right to wages for his labor; a right to his own wife and children; a right to liberty and the pursuit of happiness; and a right to worship God according to the dictates of his own conscience.

Interestingly enough, however, this deep religious artery can

also lead Bibb to the shallower vein of melodrama and the
borrowed sentimentality of the standard anti-slavery verse.

> Oh! I have often wept over my condition, while saunter-
> ing through the forest, to escape cruel punishment.

> "No arm to protect me from tyrant's aggression;
> No parents to cheer me when laden with grief.
> Man may picture the bounds of the rocks and the rivers,
> The hills and the valleys, the lakes and the ocean,
> But the horrors of slavery, he never can trace."

Yet this artificial tone is quite rare in Bibb.

A very interesting aspect of this question of tone is the way
that Bibb is able to devote most of Chapter II to his famously
readable, almost light, description of the typical slave's belief
in superstition and conjuration. Initially the subject develops
from Bibb's quiet indictment of how the slaveowners deprive
their slaves of religious instruction on the Sabbath and generally keep the slaves ignorant; but it soon blossoms on its
own terms, especially when Bibb begins discussing his own
adolescent adventures with conjure powders and witchcraft.
For example, he relates how one conjurer, for a small sum
of money, "agreed to teach me to make any girl love me that
I wished."

> After I had paid him, he told me to get a bull frog, and
> take a certain bone out of the frog, dry it, and when I
> got a chance I must step up to any girl whom I wished to
> make love to me, and scratch her somewhere on her
> naked skin with this bone, and she would be certain to
> love me, and would follow me in spite of herself; no
> matter who she might be engaged to, nor who she might
> be walking with.
>
> So I got me a bone for a certain girl, whom I knew
> to be under the influence of another young man. I hap-

pened to meet her in the company of her lover, one Sunday evening, walking out; so when I got a chance, I fetched her a tremendous rasp across her neck with this bone, which made her jump. But in place of making her love me, it only made her angry with me. She felt more like running after me to retaliate on me for thus abusing her, than she felt like loving me.

Light and comic, these anecdotes at their best tend to entertain rather than morally arouse us; at their very least, they obscure all anti-slavery thoughts and feelings in us as they come so much alive on their own, human interest level. Needless to say, it is clear that Bibb is not a bitter, passionately driven man, pouring out vituperative polemic against the evils of his life in slavery, as did a narrator like Lewis Clarke. In fact, it is rather significant that conjuring and courting women not only obscure the anti-slavery purpose of the narrative for us, but they actually did, at the time of their occurrence, obscure Bibb's own desire to escape slavery. Thus he relates this "frog bone" episode immediately after a paragraph declaratively exclaiming at its conclusion how much "I was an unhappy slave!" And he introduces the anecdote with an equally significant statement. "But my attention was gradually turned in a measure from this subject" of escaping slavery, he tells us, "by being introduced into the society of young women. This for the time being took my attention from running away, as waiting on the girls appeared to be perfectly congenial to my nature."

Despite his generally human and religiously philosophic approach to life—even life under slavery—there was one aspect of slave life which very much disturbed Bibb. This was the fact that slaves were completely deprived of religious instruction and religious sanction for marriage. Immediately after Bibb's anecdote of the "frog bone," we learn that his interest in pretty girls soon led him into a serious romance which resulted in marriage to Malinda, despite the fact that

Bibb "had no intention of courting or marrying her, for I was aware that such a step would greatly obstruct my way to the land of liberty." Nevertheless, the emotional beauty of their feelings for each other conquered the practical considerations, and the two were "married"—a circumstance which now poignantly haunts Bibb more than any other evil of slavery that he will treat in his *Narrative*.

The pain here is both personal and religious, and stems from the fact that there "is no legal marriage among the slaves of the South." Religiously this bothers a man like Bibb, just as it bothered most fugitive slave couples who, "as soon as they get free from slavery . . . go before some anti-slavery clergyman, and have the solemn ceremony of marriage performed according to the laws of the land." So intense is this revulsion at the lack of religion which slavery enforces, and the mock religion which it sometimes allows, that many fugitive couples who have been baptized by a slaveholding minister "repudiate it after becoming free, and are rebaptized by a man who is worthy of doing it according to the gospel rule." Indeed, Bibb even made as one of the conditions of marrying Malinda that both would dedicate themselves to pursuing a religious life and to effecting the escape North which would make such a life possible. "I was religiously inclined," he tells us about his view of marriage, and "I intended to try to comply with the requisitions of the gospel, both theoretically and practically, through life."

As a personal extension of his religious sense of marriage, Bibb finds slavery "marriages" abhorrent because of the ugly degradation which they bring to a sacred institution; and, as he begins to discuss this, his tone takes on a far sharper note.

> A slave marrying according to law, is a thing unknown to the history of American Slavery. And be it known to the disgrace of our country that every slaveholder, who is the keeper of a number of slaves of both sexes, is also the keeper of a house or houses of ill-fame. Licentious white

men, can and do, enter at night or day the lodging
places of slaves; break up the bonds of affection in families; destroy all their domestic and social union for life;
and the laws of the country afford them no protection.

Nor does Bibb leave his harsh denunciation on such a general
note. He then enumerates and dramatizes the pain which this
brought to him, and these are clearly the most compelling and
personally involved passages in the whole narrative. Soon
after the "marriage" was settled, Bibb was bought by the slaveholder who owned Malinda. Far from being a welcomed event,
this only proved to be the ultimate anguish which slavery could
inflict on a man. For now Bibb, deeply in love with Malinda,
was forced to witness daily the degradation and cruelties which
slavery inflicted on the body of his wife.

On this same plantation I was compelled to stand and
see my wife shamefully scourged and abused by her
master; and the manner in which this was done, was so
violently and inhumanly committed upon the person of a
female, that I despair in finding decent language to describe the bloody act of cruelty. My happiness or pleasure
was then all blasted. . . .

Furthermore, once the two become the parents of a delicate
little daughter, Frances, the emotional pain for both of them
becomes unbearable, and Bibb's tone poignantly reflects this.
Since Malinda had to labor in the fields and Bibb himself was
constantly at work around his master's house, Frances had
to be left at the unmerciful hands of Bibb's master and mistress, a woman "whom I have known to slap with her hand
the face of little Frances, for crying after her mother until her
little face was left black and blue." As he dramatically recalls
one incident,

I recollect that Malinda and myself came from the field

one summer's day at noon, and poor little Frances came
creeping to her mother smiling, but with large tear drops
standing in her dear little eyes, sobbing and trying to tell
her mother that she had been abused, but was not able
to utter a word. Her little face was bruised black with
the whole print of Mrs. Gatewood's hand. The print was
plainly to be seen for eight days after it was done.

Finally, the realization of just what slavery means to women
and children—especially as he thinks of his daughter and wife
still in slavery while he is free—leads Bibb to poignantly wring
out his bitter despair when he next hears the word "slave."

It calls fresh to my mind the separatism of husband and
wife; of stripping, tying up and flogging; of tearing children from their parents and selling them on the auction
block. It calls to mind female virtue trampled under foot
with impunity. But oh! when I remember that my daughter, my only child, is still there, destined to share the fate
of all these calamities, it is too much to bear. If ever there
was any one act of my life while a slave, that I have to
lament over, it is that of being a father and a husband
of slaves.

This is the one searing moment of anguish which Bibb feels
deeply in the *Narrative*, and it forms an interesting contrast to
his generally philosophic acceptance of slave life as it relates
to him personally. But when the issue is religion or the tender
affections of his family, we find a much more poignant, emotional narrator flashing pain and anguish across the whole page.

Clarke's incisive power, Bibb's religious dedication: these
are the kinds of tones which uniquely personalize these narratives and make them so interesting to us. For even as they
are basically didactic and devoted to giving us historical material on the conditions of slavery in the South, still they represent the honest thoughts and feelings of a unique and essentially
"unprofessional" ex-slave writer, and these narratives are actu-

ally the only place in American literature where we can go and listen to these men on such an intimate and honest basis.

"Written by Himself"

In some ways Bibb's *Narrative* is of interest for a second, even larger reason than its philosophic yet poignant tone. This interest begins with the *Narrative's* "Introduction" and leads us to a discussion of one of the major aspects of these narratives as a genre: the importance attached to the fact that each narrative was hopefully written by the ex-slave himself.

As we examine the "Introduction" by Lucius C. Matlack, we find it is a classic example of the sort of realistic "documenting" that was the hallmark of the early abolitionist press and its fugitive slave narratives. After the polemical and dramatic qualities of Bibb's story have been alluded to, with the narrative itself defined as "a revolting portrait of the hideous slave system, a thrilling narrative of industrial suffering, and a triumphant vindication of the slave's manhood and mental dignity," Matlack sets about the characteristic task of establishing the veracity of the work.

For these narratives there were two major aspects of the work to be verified. The first, obviously, was that which contained the facts, events and incidents which made up the bulk of the plot. It was sometimes important to prove or support the narrator's stories of whippings and beatings and the various parts of the South in which he had experienced them. The second aspect was even more important. This was the attempt to prove that the narrative was, indeed, written by an ex-slave who had undergone these sufferings. Not only did this "Written by Himself" quality mean that the graphically described accounts were real, but it showed also that, despite the myths that Negro slaves were unintelligent and unable to learn anything significant, this ex-slave had learned deeply and broadly enough to become a capable and often adept writer.

Such an ex-slave was obviously a living truth to discredit

the myth of the Negro's inherent intellectual inferiority, just as the fugitive slaves who could give abolitionist addresses were tangible proofs before a tangible audience that these men had attained a considerable degree of oratorical skill. Yet, unlike having an orator who stood directly and physically before the listening audience and who therefore was his own testimony to his skills, all the reader had with a fugitive slave narrative was the book in front of him; and thus there obviously was a greater possibility of skepticism and disbelief about just how much the slave had, in fact, written "by himself." Indeed, this skepticism was understandably heightened by the reiteration from every narrator of just how completely the South tried to keep the slave from learning to read or write on any level. Hence the doubt in the readers' minds when faced with a literate and moving book by a man who only several years earlier had fled from a region and institution of enforced ignorance.

There were, furthermore, two other considerations which added to the skepticism: the question of fraudulent, hoax "narratives" and the problem of having amanuenses help various of these slaves write their stories. As for the first consideration, this understandable doubt had been reinforced by a large number of wholly fraudulent "slave narratives" which had been written by whites and passed off upon the unwary public as genuine works of actual ex-slaves. The earliest major example of this kind of hoax was *The Slave; a Memoir of Archy Moore*, which we mentioned briefly above. Published anonymously in Boston in 1836, it was at first received by the growing anti-slavery readership as a dynamic, genuine account of an ex-slave's life. Later, however, it was identified by Richard Hildreth, a noted American historian of the period, as a purely fictional account which he had created.

Two years later the most dramatic forgery in this vein was published in New York. It was the *Narrative of James Williams, an American Slave, Who Was for Several Years a Driver on a Cotton Plantation in Alabama*, dictated by a Negro

known as James Williams and recorded by one of the leaders
of both the abolitionist movement and contemporary literature
as well, John Greenleaf Whittier. Unlike the attempt by the
white historian Hildreth to simulate a Negro slave's experience
in Florida, Whittier had no such design. Indeed, all the inven-
tion came from Williams' own fertile imagination. Whittier saw
himself as merely the anonymous "translator" who was helping commit to print a story that the various New York abolitionists deemed as an extremely valuable piece of propaganda,
valuable because of its strikingly graphic detail in enumerating Southern atrocities at which Williams claimed to have
been present.

When the book first came out, it was widely circulated across
the country as major emancipation material. So highly was it
regarded by the American Anti-Slavery Society, in fact, that
a copy of it was sent to each member of Congress. In time,
however, it attracted attention in those Virginia and Alabama
counties where Williams claimed he had been held in slavery.
Residents of the various areas challenged the truth of Williams' accounts, and the executive committee of the Society
initiated a complete investigation. When the evidence finally
proved conclusively that Williams' recital of cruel experiences
was false, the committee, which had staked its reputation on
the veracity of the experiences in question, was forced to yield,
and the book's circulation was suspended.

Needless to say, the controversy over the Williams *Narrative* was the sensation of the year in the anti-slavery press: a
publicity and notoriety which was broadened by the fact that
the *Narrative*'s initial reception by the public was most enthusiastic. The book had, in fact, gone through three editions before
it was ordered suppressed. The result, of course, was that the
veracity of these Anti-Slavery Society narratives suffered considerable damage throughout the country, and this was a major
reason for the sort of detailed authentication which we find
in the "Introduction" to Henry Bibb's *Narrative*.

As for the second consideration, the general reader's doubts made their most natural appearance when facing those slave narratives whose title pages admitted that they were aided by an educated amanuensis. Such a book was Lewis Clarke's *Narrative*, and, as we look back at it now, we can see just how involved and formidable these doubts could become.

> For the facts contained in the following Narrative, Mr. Clarke is of course alone responsible. Yet, having had the most ample opportunities for testing his accuracy, I do not hesitate to say, that I have not a shadow of doubt, but in all material points every word is true. Much of it is in his own language, and all of it according to his own dictation.

This is how J. C. Lovejoy concludes his "Preface" to Clarke's *Narrative*, and in this conclusion is the reader given his only direct statement as to the authorship and composition of the narrative. Yet what is meant by "much" of Clarke's own language, and just what sort of relationship is described by "his own dictation" are two of the questions which seriously make a reader wonder how much credence he can give to calling such a book a "slave" narrative.

As Lovejoy tells us further in the "Preface," when he "first became acquainted with Lewis Clarke in December, 1842," Clarke's education and articulateness were so limited that his evidently active mind could be described by noting only that "trains of thought were flowing through it, which he was utterly unable to express." Similarly, concerning a slightly prior period in August, 1841, Clarke himself explains in his *Narrative* the failure of an attempt to escape by him and another slave. In the attempt, Clarke was to pass as a white man on their way North, but the problem which they faced, he admits, is that "I did not know the roads, and could not have read the guideboards." Thus the question now arises: if this was Clarke's ability to read and express in 1841 and 1842, then how much of his *Narrative*, written by the time of Lovejoy's

"Preface" in April, 1845, can we assume to be Clarke's own language and formulation? For if this was the scope of his education three years prior to his story's completion, then how do we account for his ability to quote Edmund Burke on Warren Hastings? his ability to call his mistress a "monster-woman" and a "she-spirit . . . come up from hell" and her son a "little, peevish scion of slavery?" his ability to talk about someone's claim, "dated 'ante natum' "? In short, just what does "dictation" mean here?

When we hear Clarke tell how "we did not . . . escape the avaricious grab of the slaveholder" on page ten, we are not only bothered by the "largeness" of his three year old vocabulary, but we are further intrigued by the similarity of the expression to Lovejoy's statement in the "Preface" that Clarke "is what he professes to be,—a slave escaped from the grasp of avarice and power." The meaning of "dictation" seems to be getting a little clearer.

And yet, even such evidence does not really solve the question of authorship here, but only presents us with a rather delicate problem. For even if we can state that much of the diction and tone in the *Narrative* can be found in the "Preface," whose five paragraph length is anything but conclusive, this establishment of similarity does not clarify very much for us. For while we might tend to think that it shows that Clarke did not actually affect the tone and style of his "Narrative" very much; and that Lovejoy, in fact, wrote most of it, using Clarke's dictated outline as a bare skeleton; we are hardly in a position to be so conclusive. For it is just as possible that Lovejoy had not so much conditioned the composition of Clarke's "Narrative" as he had conditioned Clarke himself. Three years under a man as intensely religious in conviction and language as is Lovejoy, then, could have done a great deal towards formulating a young, hurt slave's vision of a harsh world into the Christian man's vision of the universe. Thus it is quite possible that even though the style and tone of the "Narrative" resemble very closely the style and tone of the

"Preface," the "Narrative" is still basically the work of Lewis Clarke—a new "Lewis Clarke," who owes obvious debts to the tutelage of J. C. Lovejoy.

Finally, there is still a third possibility, and that is that the religious and forceful Lovejoy has, himself, been influenced by the burning fire and bitterness of Clarke, which would account for the strange mixture of scornful, witty vituperation here with a parallel quantity of Christian patience and tolerance, which so much of the abolitionist, sentimental literature exhibits. This would account for the contrast between Clarke's extensive and devastating description of Mrs. Benton as "one of the *cat-handed*, snake-eyed, brawling women, which slavery produces" and his final, seemingly "tacked on" tone towards her when he tells us that "I hope and pray that Mrs. B. will repent of her many and aggravated sins before it is too late," a point which we have already discussed above.

In the final analysis, however, we have no way of definitely solving this problem or quelling our doubts. This is especially true in many of these narratives because they are the sole work by the ex-slave author, so that we have no opportunity to compare his style and thoughts here with that in any other work. Thus, since no diaries or Clarke-written manuscripts exist to give us an idea of the "dictation" process, our search for definite authorship here can go no deeper than this sort of supposition. For this and related reasons, we can realize the urgent need for the documented authentication which so massively overwhelms the "Introduction" to the *Narrative of the Life and Adventures of Henry Bibb*.

As we return now to Matlack's "Introduction," we see immediately how much attention and concern have been devoted to this verification effort. Immediately after he has discussed the narrative value and power of this "revolting portrait," etc., Matlack quickly adds in the very next sentence that "all this is associated with unmistakable traces of originality and truthfulness." It is this which he will now attempt to prove.

"To many," he begins, zeroing in on the basic problem, "the

elevated style, purity of diction, and easy flow of language, frequently exhibited, will appear unaccountable and contradictory, in view of his want of early mental culture." However, to those thousands who have heard Bibb speak in public and have "listened with delight to his speeches on anniversary and other occasions," it is clear that the man is indeed an original and polished speaker.

"Moreover," Matlack continues, he, Matlack, is well acquainted with Bibb's handwriting and style since he has "examined and prepared for the press" the whole manuscript; and therefore he will vouch for Bibb's authenticity. "Many of the closing pages of it," in fact, "were written by Mr. Bibb in my office." All Matlack himself has done to it is the work "of orthography and punctuation merely, an arrangement of the chapters, and a table of contents—little more than falls to the lot of publishers generally." Obviously, then, "no alteration of sentiment, language or style, was necessary to make it what it is now, in the hands of the reader."

Yet this discussion is not all. In fact, it is merely the beginning. Now, and for the succeeding nine pages, it "is only necessary to present the following documents to the reader" in order to sustain Matlack's assertion of the "fidelity of the narrative." At this point, a whole briefcase full of letters is placed before us, sought out and collected by a "Committee appointed by the Detroit Liberty Association to investigate the truth of the narrative of Henry Bibb, a fugitive from Slavery." The letters themselves are all from Southern personages who knew or came in contact with Bibb in the South, and all of them verify the truth of the incidents which Bibb relates. Bibb's ex-master in Kentucky, William Gatewood; his jailor in the Louisville work-house, W. Porter; William Gatewood's son, Silas; a slave catcher in Kentucky from whom Bibb escaped, Daniel S. Love. All are here, and all provide (some in spite of themselves) concrete proof of the truth of Bibb's narrative.

Nor does Matlack take the chance that the importance of

these letters will be lost upon us; for immediately after reprinting them verbatim, he then lists them in numerical order and
expositorially reiterates the major significances of each. He is
taking no chances here, just as his whole "Introduction" has
been this scrupulously detailed and specific. Verification of a
slave narrative was deemed that important.

Parallel "white" narratives

One further point is of interest to us, and this concerns
the development of "white" narratives of the South which generally paralleled the fugitive slave publications. So fruitful and
popular were the slave narratives and their stark portrayal of
slavery's cruelty in the South that the Abolitionist press found
itself extending the genre and publishing narratives of the harsh
South as experienced by white men whose sympathies were
with the slaves and who therefore suffered the same cruelties
that the slaves themselves underwent. Significantly enough,
these white narratives shared the same format, details and
approaches as the fugitive slave group, and were, in fact, published under the same auspices and sponsorship of that group.

The best example of this offshoot abolitionist literature is
the *Trial and Imprisonment of Jonathan Walker, at Pensacola,
Florida, for Aiding Slaves to Escape from Bondage*, which was,
significantly enough, published "at the Anti-Slavery Office, 25
Cornhill, 1845," exactly as were Frederick Douglass' and
Lewis Clarke's narratives. Basically the plot in the Walker
narrative is quite simple, and deals once more with the escape
of slaves from bondage in the South. Needless to say, its purpose is also the same as that of the slave narratives.

As initial background we learn that

Late in the fall of 1843, I left my home in Harwich,
Mass., and took passage on board of a vessel bound for
Mobile, where I spent the winter and spring—mostly in
working at the ship-wright business, which is my trade.

And we learn as well that, not only did he go there only for business reasons, but that even now he harbors no hostility or resentment towards the South.

> I look upon the southern States as the most favored part of my country, which nature seems to have done and to be doing much for, than for the northern States. Their soft and genial climate, their rich and luxuriant soil, their long and uniform summers... all far exceed those of New England, in my opinion. . . .
> Neither are the customs of the people there more repugnant to my feelings than the customs of the northern people generally, with the exception of what belongs to the system of slavery.

Hence we are given a fairly "objective" narrator to carry us through his Southern experiences.

At the same time, despite this "objective" format, what we are facing here is essentially abolitionist polemic couched in narrative form, and that, of course, was the reason for its publication. Most significant is Walker's early statement about his grammar and syntax, in which he acknowledges early that

> Having never been favored with an education, and laboring under the disadvantage of writing hastily... the narrative will not be so attractive as it otherwise might be.

For what strikes us most about this piece is that it is the typical "apology" which was popularly utilized by the fugitive slave orators whom we looked at above. Walker, then, is clearly in the abolitionist polemical tradition.

The plot itself deals with Walker's experiences around the Gulf of Mexico to Pensacola, Fla.: how he sailed from Mobile to Pensacola on June 2, 1844 "for the purpose of raising a part of the wreck of a vessel sunk near the latter place, for the sake of getting the copper that was attached to it;" how he then made the acquaintance of four slaves who asked him to help them flee to the Bahamas; how he was finally caught and punished before he could accomplish his mission. And yet, what is of greatest interest in Walker's account is not the man himself, or the act he performed, or even the branded "SS" that was burned into his right palm as civil punishment for his crime. Instead, we are struck by the terse, unedited diary which he kept while in the Pensacola jail: a journal whose stark simplicity effectively captures for us the people and atmosphere around that jail.

The diary begins with a description of the jailer and his family, who live in the upper story of the two-story brick building which makes up the jail. In some sense this is the programmed list of the Dramatis Personae who are to follow and act out their natures across the diary's pages.

> The family consisted of F.T. the jailer—L.T. his wife, and six children; a mulatto woman and her child, five or six months old,

and immediately we are given a greater insight into the characters and the nature of their interaction.

> Of course the work about the yard and kitchen devolved upon the slave woman, who, by the bye . . . had been brought up in the family under the lash, as the only stimulant, which, as a natural consequence, had instilled the most bitter hatred and carelessness, with other kindred qualifications.

The scene is thereby set; the characters introduced. The show now begins.

> July 19. When I was committed, there was one slave man in the adjoining room, for what I know not.
>
> 22. L.T. whipped the cook.

24. L.T. whipped the cook.
25. I wrote to Benj. D. Wright, counsellor at law, requesting an interview. L.T. whipped the cook twice.
28. Four of the slaves who had left with me were brought here and put in the adjoining room. L.T. whipped the cook.
29. My health a little improved; could sit up half the day. Wrote to my wife.

Aug. 1. L.T. whipped the cook.
4. L.T. whipped the cook.
5. The four fugitive slaves in the adjoining room whipped fifty blows each, with a paddle.
8. Were taken out; with much difficulty could walk, being very sore. Cook whipped twice, once by L.T. and once by F.T.
12. A fugitive slave man caught and committed. L.T. whipped the cook.
14. L.T. whipped the cook.
17. L.T. whipped the cook four times. Mistress dreadfully cross.
19. L.T. whipped the cook.
21. L.T. whipped the cook twice.
22. The slave man committed on the 12th, taken out and sent to Alabama.
28. L.T. whipped the cook; children got some too; lots of scolding dealt out, in both English and French. Slave woman committed; had been brought from New Orleans by mistake on board steamboat.
30. L.T. whipped the cook. L.T. confined; brought forth a fine boy.

At this point maternal duties induce L.T. to bow out of the court yard drama: whipping only occasionally, and by proxy (e.g., "Sept. 12. Cook whipped severely by L.T.'s brother, at her request.") until once more she is able to re-enter the lists and carry on as the real trooper she is, until the end of the diary on November 20.

The notations are tersely jotted down, and their very simplicity tends to underplay the situation at the jail. Walker's skeletal accounts might even seem comic for the way that they accept the many beatings and punishments which they describe so matter-of-factly, were it not for the fact that we can readily see past Walker's casual style and recreate for ourselves the amount of brutality and emotional violence rampant. Indeed, this ability to make *us* recreate the cruelties is a very effective technique for accomplishing what all of these narratives set out to picture, and this is why this genre was so important during the 1840's. Indeed, it was a dominant mode of expression of the anti-slavery literary scene when William Wells Brown arrived, and Brown was greatly influenced by it.

CHAPTER SEVEN

Narrative of William W. Brown, A Fugitive Slave

When we come to discuss Brown's own *Narrative* now, we need to remember that we are dealing as much with a genre and a tradition as with an individual piece of writing. The slave narrative, as we have seen, had a definite purpose and fixed format. Furthermore, since it stressed realism and a chronological structure, each slave's narrative tended to echo its predecessors since the realistic experiences of each slave had much in common, especially as they occurred in a birth-to-manhood, "Bildungsroman" format. This, of course, limited individuality in any single slave narrative and was, actually, one reason why Brown eventually felt the need to break free from its confinements and seek to write his "story" within the freerer formats of the novel and the play.

At the same time we have also seen that uniqueness and originality were possibilities within the fairly rigid structure and purpose of the narratives. Each slave narrator did have individual experiences which were his alone and reflected the unique environment and personality of that narrator. Furthermore, each narrator had his own tone of voice, his own way of perceiving and relating those experiences, and this was another avenue for unique narrative expression.

Needless to say, Brown's *Narrative* partook of both these strains, especially the traditional elements. Coming two years after Douglass' and Clarke's narratives, and with Brown himself coming into the Massachusetts Anti-Slavery Society in 1847 as the direct successor to Douglass, Brown's *Narrative* had a great many aspects that were common to the slave narrative genre and that genre's own close relation to the antislavery orations of the period.

Traditional Elements in the Narrative

J. C. Hathaway's "Preface" to the *Narrative* suggests to us the general nature of Brown's story, and in many ways it is indicative of the traditional polemic which the *Narrative* does contain. "The friends of freedom may well congratulate each other on the appearance of the following Narrative," he begins. "It adds another volume to the rapidly increasing anti-slavery literature of the age." Indeed, like the songs of a nation, such a book as Brown's "goes forth noiselessly upon its mission, but fails not to find its way to many a warm heart, to kindle on the altar thereof the fires of freedom, which will one day break forth in a living flame to consume oppression." Actually, Hathaway's "Preface" goes even further than the typical narrative's preface and concludes with an exhortative call to arms for all sincere Christians to join the abolitionist movement.

> Reader, are you an Abolitionist? What have you done for the slave? What are you doing in his behalf? What do you propose to do? There is a great work before us! Who will be an idler now? This is the great humanitary [sic] movement of the age, swallowing up, for the time being, all other questions. . . .
> Are you a Christian? This is the carrying out of practical Christianity; and there is no other. . . . Do you love

God whom you have not seen? Then manifest that love,
by restoring to your brother whom you have seen his
rightful inheritance, of which he has been so long and so
cruelly deprived. . . .

It is a vast work—a glorious enterprise—worthy of
the unswerving devotion of the entire life-time of the
great and the good.

The *Narrative*, as Hathaway sees it, is to be a book strong in
the anti-slavery tradition; and in many ways he is correct.

There are, first of all, the normal holdovers from the anti-
slavery oratory which Brown and the other fugitive slaves had
dedicated so much of their lives to. One aspect of this was the
conscious use of the anti-democracy irony with which we have
become familiar, and some of it is quite directly, quite rhetorically made. In discussing his attempt to flee to Canada with
his mother, Brown mentions how tired he occasionally became
and exactly what thoughts stirred him to continue. Since "I
was, almost constantly on my feet," he notes, he sometimes
"felt as though I could travel no further." However, the ironic
truth of what freedom-espousing America really meant to a
slave spurred him to greater determination.

But when I thought of slavery, with its democratic whips
—its republican chains—its evangelical bloodhounds,
and its religious slave-holders—when I thought of all this
paraphernalia of American democracy and religion behind me, and the prospect of liberty before me, I was en-
couraged to press forward, my heart was strengthened,
and I forgot that I was tired or hungry.

The lyric optimism of Canada ahead, then, is contrasted with
the staccato heaviness of America's tortures, and those tortures themselves are described through point-blank ironic

juxtaposition of democracy to whips, religion to bloodhounds, etc. The moment is effective, especially in its use of oratorical directness.

At the same time, Brown is quite subtle with this at times, letting the irony carefully develop its message instead of allowing himself to expositorially "shout" the truth to us; and here we begin to see the budding artist at work. His description of the same abortive flight to Canada reads delicately like an account of Moses fleeing the oppressive land of Pharaoh for the freedom of the promised land, but this doesn't really strike us at first because we are used to this sort of subject and tone, for America has always been pictured as the promised land of safety and asylum for those troubled peoples fleeing the oppression of foreign countries. The Statue of Liberty's credo, therefore, hazily conditions our vision of the scene before us. It is a startling shock, then, when we suddenly realize that America is actually the "land of oppression" here and that Brown and his mother are fleeing to Canada to achieve the traditional American dream of "our own FREE HOME."

"We traveled on that day," Brown tells us of their eleventh day of flight, "through a thickly settled country, and through one small village. Though we were fleeing from a land of oppression, our hearts were still there." While the truth of this "oppressive land" sinks in, he mildly discusses his feeling of sadness at leaving his sister and two brothers behind, and then he comes forward again and forces us to see the truth directly —even going so far as to burst the bubble of freedom in Canada with a dramatically sudden, concrete proof of American oppression.

> But with all this depression of heart, the thought that I should one day be free, and call my body my own, buoyed me up, and made my heart leap for joy. I had just been telling my mother how I should try to get employment as soon as we reached Canada, and how I intended to purchase us a little farm, and how I would

earn money enough to buy sister and brothers, and how happy we would be in our own FREE HOME—when three men came up on horseback, and ordered us to stop.

The pair are captured and returned to St. Louis, and the "Canadian Dream" is poignantly shattered for a sensitive boy and his mother. Powerful restraint, contrast, suspense, pathos— all are here, and all show Brown's ability to transcend the normal narrative "routine" and develop himself as a dramatic artist within the folds of this chronological genre.

Along with the anti-democracy irony, of course, Brown also included a large amount of the traditional anti-Christian irony. There is a certain subtlety here at times, as when Brown relates early in the narrative how Dr. Young suddenly "got religion," hired a preacher to come to the plantation, and had family worship both mornings and nights. Brown then recalls how one morning he, Brown, spilled and broke a glass pitcher during the service. No response was made while the service was still going on, but when it was over Brown was immediately beaten by the irate Young—a mute reminder of just how irrelevant professed Christianity became in the South when it came into the practical context of slavery and its treatment of the slaves.

Aside from such infrequent, underplayed moments, however, most of the anti-Christian irony is very directly, very forcefully handled. So pressing is this hypocritical contradiction between the compassion which Christianity professes and the inhuman cruelty which its slaveholding adherents actually perform, that Brown almost immediately follows his prior example of Young's post-service beating with an even more obviously ironic example. Thus he notes on the next page how another local "gentleman," sometime earlier, had "tied up a woman of his, by the name of Delphia, and whipped her nearly to death; yet he was a deacon in the Baptist church, in good and regular standing." And later, Brown makes the same point in equally direct fashion. Relating the unsuccessful flights to

Canada by his mother and himself, he recalls how they were captured by three Illinois men who had seen the advertisement for the two slaves, offering two hundred dollars for their return to St. Louis. During that first night he and his mother were kept in a closely guarded room in the leader's house, and Brown again notes—and comments on—the irony of slavery being aided and practiced by seemingly "devout" Christians. "Before the family retired to rest," he notes,

> they were all called together to attend prayers. The man who but a few hours before had bound my hands together with a strong cord, read a chapter from the Bible, and then offered up a prayer, just as though God sanctioned the act he had just commtited upon a poor panting, fugitive slave.

Indeed, Brown's most forceful discussion of this contradiction comes toward the end of the *Narrative* when he consciously brings this whole underlying theme into direct, explanatory focus. It is not uncommon, he tells us, to pass an auction stand in St. Louis and hear a slave being sold and advertized as one who is "a good cook, good washer, a good obedient servant. She has got religion!" This leads Brown to rhetorically ask why the auctioneer should stress the slave's religion this way, and his answer is bluntly to the point.

> I answer, because in Missouri, and as far as I have any knowledge of slavery in the other States, the religious teaching consists of teaching the slave that he must never strike a white man; that God made him for a slave; and that, when whipped, he must not find fault—for the Bible says, "He that knoweth his master's will and doeth it not, shall be beaten with many stripes!"

The ironic prostitution of Christianity is obvious, and so is the dominant motive behind it. Not only is there a warped sense of power released here and sanctioned by distorted Biblical "authority," but, even more important, "slave-holders find such religion very profitable to them."

One final and somewhat lesser holdover from anti-slavery oratory is Brown's use of borrowed verse, an aspect of his writing which we will look at in much greater detail later. After his mother and he are returned to St. Louis, for example, and his mother is now being sold into the greater cruelty of plantation slavery, Brown describes the deep pathos and pain in their moment of parting. Then, as a final note, he dips into the softness of poetry and recalls how, as he saw her boat leaving,

I could but feel that I had lost

> "_____ the glory of my life,
> My blessing and my pride!
> I half forgot the name of slave,
> When she was by my side,"

Along with approaches from the oratorical tradition here, there are naturally many elements in the *Narrative* which mark it as clearly within the slave narrative genre itself, as opposed to that of anti-slavery oratory. There is, to begin with, the standard enumeration of cruelties and hardships under slavery. The lack of family stability makes its standard appearance, as Brown begins the narrative by noting scathingly how he was born in Lexington, Ky. and how "The man who stole me as soon as I was born, recorded the births of all the infants which he claimed to be born his property, in a book which he kept for that purpose." Compounding this "theft" and the family fragmentation which it symbolized was the condition of the rest of Brown's "family." "My mother's name was Elizabeth," he tells us, and she had seven children, "viz: Solomon, Leander, Benjamin, Joseph, Millford, Elizabeth, and myself." Yet

"No two of us were children of the same father." Likewise, there is a certain amount of direct recounting of cruelties at the hands of his master and the overseer Cook, as we will see a bit later.

Furthermore, Brown is also capable of delving into general, "shotgun" enumeration, firing scattered broadsides at the slavery system as a whole or at one symbolically large target. For example, after beginning Chapter IV with a favorable account of his period with Elijah P. Lovejoy in St. Louis, Brown moves suddenly and abruptly to a discussion of slavery's "barbarity," as if to counteract the pleasant warmth which Lovejoy tended to bring to the scene. "Though slavery is thought, by some, to be mild in Missouri," he begins, and then out pours a flood of factual indictments of St. Louis slavery. "It was here that Col. Harvey, a United States officer, whipped a slave woman to death. It was here that Francis McIntosh, a free colored man from Pittsburgh, was . . . burned at the stake." Indeed, "It was here . . . ," and suddenly we are there, and Brown's major purpose has been achieved. He has involved and brought us graphically onto another scene of slavery's essential cruelty: the basic "raison d'être" of every slave narrative.

The Narrative's Uniqueness

Dominating these general points of anti-slavery polemic and narrative, however, are several unique aspects of the *Narrative*. There are, first of all, various unique "asides," small comments which spring in and out of the narrative with little emphasis by the narrator, but comments which catch our eye because they generally don't appear in the other narratives at all. Such an aside is Brown's dismissal of a New England overseer, whom he had suffered under, with the comment that "The Yankees are noted for making the most cruel overseers." Three pages later, in order to make this generalization effectively reach the reader, Brown reinforces it with a discussion of a Mr. John Colburn, one of the men who "rented" him. Colburn "was from one of the free states," Brown tells us, "but a more inveterate hater of the Negro I do not believe ever walked God's green earth."

There is, also, Brown's poignant concern over his name and its importance to him as a tangible aspect of his identity. Discussing his early days in slavery, he recalls how, when a nephew of Young was brought as a baby to live on the farm, both had the same name, "William." Though the baby was only a few weeks old and Brown ten or twelve years of age, Brown's mother was ordered to change his name. Brown's discussion of this is interesting, for it shows how strongly and deeply he felt about it. "This, at the time," he tells us, "I thought to be one of the most cruel acts that could be committed upon my rights; and I received several severe whippings for telling people that my name was William, after orders were given to change it." Significantly enough, as he later relates his thoughts while fleeing to Canada, Brown returns to this question and notes how the question of changing his name back to William constantly kept occurring to him. Indeed, as if to intensify the point, he even fuses the two identity searches together in assessing his thoughts while traveling North: "So I was not only hunting for my liberty, but also hunting for a name."

Of greater significance than such asides, however, are two major aspects of Brown's story: his experiences in the service of the slave-trader Walker and the uniquely dramatic way in which he has learned to recount his experiences in general. His most individual material, then, is composed of the inside knowledge which he gained as Walker's assistant on a trip from St. Louis to New Orleans with a cargo of slaves. Of greatest historical interest is his description of how he had to "prepare the old slaves for market" on the steamboat going South—an original account which exists nowhere else in American literature. "I was ordered to have the old men's whiskers shaved off," he tells us,

and the grey hairs plucked out where they were not too
numerous, in which case he [Walker] had a preparation
of blacking to color it, and with a blacking brush we
would put it on. This was new business to me, and was
performed in a room where the passengers could not see
us.

Furthermore,

These slaves were also taught how old they were by Mr.
Walker, and after going through the blacking process they
looked ten or fifteen years younger; and I am sure that
some of those who purchased slaves of Mr. Walker were
dreadfully cheated, especially in the ages of the slaves
which they bought.

For the most part Brown does not merely content himself
with this sort of neutral, matter of fact description of his experiences. Rather, he usually uses these experiences to enumerate, document and dramatize slavery's evil as a whole.
Thus he notes how, despite all Walker's care in keeping his
slaves chained and pacified, "We lost one woman who had
been taken from her husband and children, and having no
desire to live without them, in the agony of her soul jumped
overboard, and drowned herself," and the unadorned anguish
and tragedy which slavery unendingly brought fiercely sinks
into us.

Nor does Brown always let the enumeration stand and convince by itself. Often he is directly didactic—forcefully addressing the reader as he emphasizes the moral lessons to be
learned. In a representative example Brown records how
Walker bought a beautiful quadroon, had her put into a private stateroom on the boat, and sought to seduce her there.
Eventually he proposed that she come back with him to St.
Louis, where he would establish her as housekeeper on his
farm; and he underscored this offer with the threat that, if she

refused, he would sell her to a Deep South cotton plantation.
She finally agreed, and Walker initially lived up to his part of
the bargain, at which point Brown breaks into the story and
addresses us directly, exclamation point in hand. "But, mark
the end!" he cries out. "Since I have been at the North, I have
been credibly informed that Walker has been married, and,
as a previous measure, sold poor Cynthia and her four children (she having had two more since I came away) into hopeless bondage!"

So strongly do Brown's experiences with Walker bother
him, and so determined is he to scourge slavery itself through
his recollections of Walker, that he even delves into direct
documentation. After having discussed his experiences with
Walker in so much detail earlier in the narrative, Brown now
meets him again and decides to impress upon us the validity
of his earlier points. "For fear that some may think that I have
misrepresented a slave-driver," he tells us, "I will here give an
extract from a paper published in a slaveholding State, Tennessee, called the 'Milennial Trumpeter.' The extract itself
is clearly abolitionist in its perspective, describing 'these vile
slave-drivers and dealers' who 'are swarming like buzzards
around a carrion.'" Forcing its opponent into a corner, the
extract asks explicitly "Who is a Negro-driver?" and pours its
two-fisted soul into the answer

> One whose eyes dwell with delight on lacerated bodies
> of helpless men, women and children; whose soul feels
> diabolical raptures at the chains, and hand-cuffs, and
> cart-whips, for inflicting tortures on weeping mothers
> torn from helpless babes, and on husbands and wives
> torn asunder forever!

Related to our discussion of Walker, yet clearly in a cate-
gory all its own, is Brown's second major feature here: his
strong sense of concrete plot and his ability to create a unified,
dramatic moment. Significantly, even in Chapter One, where

we would normally expect enumeration and dramatization of Brown's own problems with the overseer Cook, he immediately tells us the heroic saga of a slave named Randall and the dramatic confrontation which he had with Cook.

Being called on to submit to an unjustified whipping,

> Randall stood silent for a moment, and then said, "Mr. Cook, I have always tried to please you since you have been on the plantation, and I find you are determined not to be satisfied with my work, let me do as well as I may. No man has laid hands on me, to whip me, for the last ten years, and I have long since come to the conclusion not to be whipped by any man living."

The voice is calm and precise, representing the restraint that springs from power and a strong man's sense of himself. The conflict is begun.

> Cook, finding by Randall's determined look and gestures, that he would resist, called three of the hands from their work, and commanded them to seize Randall, and tie him. The hands stood still;—they knew Randall—and they also knew him to be a powerful man, and were afraid to grapple with him.

The physical confrontation has arrived and the tension mounts, until Randall forcefully puts matters into honest perspective and the enemy slinks off.

> As soon as Cook had ordered the men to seize him, Randall turned to them, and said—"Boys, you all know me; you know that I can handle any three of you, and the man that lays hands on me shall die. This white man can't whip me himself, and therefore he has called you to help him." The overseer was unable to prevail upon

them to seize and secure Randall, and finally ordered them all to go to work together.

The heroic, "frontier" voice of power and self-respect has triumphed—a triumph of determination and self-integrity which Brown and his readers empathetically share with Randall. For he is almost an archetypal figure of the American frontier, even in his diction, and he reflects how deeply free and self-reliant Brown as an ex-slave now was. Most important, it shows how effectively Brown could see and recount such moments in controlled, dramatic terms.

At the same time, Brown also effectively dramatizes his own experiences—both those in which he is personally involved and those which he witnesses from a vantage point. There were, basically, two sorts of dramatization available to the slave narrator. On the one hand, there was the dramatization of that pain and violence inflicted directly on the narrator himself. And while this lost the detached perspective and thus much of the detailed recording possible in the second type, neverthe-less, because the violence is happening to *our* narrator—with whom we have come to empathize and emotionally identify—this form of dramatization is quite effective. Thus we person-ally wince as Brown dramatically recalls how he was assaulted by a St. Louis slave-holder.

McKinney not being able to find me on his arrival, left the office in a great rage, swearing that he would whip me to death. A few days later, as I was walking along Main Street, he seized me by the collar, and struck me over the head five or six times with a large cane, which caused the blood to gush from my nose and ears in such a manner that my clothes were completely saturated with blood.

On the other hand, there was also that cruelty and mistreatment which was meted out to fellow slaves within the narrator's presence. Effective here was not only the amount of immediacy which the narrator had for graphically and realistically describing the sound of the whip lash, the sight of the mutilated back, the screams of agony and pain. But also contributing to the effectiveness was the narrator's ability to see and record all this so clearly because he was not physically involved. As sensitive observer of the scene, therefore, not only could he see the horrors, but he had a perspective secure enough to sensuously report them in complete detail. Such a description is Brown's dramatic account of his mother's early morning whipping at the hands of Cook, an account which appears as early as the third page of the narrative. With the morning hardly begun, Cook suddenly began whipping her.

> She cried, "Oh! pray—Oh! pray—Oh! pray—these are generally the words of the slaves when imploring mercy at the hands of their oppressors. I heard her voice, and knew it, and jumped out of my bunk, and went to the door. Though the field was some distance from the house, I could hear every crack of the whip, and every groan and cry of my poor mother. I remained at the door, not daring to venture any further. The cold chills ran over me, and I wept aloud. After giving her ten lashes, the sound of the whip ceased, and I returned to my bed and found no consolation but in my tears.

This is the kind of dramatic power which is the great triumph of Brown's *Narrative*, and it is this dramatic ability in 1847 which soon led him to scale the dramatic heights of the first Negro novel and the first Negro play.

CHAPTER EIGHT

Growth of the Artist:
The Early Days

In order to understand the growth and development of a "first" novelist, who seems to spring up and flower from an environmental underbrush, the literary historian usually has very little secondary source material to bring to his study. Instead, he needs to rely on as complete a knowledge of the novelist as he can get, which finally means all the pertinent literary and personal background of the writer up to the time of the novel's publication. A study of William Wells Brown and the first Negro novel *Clotelle* is no exception.

The novel itself in this case is *Clotelle: A Tale of the Southern States*, published in Boston in 1864. And though Brown's "firstness" as a novelist lies in the 1853 date of his first *Clotel; or, The President's Daughter*, published in London, it is the 1864 edition which gives us our understanding of the artist who is finally pleased enough with his work so that he does not revise it again, and does, in fact, copyright and publish it himself three years later as *Clotelle; or, The Colored Heroine.*

However, compiling personal data on a mid-nineteenth century American Negro author is a difficult, and often fruitless, task for the literary historian and critic. Generally the man in question was an escaped slave, which meant that much of

his early life was spent in slavery—a place where the same
biographical data were kept of slaves as were kept of pedi-
greed cattle and other "property," with the added complication
being that the master himself might have sired much of his
stock and thus had personal reasons for concealing pertinent
background information. Furthermore, the typical slave himself could not write at this period in his life and thus did not
even have a chance for a sketchy journal of his own; so that
if he found himself sold very often or sold very young, he
really had little knowledge of his pertinent early life. What
little idea he did have, moreover, is only of limited value to
us because it is so personal and subjective. Thus the slave
narratives as a genre are extremely valuable for an idea of a
general slave's general early life, but they can never discuss
the individual life of the narrator in any great detail, especially
the early youth. Such is the case with Brown.

Brown, however, was a voluminous writer; and except for
our inability to locate his first play, *Doughface,* and the equally
uncertain serialization of *Clotelle* as *Miralda* in a New York
newspaper, we do have a good deal of material of his to judge
him by. Thus in order to understand how *Clotelle* was written
and what sort of novelist its final version represented, we have
both the novel itself and all the other pieces of major writing
which Brown had produced before it. While that period of
Brown's life in which *Clotel* and *Clotelle* were written is almost completely untouched by the literary biographer and
historian, therefore, we do have enough previous and contemporary material by him from which to make intelligent sur-
mises as to the novel's genesis and development.

Admittedly, because so much of Brown's work is so uneven
in itself, and because his earlier work is of such different types
from piece to piece, at times this approach to him seems almost formless and haphazard. Nevertheless, there are recurrent patterns of thought and expression which habitually occur
in these works, and it is to understand these patterns and their

ultimate bearing on *Clotelle* that these next three chapters are dedicated.

If we can define an artist as one who cares about a subject and expresses his care through a vehicle which, itself, receives much of the writer's attention, then William Wells Brown was an artist from the very beginning. For there is in all of Brown an awareness of effect, both psychological and literary, and an understanding of how certain perspectives and techniques work on an audience. Likewise, he was a writer who could distance himself from his material by adopting a perspective and tone of detachment and irony, letting the story tell itself with only an occasional nudge from polemic or the heavy jolt of direct sarcasm. He was, in short, a man of both mission and method.

That he was not an overly sophisticated novelist is not at issue here, for Brown was master of the didactic and rhetorical, and this is artistry enough. Not only were there many elements of the novelistic form which he never had the time or opportunity to master, but his life as a whole militated against the sense of structure and unity which a polished novelist needs. For Brown was hired and sold constantly as a slave youth, and likewise chose to travel even more extensively as a free man; and essentially this sort of personal life provided him with little chance for developing a sense of structure and personal or literary order that was anything more than episodic and chronologically narrative. And yet, the wonder is not so much that he was as structurally limited as he was, but that he wrote as well as he did despite that limitation. This, in essence, is William Wells Brown's claim to literary acknowledgement.

In 1847 Brown appeared in print for the second time with his *Narrative of William W. Brown*. Included in the front of the book were several statements by various friends and reviewers commenting on his work, two of which are significant to us as we look now at the early apprentice novelist. Edmund Quincy heads the list with an interesting assessment of Brown's description and tone in the *Narrative*. As he notes in his letter to Brown,

> Your experiences in the Field, in the House, and especially on the River in the service of the slave-trader, Walker, have been such as few individuals have had;— no one, certainly, who has been competent to describe them. What I have admired, and marvelled at, in your *Narrative*, is the simplicity and calmness with which you describe scenes and actions which might well "move the very stones to rise and mutiny" against the National Institution which makes them possible.

This is a very relevant insight. For what Quincy has seen here in "simplicity and calmness" is the ability of the artist to remove his personal feelings from the scene which he cares so much about. Most often in this early Brown and the antislavery writers in general, this sense of distance was achieved through a wide spectrum of ironies, most of them based on the incongruities inherent in having a system of slavery in "Christian" and "democratic" America. Yet there is something unique in Brown's non-ironic tones of distance and balance here, something which suggests a man able to see two sides of an issue or a dramatic moment as well as a man merely able to step away from a situation and let a one-sided sense of irony perform the work which his didacticness usually undertook. This calmness which Quincy saw, then, is essentially the artist's control over his emotions.

Related to this perspective and tone is Brown's ability to see events and characters concretely and pictorially. We note

J. C. Hathaway's comment on Brown's style in the "Preface" of the same *Narrative*.

> Many harrowing scenes are graphically portrayed; and yet with that simplicity and ingenuousness which carries with it a conviction of the truthfulness of the picture.

Objective, calm, clear and concrete: these are the basic attributes of much of Brown's work, as both Quincy and Hathaway noted.

At the same time, however, Brown's prior work with the temperance and anti-slavery movement had taught him far too many emotional and rhetorical devices for him to abandon all this for a flat, descriptive tone. Hence he is perpetually plagued by a tear-jerking sense of melodrama and the "alas! alas!" sentimental verse of the English Romantic and Sensibility poets. This, in fact, is a whole aspect of his literary personality, and we will deal with it as such in its place. Indeed, we will find that he is often glibly over-emotional in some of his verse and "song" effusions, sentimental techniques which he was only borrowing from the vast majority of the polemicists and writers around him; and we will note further how he often could not control this style once he got into the middle of it. At the same time, however, we will need to realize that he consciously, artistically chose to enter this medium on those occasions, and that quite often he was able to transcend the overdrawn sentimentality of the medium and achieve an effect which was completely his own. Indeed, this ability to select and develop a large range of voices and perspectives on the basis of effect desired was very much a part of Brown's art.

Thus we will find that Brown will be torn between these two major aspects of his style: the clear-sighted, honest description and the artificial, melodramatic sentiment and theme. His struggle with structure will also come into our final assessment of him as a novelist, but that is getting ahead of our story. For our story must begin in 1847 with the publication of *A Lecture Delivered before the Female Anti-Slavery Society of Salem.*

Salem Lecture

The first published piece of writing which we have by Brown, now, is this *Salem Lecture* of 1847; and it is to this which we first must turn. Originally given as an anti-slavery address, it was reported in pamphlet form by Henry M. Parkhurst and is of interest to us for much of its content and argumentative technique.

The first aspect which strikes us in the lecture is the breadth and universality of its topic and perspective. "My subject for this evening," Brown tells us in the beginning, "is Slavery as it is, and its influence upon the morals and character of the American people." Reiterating this point a little later, he shows just how wide his interest is when he defines "the influence of Slavery" as one "not only upon the morals of the Slaveholding South, or of the Slave, but upon the morals of the people of the United States of America." As good as his word, Brown then devotes the address to discussing in full the moral effect which slavery has had upon all three segments of the country's population; and it is in this discussion that we can clearly see his penchant for detached perspective and a historical tone— a position which allows him a more rational and commanding effect on his readers than he would have had, had he merely indulged in anti-Southern polemic or pro-Negro sentimentality.

Within the framework of this large structure, now, we find several of Brown's early techniques. There is, first of all, the conventional anti-slavery use of Christian and Constitutional irony, where all the horrors and indignities of slavery are pointedly juxtaposed against all the beautiful promises of this country's premised ideals. A religious Christian himself, as we note in the tone of his *Narrative*'s "Dedication" to Wells Brown ("I was a stranger, and you took me in. I was hungry,

and you fed me. Naked was I, and you clothed me."), Brown
is constantly noting how the ministers of both North and South
own slaves, sell them for church fund raisings, and so on. Yet
it is significant to note that Brown here does not merely content himself with stating these ironies. For even this early in
his career he is able to concretely picture them for us in the
manner which J. C. Hathaway saw as the "graphic portrayal"
of "simplicity and ingenuousness." In a typical moment, for
example, Brown tells us how

> . . . you can see the master going into the church on the
> Sabbath, with his Slave following him into church, and
> waiting upon him,—both belonging to the same church.
> And the day following, the master puts his Slave upon the
> auction-stand, and sells him to the highest bidder.

No polemic or melodramatic effusion is needed; the irony
speaks for itself in statuary form.

Equally concrete and equally typical of Brown's writing is
his use of historical "documents" in his polemical presenta-
tions. This is one of his more interesting—and pervasive—
techniques, and it will be found in almost everything he will
write and publish. In his plan to indict slavery and its brutal
effects on Southern white morals, therefore, Brown cites newspaper advertisements essentially as "symbols of the times."
They deal mostly with cock-fights, bull, bear, and dog fights:
all basic testaments to the Southerners' mode of violent self-
expression and amusement. Yet their range is such throughout
the lecture that they can move from the citation of a formal,
businesslike advertisement to sell a slave mother and three
children, "By virtue of a deed of trust made to me," to a more
rousing "record" of the South's interest in violent outdoor,
audience participation sports:

> A Bull Fight, between a ferocious bull and a number of
> dogs, will take place Sunday next, at 4¼ o'clock, P.M.,

on the other side of the river, at Algiers, opposite Canal
Street. After the bull fight, a fight will take place between
a bear and some dogs. The whole to conclude by a combat between an ass and several dogs.

Amateurs bringing dogs to participate in the fight will
be admitted gratis.

—*New Orleans Bee*

As interesting as the advertisements is the technique per se
of choosing Southern advertisements by which to damn the
South. As Brown tells us, "I do not present to you the assertion of the North; I do not bring you the advertisement of the
Abolitionists, or my own assertion; but I bring before you the
testimony of the Slaveholders themselves,—and by their own
testimony must they stand or fall." In fact it is significant to
note that William Lloyd Garrison's incisive attack on the
Colonization Society in his 1832 pamphlet, *Thoughts on African Colonization*, used exactly the same objective, physically
detached format, as Garrison spent a great part of 1831 in
the files of the Colonization Society's own library. As we can
see, Brown has learned the approach well from his anti-slavery
mentor. Even more importantly, this use of advertisements
and other "documents" will, from this moment on, form another major aspect of his writing, as he will continually call
on this kind of material to evoke everything from pathos to
indignation.

However, Brown's writing in the *Salem Lecture* is not so
easily "typed" and dismissed. For, just when we think that we
can account for his "graphic portrayal" in terms of episodic
concrete moments, such as those which Hathaway saw in the
Narrative, and in terms of historically rendered "documents"
which he developed from his Abolitionist work, we are con-
fronted with a concrete-symbolic-whimsical moment which
seems to just brilliantly explode from Brown's own creative
imagination. Thus toward the end of the lecture we find the
exotically strange and hyperbolic example of the slave's non-

American position in this country—an example which concretely, yet symbolically, juxtaposes slave with nation in order to show how little the former is able to enroll in the latter.

> Wherever the stars and stripes are seen flying upon American soil, I can receive no protection; I am a slave, a chattel, a thing. I see your liberty-poles around in your cities. If to-morrow morning you are hoisting the stars and stripes upon one of your liberty-poles, and I should see the man following me who claims my body and soul as his property, I might climb to the very top of your liberty-pole, I might cut the cord that held your stars and stripes and bind myself with it as closely as I could to your liberty-pole, I might talk of law and the Constitution, but nothing could save me unless there be public sentiment enough in Salem. I could not appeal to law or the Constitution; I could only appeal to public sentiment.

Clearly there is something more here than the typical Negro slave narrator or the typical anti-slavery polemicist. It is a fusion of the two, somehow, with a touch of both whimsy and a very biting symbolism. In fact, though it is a unique moment for Brown at this early stage in his writing, it nevertheless shows us how graphic and significant his writing and thinking could be. For one magnificent moment then, the early William Wells Brown has directly partaken of the world of art.

Having digressed to look at this exceptional moment of dramatic artistry, however, we need now to return to the more basic discussion of the apprentice writer. Two further points therefore need to be made about the *Salem Lecture*. The first deals with "borrowed verse" and the great use which Brown makes of it to evoke emotion and a unified sensibility of sorts in his addresses and writings. And the second deals with his obvious weakness in handling the dialogue and characterization which will later be the bases of his novels and plays. Indeed, the two points are interrelated. Nor is this mere coincidence. For essentially it is because the verse and sentiments involved here (and in the mouths of his major characters in *Clotel, The Escape,* and *Clotelle) are* borrowed that Brown does not really know how to handle them.

Like most of his contemporaries, therefore, Brown liberally uses small quotations of poetry to enhance or strengthen his didactic points. At the end of his rhetorical question about whether the American people shall be behind the Old World's people—fighting words to a country which considered itself to be a moral "leader" as early as it had finished building its "city on the hill"—the orator in him chooses to lapse into ballad stanzas in order to rhythmically emphasize his point.

> Shall every flap of England's flag
> Proclaim that all around are free,
> From furthest Ind to each blue crag
> That beetles o'er the western sea?
> And shall we scoff at Europe's kings,
> When Freedom's fire is dimmed with us;
> And round our country's altar clings
> The damning shade of Slavery's curse?

The point is gracefully, if artificially, made, as it was made constantly during the period by every kind of effective writer. For this sort of "borrowed" verse was a conventional form of emphasis throughout most of the nineteenth century in English and American writing.

However, the technique has a limited application, which depends on the probability that such a speech could, indeed, have been found in the mouth of the person who, we are told, is speaking it. Thus when Brown calls up the poetic moment here, we realize that he does so as an intelligent, literary orator, delving into an artificial tongue for a special effect. At the same time, the technique becomes treacherous when the orator attributes such verses to a realistic person in a realistic setting. The question of appropriateness of dialogue and characterization now raises its aesthetic head.

Brown, however, seems unaware of the difficulty; and this is a good early example of what will finally be one of his major flaws as a creative writer of plays and novels. Hence he gives us now a hoi polloi, wharf-side setting in Liverpool, where the various poor and ignorant members of merchant-life England congregate before our eyes, without Brown's realizing the limitations which this now imposes on the sort of dialogue which will come from this setting.

Only a short time since an American man-of-war was anchored in the bay opposite to Liverpool. The English came down by the hundreds and thousands. The stars and stripes were flying; and there stood those poor persons that had never seen an American man-of-war, but had heard a great deal of American democracy. Some were eulogising the American people; some were calling it the "land of the free and the home of the brave." And while they stood there, one of their number rose up, and pointing his finger to the American flag, said:

> "United States, your banner wears
> Two emblems,—one of fame;
> Alas, the other that it bears,
> Reminds us of your shame.
> The white man's liberty entyped,
> Stands blazoned by your stars;
> But what's the meaning of your stripes?
> They mean your Negro-scars."

Somehow, the complex meter, the elaborate and inventive diction, the symbolic genesis of the poem, and the poetic verse form itself do not seem realistically available to the tongue of "one of their number." It seems a small point at first, but it is not at all so.

For there were two methods of impressing an anti-slavery audience for a fugitive slave orator. The first lay in detailing and enumerating the horrors and cruelties of slavery, giving the audience the harsh, concrete facts of Negro slave experience. This is why such a premium was put by Garrison and Gerrit Smith on dark-skinned Negroes who had lived in the South. And this is why, also, that Garrison kept telling Frederick Douglass to just "tell your story." The other method of impression was predicated upon the first. Its power lay in its ability to show how far a slave had progressed from his crude, ignorant beginnings. The ability to speak fluently and rhetorically, to cite verse and to luxuriate in warm metaphors, therefore, was an impressive testament in its own right. In fact, both these methods were to be found in that major hope that every slave narrative could be "written by himself." For not only were the realistic facts thereby authenticated on the one hand, but the artistic ability of the slave being able to emphatically present these facts was a major virtue in its own right.

Hence he is caught between the two poles here. Instead of sticking to the realism of an English setting and a Liverpool speaker, he enhances the speech through very artificial, "borrowed" verse, without realizing that it is really his own mouth, and not the Liverpool man's, from which these complex stanzas flow. By seeking art in the wrong place, then, Brown has shown a certain weakness in the art of selection and his unawareness of the question of "appropriateness" in dialogue and characterization. Unfortunately the child *is* father to the man, and this flaw will later go on to seriously mar all three of Brown's major fictional works.

The Narrative

We come next to a discussion of the *Narrative* of 1847. Having already noted Messieurs Quincy and Hathaway's suggestions as to its simplicity and calmness of tone, we will immediately begin our discussion along that line of inquiry.

On the one hand both Quincy and Hathaway are quite correct in their analysis of Brown's tone. For there is a flatness and detachment to be found in his *Narrative* which is rare in the slave narratives in general. We note, for example, the flat, unemotional description at the conclusion of Chapter I, where a moment of great anguish and agony is somehow cut short by a tersely detached, reportorial tone of voice. It is different from a Hemingway tone, because Brown is actually trying to explain just how early in the morning punishment can begin for a slave, whereas Hemingway purposely uses irrelevancy for an effect; yet we are nevertheless amazed at how severely the tone truncates the emotional artery which only moments before had been gushing pain across the whole page.

> . . . the overseer commenced whipping her [Brown's mother]. She cried, "Oh! pray—Oh! pray—Oh! pray"— these are generally the words of the slaves when imploring mercy at the hands of their oppressors. I heard her voice, and knew it, and jumped out of my bunk, and went to the door. Though the field was some distance from the house, I could hear every crack of the whip, and every groan and cry of my poor mother. I remained at the door, not daring to venture any further. The cold chills ran over me, and I wept aloud. After giving her ten lashes, the sound of the whip ceased, and I returned to my bed and found no consolation but in my tears. It was not yet daylight.

Ten pages later we meet a similar reportorial tone at a moment normally calling for greater emotional handling. There we note the incredibly terse and bland final paragraph of Chapter II, which, in its entirety, is all Brown has to say about the complete dissolution and fragmentation of his family.

> While living at the Missouri Hotel, a circumstance occurred which caused me great unhappiness. My master sold my mother, and all her children, except myself. They were sold to different persons in the city of St. Louis.

Period. That is all there is; for the next chapter goes off elsewhere, never to return to the subject again. At this point now, we are partially plagued by certain questions about the tone. On the one hand, it seemingly might be the paragraph of an occasionally tired, grind-the-facts-out slave narrator telling his story. Or, on the other hand, it might be that the episodic structure of the *Narrative* as a whole has clouded Brown's vision as to which moments deserve emphasis and which moments do not. Whatever the reason, it is a strangely terse piece of personal history.

Furthermore, if Brown could be detached about his close family and friends, he could be equally detached and unemotional about himself. We note, for example, his mention of a beating which he received in St. Louis, which required five weeks to heal, and we are struck by the fact that he sees it solely in terms of his regret that the five weeks' recuperation period cost him his job in town. Relatedly, we note his calm and extremely rational response to the kind of pack dogs which traditionally set runaway slaves such as Lewis Clarke and Henry Bibb into searing tones of vituperation or pathos. Brown, instead, tells us that

> As soon as I was convinced that it was them ["the bloodhounds of Major Benjamin O'Fallon," used "to hunt runaway slaves with"], I knew there was no chance of escape. I took refuge in the top of a tree, and the hounds were soon at its base, and there remained until the hunters came up in a half or three quarters of an hour afterwards.

And when this same note of acceptance marks his description of his capture a second time, later in the narrative, we realize that Brown has, indeed, developed a new tone for the slave narrative.

At this point now our earlier questions return to re-plague us. We begin to wonder whether this is a distinctively achieved new tone for the slave narrative, or whether it simply represents ignorance and mishandling on the part of the narrator. Is this a consciously chosen speaking voice, or merely the highest branch of expression to which the newly freed slave had been able to climb? With this doubt in mind, we now begin to notice the various tones throughout the narrative.

We are drawn, for example, to the savage tone of the opening two sentences:

> I was born in Lexington, Ky. The man who stole me as soon as I was born, recorded the births of all the infants which he claimed to be born his property, in a book which he kept for that purpose.

and to the fiercely bitter ironies spilled throughout the narrative as a whole:

> In his fits of anger, he would take up a chair, and throw it at a servant; and in his more rational moments, when he wished to chastise one, he would tie them up in the smoke-house, and whip them; after which, he would cause a fire to be made of tobacco stems, and smoke them.
> This he called "Virginia Play."

More important than these spot examples of versatility is a key dramatic moment which contains several different tones artistically used side by side. The moment begins and ends with a flat, factual tone, even as its pathos is celebrated in the middle through evocative emotion and borrowed verse; and it takes simply one example like this to convince us that Brown is very much in control of his narrative tones. "Soon after we left St. Charles," he begins,

> the young child grew very cross, and kept up a noise during the greater part of the day. Mr. Walker complained

of its crying several times, and told the mother to stop the child's d- - - -d noise, or he would. The woman tried to keep the child from crying, but could not. We put up at night with an acquaintance of Mr. Walker, and in the morning, just as we were about to start, the child again commenced crying. Walker stepped up to her, and told her to give the child to him. The mother tremblingly obeyed. He took the child by one arm, as you would a cat by the leg, walked into the house and said to the lady,

Madam, I will make you a present of this little nigger; it keeps such a noise that I can't bear it."

"Thank you, sir," said the lady.

The mother, as soon as she saw that her child was to be left, ran up to Mr. Walker, and falling upon her knees begged him to let her have her child; she clung around his legs, and cried, "Oh, my child! my child! Master, do let me have my child! oh, do, do, do. I will stop its crying, if you will only let me have it again." When I saw this woman crying for her child so piteously, I shuddered —a feeling akin to horror, shot through my frame. I have often since in imagination heard her crying for her child:—

"O, Master, let me stay to catch
    My baby's sobbing breath,
His little glassy eye to watch,
    And smooth his limbs in death,
And cover him with grass and leaf,
    Beneath the large oak tree:
It is not sullenness, but grief—
    O, Master, pity me!

- - - - - - - - - - - - -

Then give me but one little hour—
    O! do not lash me so!
One little hour—one little hour—
    And gratefully I'll go."

We have here, now, a moment of real artistry and tonal structure. It begins with a sense of restrained power and tension in its detached tone and yet hesitant meter. Then, reaching the moment of crisis in which a child is taken away from its mother, it once more underplays the terrible emotion involved through a starkly dehumanizing cat simile and the even more callous, yet ironically chivalric, piece of insensitive dialogue. All of this is portrayed without a flicker of the narrator's emotion.

Then the flood gates burst—for both the mother and the narrator. Couched in a delicate and poignant simplicity, the mother's feelings involve us as only a single-mindedly distraught mother's words could. Then, as the moment rises to its emotional climax, the narrator paraphrases the mother's plea with a piece of borrowed verse that manages to keep the same feeling of simplicity even as it soars on the wings of a polished ballad stanza form.

Having reached this peak, the moment now concludes with the same factual, reportorial note with which it began, and the episode is all over.

> Mr. Walker commanded her to return into the ranks with the other slaves. Women who had children were not chained, but those that had none were. As soon as her child was disposed of, she was chained in the gang.

After the borrowed verse and genuine pathos, this return to the unemotional tone is somehow very effectively unnerving. For after the tears and the pain, something incredibly poignant happens when dry-eyed order is clamped down over the moment and it becomes just another museum horror soundlessly exhibited in a plain glass case.

Clearly Brown is in complete control of both halves of the tonal coin here, able to move deftly and strikingly between the poignantly emotional and the sparsely detached without even the slightest grinding of gears. By 1847, then, we have a strongly developing dramatic artist in our midst.

"The American Slave-Trade"

Brown's third piece of published writing was his article on "The American Slave-Trade," appearing in *The Liberty Bell* of 1848. Strictly a piece of anti-slavery propaganda, as we noted above, and included as one of thirty-nine abolitionist pieces, its major interest for us is the core of this short piece and the fact that it attains all its vitality and power from its reliance on first-person, realistic description. "I shall never forget a scene which took place in the city of St. Louis, while I was in slavery," he begins, and the rest of the article is devoted to the concrete and artistically handled narration of that moment when he saw a slave husband and wife sold away from each other on an auction stand.

Despite its briefness, there are two aspects of this article which are of major interest to us. The first, of course, is Brown's reliance upon an anecdote and personal experience as a touchstone for his public message—a reliance which continues and reinforces the episodic structure which will so strongly make itself felt in his later fictional work. At the same time, of perhaps greater interest is his adroit, dramatic handling of his narrative perspective, with what strikes us today as almost the precision and focus of the television camera. "My eyes were intensely fixed on the face of the woman, whose cheeks were wet with tears" is his initial perspective, and from this incisive close-up he manages to capture all the heart-rending pathos to be found in a slave woman's realization of her helpless degradation and ultimate loss of her husband.

Next Brown draws near to the husband, who has already been sold, and overhears him trying to convince his new master to buy Fanny so that they will not be separated. Not only is this a microphone close-up, as Brown directly hears the slave begging his new master to purchase her because she "is a good cook, a good worker, and her last mistress liked her very much," but it is visually intimate as well. "I watched the countenance of the man while the different persons were bidding on his wife," he tells us. "When his new master bid on his wife you could see the smile upon his countenance, and the tears stop; but as soon as another would bid, you could see the countenance change and the tears start afresh. From the change of countenance one could see the workings of the inmost soul."

Finally, with the auction over and the couple ripped apart forever, Brown captures their tears of realization and the husband's final words to his wife. Then, most effectively, he reinforces the pathos which he has been eliciting from us by showing how the same pathos was to be found at the moment of crisis itself in the eyes of the various onlookers at the scene. Shifting his perspective once more then, he visually zeroes in on faces of those witnessing the tragedy, and notes how "I saw the countenances of a number of whites who were present, and whose eyes were dim with tears at hearing the man bid his wife farewell."

It seems so simple, and yet this shifting, incisive focus is very effective and technically impressive. It is, in fact, the essential format of all drama, and thus is a very favorable foreshadowing of Brown's later ability to write a novel and play which will be able to transcend the narrow, limited perspective of the single, didactic narrator and which will move instead towards a dramatic structure which allows for different characters, different voices, and the kind of sustained dramatic conflict which different human perspectives bring. The portrait of our artist is beginning to take form.

The Anti-Slavery Harp

Brown's next major publication was *The Anti-Slavery Harp* of 1848. The purpose of this book is clearly stated by him in the preface, when he tells us that "The demand of the public for a cheap Anti-Slavery Song Book, containing Songs of a more recent composition, has induced me to collect together, and present to the public, the songs contained in this book." The book itself is merely a collection of harsh, brutal or sentimental songs of hardship and woe—some of them made all the more glib by the too-easiness of their rhyme and meter. As "O, Pity the Slave Mother" tells us,

> I pity the slave mother, careworn and weary,
>   Who sighs as she presses her babe to her breast;
> I lament her sad fate, all so helpless and dreary,
>   I lament for her woes, and her wrongs unredressed.

Sharing the spotlight with this sort of sentimentality are the tiresome harshness to be found in "The Bondsman" and the pulsating shout of such slogan marches as "Emancipation Song." On the other hand, however, there are several interesting verses here. "What Mean Ye?", for instance, has God speaking four of its stanzas, while the vividly metaphorical song "The Bigot Fire" is a brilliant piece of topical allusion treated in mock dialogue.

Despite the interesting and sometimes exciting elements to be found in several of these songs, however, the major significance of the book for us lies in the fact that Brown has had no hand in composing any one of them. There is a list of authors at the conclusion of the collection, and it makes clear the fact that Brown was not a writer of any of the lyrics. Thus the collection as a whole is only of limited value to us; for while it shows us that Brown was important enough to the anti-slavery movement to be in a position to collect these songs under his editorship and name, we not only have no evidence of him as a writer, but we can't even ascertain just what editing or selecting he did here.

And yet, despite these major drawbacks, there are certain significant aspects to this pamphlet. First of all, once again we find Brown caught up in an episodic structure. And though he was only editing here, the point is that he was nevertheless compiling "documents" of a sort, as he had previously done in his three earlier publications. This is important for us to note because this early practice in such a loose structure will soon be carried over, as we have already noted, to Brown's more artistic works.

Secondly, not only has Brown had more practice in general "compiling," but he has now had practice compiling songs as if they and the borrowed verses he compiled were real emotions. Having understood this relationship between emotional moments and borrowed materials to express those emotions, then, we will not be surprised to find all of Brown's major characters in *Clotel* and *Clotelle* intoning romantic verse to each other which is clearly borrowed from the late eighteenth and early nineteenth centuries' stage and parlor. Nor will we be surprised to find four major characters in *The Escape* turn the end of the play into a comic opera, as they mouth on stage whole anti-slavery songs in bald soliloquy. For, once again, this early dependence of Brown's upon borrowed emotion and borrowed expression will finally atrophy his own sense of the beautiful and poignant.

Panoramic Views

In 1849 Charles Gilpin of Bishopsgate Street, London, published Brown's next work, *A Description of William Wells Brown's Original Panoramic Views of the Scenes in the Life of an American Slave*. The cover of this sixpence pamphlet was ornamented with a typically stilted figure of a slave in chains, praying to the Lord above and the world at large. But what is most interesting about our first sight of the pamphlet is the delightfully clenched-teeth sense of irony which plays across its face.

FICTION

"We hold these truths to be self-evident: that all men are created equal; that they are endowed by their Creator with certain inalienable rights; and that among these are LIFE, LIBERTY, and the PURSUIT OF HAPPINESS."

—Declaration of American Independence

FACT

"They touch our country, and their shackles fall."

—Cowper

This wry awareness, in fact, sets the tone for the rest of the pamphlet as a whole and marks again the ironic contrast of America and Europe which Brown found so valuable throughout his writings.

Sixpence that it was, the pamphlet was basically meant as a tour guide for a collection of scenes picturing slave life in America which Brown had selected and was exhibiting in London. His collection was in response to an exhibition of a Panorama of the Mississippi River which Brown had seen in Boston in 1847, in which "I was somewhat amazed at the very mild manner in which the 'Peculiar Institution' of the Southern States was there represented." With characteristic dispatch and incisiveness, "I, therefore, commenced collecting a number of sketches of plantations in the Slave States, illustrating the life of the Slave, from his birth, to his death in bondage, or his flight from the 'Stars and Stripes' to the British possessions of North America." The result is a very striking and effective book, as once more Brown's creative sense of mission impresses us with its power and dedication.

Interesting as the tourbook is for its content, it is of greater significance to us for two basic aspects of its composition. On the one hand, we can see quite clearly how very close Hathaway was to the truth when he cited Brown's eye and concern for "graphic portrayal." For Brown has selected and arranged each of the scenes in this museum collection himself, and thus has found himself "writing" anti-slavery propaganda with a literally pictorial eye and hand. It is no wonder, therefore, that throughout his career he was able to see so many elements and anecdotes of slavery so clearly, and was then able to render them in his writing with such pictorial clarity. The tour guide is both a culmination in itself and a preparation for much of Brown's later work.

On the other hand, the tourbook, like so many other works of Brown, is also of interest because its structure is so essentially episodic. And though this now begins to seem as if we are belaboring the point, its importance will become strongly obvious in our discussion of *Clotelle*.

CHAPTER NINE

Growth of the Artist: Metamorphosis

By the end of 1849, Brown had made a fairly substantial literary mark for himself. His *Narrative* had gone through four editions in America and one in England; and he had compiled *The Anti-Slavery Harp*, contributed to anti-slavery journals, and published *Panoramic Views*. As all this began to attract the favorable attention of London newspaper publishers, he now became a regular contributor to several of their papers, devoting himself primarily to American subjects. Between lecturing throughout England and the Continent, and writing short articles in *The Daily News, The Morning Chronicle*, and *The Leader*, Brown had little time for any formal writing. It was three years, therefore, between *Panoramic Views* and his next book, *Three Years in Europe*.

Essentially, *Three Years in Europe* is a travelogue, written in journalistic-epistolary style by the author as he made his way around England and the Continent, as both representative of the American anti-slavery cause and as personal tourist in his own right. Liverpool, London, Edinburgh, Versailles: all are described pictorially, all are anecdoted in the travelogue style so typical of the nineteenth century. This is the major portion of the book, and it is of major significance for us in our understanding of the emerging artist. Here for the first time Brown was beginning to feel free from the need to polemicize all his work, and here he let himself relax and write a purely social travel book, savoring more of the casual tourist than of the dedicated polemicist. In its own small way, this was a significant step for Brown to take.

At the same time, the book is of interest to us for other reasons as well. We see again Brown's reliance on "graphically portrayed" description and note how strong this aspect of his writing is in him. More important than his kind and amount of description, however, is the structure involved in the book. In the major, travelogue section, we find a structure that has nothing more extensive than a paragraphic unity based merely on a movement through time and space, and this insight will soon figure in our assessment of Brown's structure in the writing of *Clotelle*. Furthermore, there is something even more intriguing about the structure at the conclusion of the book. In Chapters XX, XXI, and XXII, then, we suddenly find an attempt by Brown to achieve a unity of interest and treatment in each chapter which is necessarily absent from the strictly travel book chapters above. Even here, however—even where he is consciously seeking to structure a unified whole—we find what is at best a fragmented unity.

Chapter XX on "Fugitive Slaves in England" is very distinctly composed of several disparate elements: a one-page philosophic polemic on freedom and the irony that slavery is fostered in America; a two-page Who's Who introduction to the August, 1851 meeting of fugitive slaves in England; a six-page account of Brown's opening address at that meeting; a one-page account of two other addresses given there; followed by a five-page reprinting of the "Appeal to the People of Great Britain and the World" which concluded the convention. In fifteen pages which are supposedly devoted to a single, unified subject then, what we have is a structure composed of five distinctly separate subjects and documents.

This same sort of format is true of Chapter XXI also, devoted to "A Chapter on American Slavery." Beginning with an opening two-page statement of the intellectual and law-abiding superiority of England to America, it then goes on to give us another list: a three-page general sketch of William Lloyd Garrison—"the greatest writer of the Anti-Slavery field," who "is at present time but little more than forty-five years of age, and of middle size;" a three-page general sketch of Wendell Phillips—"the most distinguished public speaker" in America, whose "stature is not tall, but handsome;" two pages similarly devoted to Frederick Douglass, one to Charles Lennox Remond, one to Francis Jackson, etc., etc. In all, it is little more than a series of unrelated, uninsightful travel brochure items for the European reader who is planning to come to America and see the sights of Anti-Slavery. Of greater unity here is Chapter XXII, but this is a special case which we will discuss more fully when we come to our study of *Clotelle* itself.

The year after *Clotel; or, The President's Daughter* was published and two years after *Three Years in Europe*, Brown came out with an enlarged and revised version of the latter book. Entitled *Sketches of Places and People Abroad*, it differs from its predecessor only in length and one significant piece of direct exhortation. The first twenty chapters are exactly the same as those of *Three Years in Europe*, and the next twelve merely expand the coverage of Brown's itinerary. It is the conclusion of *Sketches*, however, which sets it apart from the earlier work, for there is a dramatic rise to the later book's conclusion which is absent from the earlier travelogue.

Hence, where *Three Years in Europe* is content to end with the *Clotelle*-like "Narrative of American Slavery" which we will discuss later (a unit all to itself, which has no relationship to the twenty-two other chapters in subject matter, form, tone or purpose, and therefore hardly a piece which could be considered a conclusion to the book as a whole), *Sketches*, by contrast, soars to great declarative heights as Brown explains why he came home at the end of his travels to "my native land. Native land! How harshly that word sounds to my ears!"

I might have remained in a country where my manhood
was never denied; I might have remained in ease in other
climes; but what was ease and comfort abroad, while
more then three millions of my countrymen were groaning in the prison-house of slavery in the Southern States?
Yes, I came back to the land of my nativity, not to be a
spectator, but a soldier—a soldier in the moral warfare
against the most cruel system of oppression that ever
blackened the character or hardened the heart of man.

The growing strength and personal assurance is readily apparent.

Sketches does, moreover, have more to offer us outside the
realm of its major content than it does within the twelve additional
chapters and Brown's personal declaration. For in part
of the introductory material we find the intriguing acknowledgement that sometime between 1852 and 1854 Brown had
become more than an anti-slavery orator: had become, in fact,
a professional man of letters. As "The Memoir" tells us,

Most of the fugitive slaves, and, in fact, nearly all the
colored men who had visited Great Britain from the
United States, have come upon begging missions, either
for some society or for themselves. Mr. Brown has been
almost the only exception. With that independence of
feeling which those who are acquainted with him know
to be one of his chief characteristics, he determined to
maintain himself and family by his own exertions,—by
his literary labors, and the honorable profession of a public lecturer.

And when Brown himself begins his preface with a typical
anti-slavery "apology" which is now being utilized to *sell*
copies of the book as well as to gain sympathy, we know that
we have a professional writer in our midst. "While I feel con-

scious that most of the contents of these Letters will be interesting chiefly to American readers," he begins,

> yet I may indulge the hope that the fact of their being the
> first production of a Fugitive Slave as a history of travels
> may carry with them novelty enough to secure for them,
> to some extent, the attention of the reading public of
> Great Britain.

It seems a small point at first glance, since the materials which
Brown has used as a professional writer for London newspapers and publishers have largely been based on his experiences
in the anti-slavery cause. But the difference between anti-
slavery agent and professional writer here is less one of content than it is of method.

Hence as we look at the over-all development of Brown's
writings during this period, we are struck by the definite growth
from the didactic to the implicit, from the literal to the fictional. After the normal polemic and autobiography of *Salem
Lecture*, the *Narrative*, and "The American Slave-Trade," we
find that *The Anti-Slavery Harp* and *Panoramic Views* offer
a very different type of anti-slavery writing, accomplishing
their didactic purpose in a far more subtle way. Three years
after the second of these, we find Brown's *Three Years in
Europe* only partially dedicated to the anti-slavery movement
and living much more for itself as a casual travel journal.
Furthermore, the final chapter of that book is devoted to a
completely unexpected short story, which is the germ seed of
much of *Clotelle*. The topic here is still the same: it is still
social argumentation about the cruelty of the slave's life. But
now it comes at us not in the directly pressed prose of the
orator-author; instead, it is filtered to us through the finely
woven threads of an intricate cloth story. Brown's venture
into the realm of the novel then, with his publication of *Clotel;
or, The President's Daughter* in 1853, will be the first time
that this indirect, fictional approach will be attempted on any

major scale by Brown. It is a culmination of his growing as an artist, and it is a major reason for his being considered a professional in "The Memoir" of the 1854 *Sketches* when there was no mention of this in the 1852 version of the travelogue. The date of this professional acknowledgement was 1854. The date of *Clotel* was 1853. This is no coincidence.

Though the purpose of his writing was still the same, there is a very definite shift from historical fact and argument to romanticized, "appealing" fiction in Brown's writings from 1848 to 1854. And this distinctly marks his movement from orator to artist. That he was a better orator-pamphleteer than he was a novelist is of little import here. What is important is that the first Negro novel was on its way and Negro expression had gained a whole new field in which to grow.

Clotel

As we approach the first version of *Clotel*, now, we are attracted initially by those elements in it which are holdovers or developments from Brown's earlier writings. We are not surprised to find that Chapter I, for example, begins with an epigraph of borrowed verse:

> Why stands she near the auction stand,
> That girl so young and fair?
> What brings her to this dismal place,
> Why stands she weeping there?

Nor are we surprised at the amount of point-blank polemic and history in it. In fact, where the later *Clotelle* will end Chapter I with a mildly sentimental discussion of the cruelty involved in the separation of the slave mother and her two daughters, Chapter I of *Clotel* concludes on a note of strongly indignant anti-Christian and anti-democracy disputation aimed at "the inhumanity, the atrocity, and the immorality of that doctrine which . . . commends such a crime to the favour of enlightened and Christian people." It follows this with an equally strong anti-democracy denunciation based on the central irony of the whole novel, as Brown notes again that the girls sold were "two daughters of Thomas Jefferson, the writer of the Declaration of American Independence." And finally the Chapter concludes with another piece of borrowed verse, rounding off its oratorical presentation.

Just within the space of Chapter I, then, we have moved from borrowed epigraphic verse to eight paragraphs of historical indictment to three paragraphs of novelistic exposition to two paragraphs of strident denunciation, finally catching our breath on another plateau of borrowed verse. Obviously Brown is still interested in the direct writing of anti-slavery material, even as he is branching off into the use of the novel as an indirect method of attack.

In fact, this is the key to understanding the nature of this first version of the first Negro novel. Accordingly, we note his many one-sided narrative discourses on the harshness of slavery and his international ironic contrasts of America and Europe, techniques which we have seen as far back as the *Salem Lecture*. Indeed, the list is endless, for basically Brown was more interested in documenting a broadside against slavery than he was in writing a novel; and once again it is the recurrent use of "documents" which seems to be the cornerstone of this massive fortress.

The very second paragraph of the novel, for example, is featured by the citation of documents to support Brown's opening statement that marriage for slaves is greatly discouraged by their white Southern masters. Not only does he state this, but he then goes on to cite verbatim, in historical thesis fashion, several reports on the matter by various Southern organizations like the "Shiloh Baptist Association" and the "Savannah River Association." Our very first moment in the novel, therefore, is one composed of historically "documented," argumentative prose. In fact, the large half of the large first chapter concludes with Brown's statement (using an editorial "we," no less) that

> We have thought it advisable to show that the present system of chattel slavery in America undermines the entire social condition of man, so as to prepare the reader for the following narrative of slave life. . . .

This early novel, then, is deemed incapable of standing alone; and throughout its entirety Brown will adhere to this premise.

We are consequently prepared to find the same sort of "advertisements" which we had been accustomed to in Brown's earlier writing; nor are we disappointed. Likewise we don't even blink when we find whole sections of Thomas Jefferson's speeches quoted directly in parts of Chapter XVII. There, while Mary (Jefferson's mulatto "granddaughter") broils in the hot Richmond sun because her mistress desires to "blacken" her to the skin shade which the mistress thinks a slave ought to bear, Brown ironically quotes some of Jefferson's anti-slavery speeches to the Virginia legislature, verbatim, for three fourths of the chapter. This is documentation with a vengeance.

"Documentation" we call it, and documentation it is. For though at first glance we are tempted to consider it merely an unconscious holdover from Brown's earlier writings, and thus only a minor aberration in his style, the fact is that he is very much conscious of this technique and very much committed to its use. At the end of an incredibly romantic, discovered-identity anecdote in New Orleans, for example, we not only note the lack of integral relationship between the moment and the novel as a whole, but we are even more interested in Brown's discussion of it in the final paragraph of the chapter. As he tells us,

> This, reader, is no fiction; if you think so, look over the file of the New Orleans newspapers of the year 1845–6, and you will see there reports of the trial.

In this single paragraph Brown has succinctly told us the nature and purpose of this first novel of his, and this is no isolated example. Historical and true, the novel is a running comment on the South and its slavery with as many real cases and anecdotes incorporated into the narrative as possible. In fact, this is one of the reasons that we have so many characters and so sprawling a geographic structure: it is simply a mathematical matter of more geography $=$ more pain $=$ more indictment.

Several similar examples of this conscious "current events" realism easily come to mind. For instance, at the conclusion of William's and Clotel's escape by steamboat from Vicksburg, Brown presents us with another verbatim advertisement describing what Clotel and William actually looked like to a suspicious correspondent of a Southern newspaper, who happened to be on the same boat with them and later learned that the two figures he saw were runaway slaves. This newspaper account is directly quoted and is clearly not Brown's writing. Again we have a documented basis given for what we would—and should—be tempted to call a novelistic creation.

A further example occurs in the very next chapter. While we are still with William, we learn of his successful skirmish with a Northern railroad conductor about how much fare he should pay since he has been made to ride in the luggage van of the train. Concluding this anecdote in which William paid for himself as freight and thus saved three quarters of the normal fare, Brown tells us again that

This, reader, is no fiction; it actually occurred in the railroad above described.

and occurred, we might add, to Brown himself in 1844 on the Mad River and Lake Erie Railroad line in Ohio.

What we finally have in *Clotel*, therefore, is not so much an artistic novel as a loosely structured skeleton of a plot on which the author can hang true and vivid anecdotes, stories, advertisements and Virginia legislature speeches; not a work of sculptured unity resting on American soil, it is actually a nineteenth century "deus ex machina" mobile, propitiously hanging from the sky.

At the same time, there is clearly a positive side to this novel, as novel, and this immediately brings us to a discussion of its structure again. For if certain critics are correct in saying that there is enough material here for a dozen novels, this is largely due to the scope and size which Brown has put into his overall structure. This is not to say that the structure is an especially good one for the novel; yet it is to say that there is a very definite sense of structuring nevertheless.

The novel essentially takes place in three cities: Richmond, Natchez, and New Orleans. We begin with the family of a mother and two girls living together in Richmond, and then watch as they are sold and split up: Clotel remaining in Richmond; her mother, Currer, being sold in Natchez; her sister, Althesa, being sold in New Orleans. What this gives Brown is the ability to probe and draw on the whole South for his anti-slavery investigation and story, for he can thereby spread his discussion of the subject over many different characters in many different areas. Given Brown's purpose here, the structure is very aptly chosen.

At the same time, however, this large scale planning does not carry over to the relationship *among* the incidents and anecdotes within that structure. For if this three-pronged narrative structure tends to be episodic to the general writer, it becomes even more so in the episodically-trained hand of William Wells Brown. Thus we jump from place to place because the author says we should and not because the material itself dictates it. But this is only half the problem. Worse still is the fact that even fictional moments here finally become handled as the realistic "documents" which Brown has become so used to handling. Hence some very promising approaches to a literary and artistic handling of material somehow become isolated, self-contained anecdotes and nothing

more. And there they sit like monstrous sequins crudely im-
bedded in a thin and tattered rope belt.

We find that Chapter XXI, "The Christian's Death," for
example, is a completely self-contained analytic thesis tucked
into a single chapter in Natchez. It begins with the Mayflower
in November of 1620, and thereafter treats, in order, the
nature of Christianity, slavery in America, emancipation,
colonization, Henry Clay, and finally some of the characters
who actually do belong in the novel. It is a historical paper
all in itself, with only a small dab of novelistic glue used to
attach it to the plot as a whole.

Chapter XXII is also a self-contained play, as Clotel rides
a stagecoach from Cincinnati to Lynchburg and we meet in
dialogue a whole new group of characters in this dramatically
isolated setting. The whole chapter—in its political, dialectical,
and humorous dialogue—is completely unrelated to the novel,
except for the fact that Clotel is inertly there on the scene.

Likewise, Chapter XXIII is a short story all in itself. It
takes us to New Orleans, introduces us for the first time to
one of Althesa's daughters, and follows her quickly into adult-
hood, where she is just as quickly sold to a profligate Southerner and almost rescued by the gallant Frenchman she loves,
who in turn is shot in the attempt. She promptly dies of a
broken heart, and the short story-chapter is breathlessly over.
Exposition, crisis, climax, denouement: all are narratively provided in a short chapter which is linked to the main novel only
through the name of the heroine in question.

And yet this is not to damn *Clotel* completely as a novel,
for there are several elements in it which are quite fascinating
and well-planned. We need to be constantly aware, as mentioned above, of just how well the overall novel functions because of its sweeping geographic structure. Natchez, actually,
is the setting for the best parts of the novel, both humorous
and didactic, and this is no coincidence. For it somehow manages to be the artistic and geographic middle ground between
the sentimental pathos of Clotel in Richmond and the romantic

melodrama of Althesa in New Orleans. Brown's structure is beginning to bear fruit.

Part of this, of course, is the fact that Natchez was not at all the kind of socially and commercially important city which Richmond and New Orleans were. For this reason it did not offer the "false" (for Brown's own abilities) opportunities for the glamor and over-sentimentality of situation, action, and dialogue which the other two cities seemed to call forth from the author. In a sense, then, his choice of cities determined what sort of material Brown presented in each; and if we feel that much of the choice was incorrect for his own talents, at least we must acknowledge that a good deal of novelistic planning went into the choices in question.

Related to this artistic choice of cities and material is Brown's choice of which characters are going to be placed in each city. For when the family of Currer, Clotel, and Althesa was sold and split up in Chapter I, Brown presented himself with a carte blanche regarding his positioning of characters. Thus it is an artistic choice which has placed the two beautiful daughters, who contain the greater emotional and sentimental possibilities for a melodramatic novelist, in romantic Richmond and New Orleans. Currer, on the other hand, is relegated to the hinterlands of Natchez, far from the traffic of bright lights and glamorous possibilities. What this means for the novel is that, when dealing with Natchez, Brown does not feel required to use artificial, melodramatic language about frilly, sentimental happenings. Instead, in Natchez he can ·devote himself to the things which he knows, rather than to the things which he thinks he should talk about.

It is in Natchez then that we find the great and important questions of Brown's time debated and discussed. Colonization versus emancipation, Negro gratitude versus man's inherent rights—the range and depth of the questions here are awesome. Likewise, situated on the Carlton farm, Brown can allow himself to describe in concrete detail and semi-realistic dialect those elements of Negro and poor white farm and home life which Brown had experienced in his own early years in slavery. In fact, many of these characters (Sam), situations (the mistaken-tooth extraction), and even repartee jokes ("Who made you?" "De overseer told us last night who made us, but indeed I forget the genteman's name.") will find themselves directly transferred to *The Escape* five years later, where, once again, they will be the freshest material in sight.

Also significant here is the fact that where Brown allots only single chapters to Richmond and New Orleans each time we visit them, Natchez very often is treated in blocks of two or three chapters. The artistry behind this structure is obvious. For Natchez, as we have noted, is the location of Brown's major debates. Hence the greater the space, the more profound and extensive the treatment. At the same time, Natchez is also the home of Brown's native dialect and humor; so that not only does this additional length of two or three chapters allow him to treat each of these two components in greater depth, but it also allows him to place them together, deftly lightening much of the serious debate with small amounts of comic relief. With all these points in mind, then, we can suddenly see just how much Brown has achieved through his attention to, and control of, overall narrative structure.

There is, now, one other moment of the novel which indicates the growing artist in Brown in a manner so unexpected that we tend to overlook it in its isolation. It is not an integral part of the novel really (very few events here are), nor does it ever recur again. And yet, for one intriguing moment, Brown forsakes disputation and well-wrought structure, and simply abandons himself to a moment of vicarious identification with some of his characters: a pack of dogs.

> Two slaves had run off owing to severe punishment. The
> dogs were put upon their trail. . . . The dogs soon took to
> the swamp . . . covered with water, waist deep: here these
> faithful animals, swimming nearly all the time, followed
> the zigzag course, the tortuous twistings and wanderings

of these two fugitives . . . sometimes scenting the trees
wherein they had found a temporary refuge from the
mud and water; at other places where the deep mud had
pulled off a shoe, and they had not taken time to put it
on again. . . . Now losing the trail—then slowly and
dubiously taking it off again, until they triumphantly
threaded it out, bringing them back to the river. . . .

It is well known to hunters that it requires the keenest
scent and best blood to overcome such obstacles, and yet
these persevering and sagacious animals conquered every
difficulty.

It is a creative piece of descriptive narrative, and it is interesting how, in this moment, Brown loses all sense of his polemic cause and racial identity. For there is a pride, a triumph,
and almost heroic note about this chase—one that can be seen
only from the dogs' point of view: the "faithful," "persevering," "sagacious" animals, now dramatically losing the
track, now successfully finding it again, until they "triumphantly" thread it out. It is an incredible moment for Brown,
one which he will not achieve again in the rest of the novel
with its clogged up concern for moral message, melodramatic
appeal, and polemical history. For just this single moment he
is the completely emancipated Ariel artist, pursuing a subject
and point of view simply because it intrigues him. The meta-
morphosis is on its way.

After *Clotel* in 1853, Brown wrote three pieces before his
next major venture into dramatic literature with *The Escape*
of 1858. Since we have no tangible remains of *Doughface*,
Brown's supposed first drama, the only extant works in this

period are *Sketches*, "Visit of a Fugitive Slave to the Grave of Wilberforce," and *St. Domingo*: all of them appearing in 1854. We have already discussed the first work at some length, so that it now behooves us to spend some time on the remaining two. For our purposes, however, little time will be needed for either.

When we come to "Visit of a Fugitive Slave," we need concern ourselves with nothing more than a look at its structure. For once again we note how it is episodic in its movement from Trafalgar Square to general anecdote to Westminster Abbey. Entering the abbey, we then episodically move past several statues and thoughts about the men so honored (Sharpe, Newton, Addison, etc.) until we finally reach Wilberforce's grave and a meditation thereon. Characteristically structured by Brown, the article impresses us again with the great deal of movement which takes place within its very limited confines.

St. Domingo, on the other hand, is a fascinating piece of presentation and perspective which we have seen in its more important aspects in our discussion of Brown as orator. What it demonstrates for us here is an extraordinarily graceful prose style, full of rhetorically stylized statements and various tonal modulations. Relatedly, it shows Brown's ability to see detachedly and objectively both sides of a man's nature and both sides of a historical struggle. Thus while he is able to celebrate the heroic Christophe in almost Classical cadences, he is also able to give Rigaud, Petion, and Boyer their due as men, even as they represent the enemy in this speech of liberation and revolution.

A beautiful piece of writing and integrated structuring, the address is unfortunately unrelated to our present inquiry. For whether its partial detachment and balanced perspective were made possible by Brown's treatment of a country and subject which he was less committed to than he was to slavery in the United States; or whether this perspective and polished style represent the maturation of his historical speaking voice as it first appeared in the *Salem Lecture*; neither the subject matter nor the tone will have any bearing on either of Brown's subsequent fiction: *The Escape* or *Clotelle*.

The Escape

As we come to the first extant Negro play, *The Escape*, we have reached the final transitional stage before the artist's ultimate emergence. Our initial impression of the work is that Brown is still essentially didactic in his motivation and means to be as factual as possible in his method and presentation. He begins his "Preface" by stating that he never meant the play to be publicly presented and therefore is not worried over its success or failure in that realm. As he notes,

> The main features in the Drama are true. . . . Many of the incidents were drawn from my own experiences of eighteen years at the South.

He then concludes the "Preface" with the standard "apology" offered by the anti-slavery orator:

> The play, no doubt, abounds in defects, but as I was born in slavery, and never had a day's schooling in my life, I owe the public no apology for errors.

In short, there is nothing in the "Preface" to make us think that this first Negro drama will be anything more than an anti-slavery discourse couched in dialogue and action. Nor are we very much mistaken. Yet what will be most significant here is the effect which dialogue and action as expressive forms will have on Brown's present and later work.

"Look on this picture, and on this" the epigraph quotes from *Hamlet*, and we realize once more that direct moral guidance is to be gained from our attention to the work, no matter how different the form and style may be from Brown's earlier work. And yet, what is so refreshing about *The Escape* is just how little moral guidance is explicitly provided us. The playwright's motives are the same here as they were in *Salem Lecture*, but the method has radically changed. In fact we find only one character in the play who is directly preaching to us, and he appears only briefly and only in the very end. Mr. White therefore, the visitor from Massachusetts who comes South to teach moral truth like a Yankee Greek chorus, is the only figure in the book who is a direct descendant from Brown's oratorical days.

For the most part, it is the nature of the work which has accomplished this change in Brown's delivery. For the matter of form and technique in the drama does not allow for the kind of outspoken, direct didactness which Brown imparted so plentifully to *Clotel* and to his anti-slavery orations before that. Drama must be seen as well as heard, and this requires action, perhaps even symbolic action. Furthermore, while the play is still "heard" to some extent, it is now heard from more than one speaker, and thus the playwright must spend as much time on making his speakers different from each other as he does on compiling the material which he wants them to speak. In short, the play form demands that an anti-slavery "crusader" now become an artist: demands that he devote as much attention to the vehicle which expresses his caring as he does to that caring itself. This is a significant step which Brown has made.

At the same time that Brown is now a "unified" artist in the sense that his work in *The Escape* is fully dramatic and not a mere combination of borrowed verses, historical declarations, compiled "documents," and fictionalized characters, we must now admit that he is not exceptionally strong as a purely dramatic artist. His progress as a writer towards the world of art and fiction has been an extremely important achievement in the world of Negro letters; however, having given this giant step all the acclaim it deserves, we must now look at the step itself to see what sort of foothold was actually gained.

We begin with a necessary discussion of the dialogue and characterization, since the play must rise or fall on that. Brown's best writing in this vein lies in his creation of native Negro dialogue which is essentially comic. The combination of familiarity with the tone and cadence plus Brown's freedom from having to earnestly make a moral point (his comedy is strictly comic relief) seems to somehow liberate him and allow him to create what he sees and hears rather than what he thinks.

Unfortunately these Negro characters are only minor figures in the play as a whole, and much of their comedy is all too reminiscent of the minstrel tradition. The essential truth then is that for most of the drama Brown has considerable difficulty with his dialogue and characterization. Part of this is his use of melodramatic verse for his major romantic characters, which is somewhat disconcerting, especially when juxtaposed against the more realistic Negro dialogue which we mentioned above. Right after the very natural dialogue of Cato, (a Negro servant) in an early farce scene, for example, when scene iii brings us to Glen (our Negro hero) in the slave quarters, we find it rather hard to believe that the pseudo-Byronic, Shakespearean tones are really his. "How slowly the time passes away," he muses.

> I've been watching here two hours, and Melinda has not yet come. What keeps her, I cannot tell. I waited long and late for her last night, and when she approached, I sprang to my feet, caught her in my arms, pressed her to my heart, and kissed away the tears from her moistened cheeks. Ah! Here comes Melinda

Yet the problem is considerably more complex than just this. For Brown not only doesn't know how people talk as a homogeneous group (i.e. both Cato and Glen are slaves on the same plantation), but he also has trouble differentiating between characters once they are in a homogeneous group. Essentially this is a question of spoken mannerisms as the basis of individualizing characters, and essentially Brown has no real ear for this at all. Hence "Oh! dear me" seems to be a characteristic expression of pain for two such disparate characters as Ned, a slave, and Scragg, the white overseer. The phrase, actually, fits in the mouth of neither of them, as Ned enters the doctor's office and tells Cato

> O! do tell me whar de doctor is. I is almos dead. Oh me! Oh dear me! I is so sick.

and Scragg, likewise, laments a lost fight with

> O, dear me! oh, my head! That nigger broke away from me, and struck me over the head with a stick. Oh, dear me! Oh!

Equally significant is the fact that Brown is further unable to distinguish between forms of speech for a single character herself: once more the question of "appropriateness." Thus he has the fragile, delicate Melinda highlight Act I, scene ii with a very masculine, Shakespearean piece of musing.

> It is often said that the darkest hour of the night precedes the dawn. It is ever thus with the vicissitudes of human suffering. After the soul has reached the lowest depths of despair, and can no longer plunge amid its rolling, foetid shades, then the reactionary forces of man's nature begin to operate, resolution takes the place of despondency, energy succeeds instead of apathy, and an upward tendency is felt and exhibited. Men then hope against power, and smile in defiance of despair.

Clearly this is not the same distraught powderpuff who only two speeches earlier had plaintively gasped, "Alas! alas! how unfeeling and heartless."

Characterization and dialogue, then, are both noticeably weak in *The Escape*, with the minor exception of the background slave figures. There are, however, several further points of interest here, such as Brown's dramatic "first" in his graphic portrayal of the "jump de broomstick" marriage scene; and we are intrigued to find him still "documenting" his art with borrowed songs, as when he has everyone from Cato to Glen and Melinda sing various songs about their freedom at the end of the play, in an attempt on Brown's part to evoke lyrical uplift in the reader-audience from the same sort of song which Brown had published in *The Anti-Slavery Harp* of ten years earlier. In fact, the correlation between *The Harp* and Brown's use of songs here is made even more explicitly "documentary" by his supplying us, in the right hand margin of the page, with the information that these lyrics in the play are happily wedded to the "Air—'Dearest Mae.'"

After we finish listing the play's minor interests and major limitations, however, we must become historical again and note that its form is finally our major concern here. For it was the dramatic play structure which gave birth to a more artistic concept of writing in Brown. When the spoken dramatic form demanded that he omit all of his historical documents and direct narrative polemic on slavery, international justice, and Henry Clay, Brown learned that he could somehow live without them. Thus, when we come to *Clotelle* six years later, we will find that it differs from the 1853 *Clotel* largely through the absence of all narrative broadside and documentation. Brown will now be content there to limit himself to the more implicit moralizing which the dramatic form of *The Escape* forced upon him. The artist will finally emerge.

CHAPTER TEN

Growth of the Artist:
Each Man His Own Daedalus

From our discussion of *The Escape* in 1858 we come finally to *Clotelle* of 1864 and the conclusion of our artist's portrait. Before we do, however, we need to mention two possible works by Brown which were written during this period and which are of significance for us. There is the possibility, first of all, that a second novel, *Miralda, or the Beautiful Quadroon* was written in this period, with the further suggestion that it was actually a serialized version of *Clotel* that ran in an unknown abolitionist newspaper. And there was, secondly, Brown's first extensive attempt at history, *The Black Man: His Antecedents, His Genius, and His Achievements*, published in 1863. Both of these have limited, though definite, interest for us and will therefore be treated in our discussion of *Clotelle* itself.

In order to understand how the final *Clotelle* was written and put together, now, it is necessary for us to break the discussion into two parts: that of structure and that of content. Although it is clear to us today that there really is no such

clear-cut separation in the process of writing, the conception
and material of *Clotelle* do, unfortunately, lend themselves to
such a bisected scrutiny.

The Structure

The first and major aspect we notice about *Clotelle's* structure is its fragmentation and lack of direction: an element
which makes itself apparent from the very beginning. Chapter
I, "The Slave's Social Circle," for example, begins our introduction to the characters and situation of the novel—or so we
think. Hence after a quiet condemnation by the narrator of the
adverse effect of the master-slave relationship upon the female
slave's morality (the two, long, first paragraphs which begin
the book), the chapter goes on to acquaint us with a mulatto
slave, Agnes; her two mulatto daughters, Isabella and Marion;
and Isabella's white lover, Henry Linwood. These introduc-
tions over with, the chapter concludes with the death of the
women's master and the announcement that all three slaves are
to be sold at auction. Structurally, the chapter could very easily have been serialized into three parts; and our technical
interest in it is furthered by the appearance of a sentence-
paragraph, used by Brown to dispose of a character's description which he seems not interested in enough to elaborate on,
nor facile enough to integrate elsewhere. Consequently the
statement that "Marion was scarcely less richly dressed than
her sister," is allowed to stand by itself as a complete paragraph.

Chapter II, "The Negro Sale," continues the plot line and
deals with the auction itself. It, too, is divided into three
discernible sections. The first third of the chapter is a historical
narrator's account of how the death of a master often meant
this sort of separation and heartbreak for the slave in the
South. The middle third is a realistic tape recording of the
actual auctioneer's sale of Isabella to Henry Linwood. And the
final third wraps up the scene by commenting on the separa-

tion of Agnes and Marion, who are sold to a slave trader, from
Isabella, who is now secure in the arms of her beloved.

Unfortunately, the movement of the book begins to go awry
here. For both the second and third parts of Chapter II deal
with Isabella's sale and her feelings during and after the auction; and this, coupled with the emphasis placed upon her and
Henry Linwood in the first chapter, now leads us to believe
that in them is our plot line to lie. We are mislead. For with
Chapter III, "The Slave Speculator," we find ourselves pursuing not Isabella and Linwood; nor even Agnes and Marion
really. Instead, we are introduced to Dick Jennings, a slave
speculator, and we dwell upon him for the first half of the
chapter. And even though he is ostensibly leading both Agnes
and Marion in his slave-gang, slight mention is paid them. Nor
is Jennings viewed from their point of view. Rather, he is
physically described in considerable detail, as if we were to get
some sort of insight or interest in him from such depth of
description, and we follow him as he leads his slaves out of
Richmond for New Orleans. Immediately afterwards we are
on the banks of the Ohio, and then aboard a riverboat, within
the space of two paragraphs. At this point we are introduced
suddenly to Pompey, Jennings' full-blooded Negro servant;
and the rest of the chapter—it is divided into halves—is spent
watching Pompey prepare some unknown slaves for market.
Marion and Agnes are nowhere in sight throughout the chapter, though we are ostensibly on their boat throughout.

Jennings, therefore, dominates the first half of the chapter,
and Pompey the second. And though each half seems as if it is
introducing us in Tolstoian fashion to an interesting character
who will develop into an important figure later in the book,
Jennings will be only a peripheral figure as we progress, and
Pompey will drop out altogether after this chapter. So that it
soon becomes clear that Chapter III and its schizoid attention
to Jennings and Pompey does not necessarily belong in that
part of the novel in which it is placed. The description of the
minor character Jennings could have taken place much later,

or not at all; and the "hair plucking" scene of Pompey's has even less dramatic relevance to the movement of the story. So that not only does this chapter spoil the movement of the plot line by its early placement in the novel, but it also raises the serious question of whether it has any place in the novel at all.

From Pompey the novel goes next to "The Boat-Race" of Chapter IV: a spectacular scene of racing riverboats, danger, explosion and disaster. It has all the earmarks of a Boucicault spectacle scene, and is, interestingly enough, just as distantly handled and unrelated to the plot of the story as was the burning ship, "Magnolia," in Boucicault's *The Octoroon* of 1859. It is all over in the first half of the chapter, and has really nothing to do with anybody or anything in the story thus far. For though the explosion takes place on the "Patriot," which is Jennings', Pompey's, Agnes' and Marion's boat, we never see or hear from a single one of them during the whole scene. "Men were running hither and thither looking for their wives, and women were flying about in the wildest confusion seeking their husbands," and "Dismay appeared on every countenance." But there is no one whom we know here, and nothing which we can see clearly and concretely. It is all over in the space of two paragraphs as "The killed and wounded were put on shore, and the Patriot, taken in tow by the Washington, was once more on her journey." The whole half-chapter is simply a throw-in spectacle scene which has no relevance to anything preceding or following it in the novel.

The second half of Chapter IV is just as irrelevant as the first—both to the first half and to the novel as a whole. For it introduces an incredible air of calm onto the "Patriot" immediately after its supposed disaster, as we find ourselves somehow watching a heretofore unknown Mr. Jones playing cards with an equally unknown Mr. Thompson over a similarly unknown slave boy, Joe, who is the stake of the game. Not only is its quiet atmosphere introduced into the novel at an implausible time, but the piece itself is nothing more than a thinly-played melodrama scene brought in by Brown to allow him the opportunity of moralizing about "the uncertainty of a slave's life." It completes the second half of Chapter IV.

By this point we have gone through four chapters of a novel which once seemed to be quite clearly about Isabella and Linwood, or maybe Agnes and Marion. Yet suddenly, within the four very separate and very disparate halves of Chapters III and IV, we have found ourselves reading about Dick Jennings, Pompey, a Boat-race, and a gambling scene— all unrelated to each other and to the rest of the novel.

Chapter V, now, continues the pattern. We are still on the "Patriot," and now two new characters are introduced: "a woman so white as not to be distinguishable from the other white women on board" and, in her arms, "a child so white that no one would suppose a drop of African blood flowed through its blue veins." After three paragraphs, this introduction and its sentimental, moral accompaniment ("No one could behold that mother with her helpless babe, without feeling that God would punish the oppressor.") are over, and the boat arrives at Natchez. There Agnes is sold to a Rev. James Wilson in the course of two quick paragraphs; Marion gets another one of those sentence-paragraphs which she seems assigned to ("During the remainder of the passage, Marion wept bitterly."); gambling and drinking are the order of the day as the boat moves on to Baton Rouge; and a second sentence-paragraph completes this geographic movement as "The next morning, at ten o'clock, the boat arrived at New Orleans, where the passengers went to their hotels and homes, and the negroes to the slave-pens." A final sentimental sigh is given for "Lizzie, the white slave-mother, of whom we have already spoken," and this incredible chapter is over. Thus, within the confines of a single chapter, entitled "The Young Mother," we find that we have discussed—in random order and with no defined length of treatment or tone of voice—no less than eight characters (three of them new) and four river towns, in a hodge-podge featured by two sentence paragraphs and two directly delivered sermons.

There is in Chapter V then a definite uncertainty of dramatic movement. For not only do we move through all the many characters and incidents noted above, but, when we come to the end of the chapter, we find that we have returned to Lizzie for the final moral of the chapter, only to discover that she will now drop out of the novel completely. So that while we may be inclined to see a certain unity in the chapter by pointing to the sense of "completeness" which the return to Lizzie brings, it is much closer to the truth to note that this final paragraph is merely tacked on and that the structure of the chapter is once more constituted by a pair of unrelated half-chapters; the introduction to Lizzie on the one hand, and a geographic sweep on the other. And finally, even if we do allow a claim of unity for the chapter, we are still hard put to justify the fact that all this unusual elaborateness of structure is being devoted to a character whom we shall never see again.

Yet the structural problem in *Clotelle*, of which Lizzie here is merely typical, goes even deeper than the rapid, pasted together handling of events and characters. For what makes this element of the structure so bothersome to us is the fact that we are never given any idea what characters will or won't be developed. For one of Brown's greatest failings is that he never gives any any hint as to how extensively he means to treat a character, or how important she will be in the future pages of the novel. Indeed, the narrative mind behind the book's movement never attempts to signal who is important and who is not, where we are ultimately going and where we are not. Hence even a character as important as Clotelle herself does not command the center of the stage until Chapter XX, and even then she finds herself offstage through much of the final third of the novel as we follow the travels and tribulations of her lover, Jerome.

Despite his work on his *Narrative* and travelogues, then, Brown seems strangely unable—or disinclined—to piece things out chronologically in his novel. Even as late as Chapter IX we are introduced to Augustine Cardinay in an insightful way which suggests that we commit him to memory, only to discover that the opening paragraph of introduction is the only one in the whole novel in which Cardinay will appear. Instead, we soon find that it is Cardinay's house boarder who is of interest to us here, at which point all sense of chronological development and structure vanishes from the chapter. Adolphus Morton, Cardinay's boarder, immediately woos and marries Marion within the space of two paragraphs, has two daughters by her in the next paragraph, and sends them both up North to school at the ages of ten and eleven in the last paragraph. Gone from memory then, as all this takes place in this strangely compressed time period, is almost everything that has gone before in the book: Cardinay, Sam, Rev. Wilson, Aaron, Lizzie and her child, the riverboat gamblers and their pawn, the boat race, Pompey, Jennings, Linwood, Isabella, and Agnes. Chapter IX, it seems, is the germ for a novel in itself and therefore develops itself oblivious to everything around it. In fact, Marion and Morton are so heavy on Brown's mind at this point that, in the middle of those three paragraphs devoted to the couple's marriage and subsequent bliss, he inserts a single sentence to the effect that Agnes had died of fever sometime before the first daughter was born to Marion. Thus Agnes— the major character of Chapter I; the mother of the two heroines, Marion and Isabella; and the grandmother, as we will soon learn, of the final heroine, Clotelle—is dismissed from life and the novel in a single sentence tucked into the marital happiness of Marion and Morton. And what is even more ironic is the fact that this same couple will share a similar fate: for after being introduced into the novel at the beginning of Chapter IX and raised to the stature of major character by the many actions he performs, Adolphus Morton now drops out of the book forever, taking his family with him. Thus Chapter X moves us back up to Richmond with Isabella and Linwood, and it is as if the first nine chapters had never existed. It is that kind of novel.

In examining *Clotelle*'s structure, therefore, we must basically be concerned with the incredible number of characters which are brought on stage in one pargraph only to be forgotten in the next, as Brown's narrative meanderings sweep on. For the basic problem in the novel is that Brown is used to the formless structure and documentation of his earlier writings and speeches; so that the movement of the novel, with its essential need for an inner logic and sense of what Tolstoy called "inevitability," is completely foreign to his prior experiences. Not only is he unable to prepare his audience for what is to come, and unable—and/or disinclined—to limit himself to only those characters and situations which will prove important, but he lacks as well a sense of chronology and dramatic build-up here.

Eventually he does show an awareness of dramatic foreshadowing as a means of structuring a novel for the reader, as when he hints in Chapter XXI at Clotelle's future by rhetorically asking

> What would have been her [Isabella's] feelings if she could have known that the child for whose rescue she had sacrificed herself would one day be free, honored, and loved in another land?

Yet, in the final analysis, *Clotelle* is like a well-lit iron mine, built around a great many interesting tunnels and shafts, all of which run out of ore long before we run out of interest in mining them. Instead of utilizing a novelistic sense of narrative order and character solidity, Brown constantly shifts us back and forth from characters we have known in Chapter I to new figures and new towns and new spectacles. All of which leads us nowhere—and/or everywhere—and leaves us, artistically, with that mixture of hollowness and appetite which Madison Avenue calls "hungry for flavor."

At the same time, however, to realize all this is not to necessarily condemn *Clotelle* out of hand, for along with "unable" there is also "disinclined." And both points here are significant.

To a large extent, then, the structure of *Clotelle* is weak because, though it had eliminated much of the broadside polemic and direct documentation of *Clotel*, it was still not meant to serve exclusively an artistic function. For in *Clotelle* as elsewhere, Brown resorted to prose fiction not so much for art's sake as for a means of crusading against slavery. Thus it is not a structurally "good" novel partially because it could not be and still serve the purpose for which it was meant. Indeed, its primary purpose was to exemplify slavery as the sum of all cruelties, and to thereby foster a public sentiment which would hasten slavery's abolition. And what was Brown's greatest artistic achievement here was the fact that he set out to accomplish this without delving into the heavy and clustered polemic of the earlier *Clotel*.

In such a light then do we understand the great many characters whom we meet in the novel—fleetingly, yet in some sense poignantly and completely. For the sufferings of one character, though real and powerful, was not seen by Brown as calculated to move an audience to social reform action as much as the various and continual sufferings of a great many characters. Similarly, the sufferings of one man in one part of the slave-holding South was not deemed as being as convincing a historical record as would be the movement throughout the South by the author through his use of so many separately distributed characters. Thus the plot is extended, the characters multiplied, and the geography enlarged in order to bring as strong a historical story as possible to bear on the evils of slavery in America.

Before we drop this discussion of structure now, there is one further aspect of it which deserves our attention. We have tended to see Brown's "scattered" structure as partially the product of intent and, more probably, the product of his earlier episodic life and writings. There is, however, one other possible influence here.

During the period around 1860 or so, it has been suggested by some critics that Brown published a somewhat changed version of the early *Clotel* as a newspaper serial entitled *Miralda; or, The Beautiful Quadroon*. Changing the name of one of his heroines from Miralda to Clotelle, Brown then published the serialized version of this story in 1864 as the final version of our *Clotelle*. Such is the theory—a theory which will probably remain unproven since there seems to be little concrete external evidence for the literary historian to work on. There are, however, several points of internal evidence which tend to substantiate this theory of serialization. There is, first of all, the very definite sense of demarcation between parts of chapters as we have seen above. Chapter I and II were clearly split into three parts each; Chapters III and IV were just as clearly divided into halves; while Chapter V attempted a kind of make-shift unity out of two easily distinguishable halves. And so it goes.

Even more intriguingly, there is a strange technical flaw in Chaper XXX which goes a long way towards authenticating the serialization theory, though none of its proponents seems to have noticed it.

> Thus far the chase was enjoyed by all, even the American rider, who was better fitted to witness the scene than to take part in it.

is the sentence with which Brown concludes the seventh of seventeen paragraphs about Jerome in Perth, Scotland. Then, with no break between paragraphs other than the normal indentation, paragraph eight of Chapter XXX begins by reminding us that

> We left Jerome in our last reluctantly engaged in the chase; and thought the first mile or so . . .

And now the question immediately arises: "our last" what? Clearly there has been some sort of break here other than that of paragraph to paragraph. And it is only logical to assume that in the suggested serialization of the novel this sentence marked the beginning of a new installment, which was not editorially deleted when *Clotelle* went to press in 1864 as a unified novel. If this is indeed the case, we now have one more reason for understanding the structure and writing of *Clotelle*.

The Content and its Sources

At the same time, there are even more definite debts which *Clotelle* owes to Brown's earlier life and writings; and it is the nature of these debts which forms the basis of our understanding the content in the novel. There are, first of all, the incidents with and the character of Dick Jennings, slave-speculator: all of which are based upon Brown's own experiences as servant to the slave trader, Dick Walker, as seen in the *Narrative*. Whole blocs of identical description and action show this. Just as Walker was a South-bound slaver who "always had the time advertised in the New Orleans papers, that he would be in Rodney, Natchez, and New Orleans" (*Narrative*, 42–3), so do we find in *Clotelle* that "Jennings had already advertised in the New Orleans papers, that he would be there with a prime lot of able-bodied slaves" (*Clotelle*, 10–11). And, just as Jennings "often bought [slaves] who were far advanced in age, and would try to pass them off for five or six years younger than they were" (*Clotelle*, 11), and for that purpose had a Negro servant named Pompey, who would drill the slaves in lying about their ages and who was told further by Jennings that "If any of them have so many gray hairs that you cannot pluck them out, take the blacking and brush, and go at them." (12); so do we find the very same function performed by Brown while a similar servant to Walker.

I was ordered to have the old men's whiskers shaved off, and the gray hairs plucked out where they were too

numerous, in which case he [Walker] had a preparation
of blacking to color it, and with a blacking brush we
would put it on. This was new business to me, and was
performed in a room where the passengers could not see
us. These slaves were also taught how old they were by
Mr. Walker, and after going through the blacking process
they looked ten or fifteen years younger. (*Narrative*, 42)

It is quite clear that Brown is writing from his own experiences in this part of *Clotelle*, even as he is rewriting parts of
his earlier, successful *Narrative*. In fact, it is a double borrowing here when we see it in this light; and, when we remember
that Walker-Jennings has been the same character in *Clotel*
and *The Escape* as well as the *Narrative*, we realize that this
is almost a quadruple borrowing of content here.

Related to this sort of "borrowing" is the similarity of a
mysterious woman treated briefly in the *Narrative* to the just-
as-quickly-seen Lizzie in Chapter V of *Clotelle*. In the midst
of a discussion about his life as a waiter on a Mississippi riverboat for a Capt. Otis Reynolds, Brown in the *Narrative* suddenly introduces to us a fascinating figure of mystery and
beauty, who just as suddenly leaves.

A few weeks after, on our downward passage, the boat
took on board, at Hannibal, a drove of slaves, bound for the
New Orleans market. . . . There was, however, one in this
gang that attracted the attention of the passengers and
crew. It was a beautiful girl, apparently about twenty
years of age, perfectly white, with straight light hair and
blue eyes. But it was not the whiteness of her skin that
created such a sensation among those who gazed upon
her—it was her almost unparalleled beauty. She had been
on the boat but a short time, before the attention of all
the passengers, including the ladies, had been called to
her, and the common topic of conversation was about the
beautiful slave-girl. She was not in chains. The man who

claimed this article of human merchandise was a Mr.
Walker—a well-known slave-trader, residing in St. Louis.
There was a general anxiety among the passengers and
crew to learn the history of the girl. Her master kept close
by her side, and it would have been considered impudent
for any of the passengers to have spoken to her. When
we reached St. Louis, the slaves were removed to a boat
bound for New Orleans, and the history of the beautiful
slave-girl remained a mystery. (*Narrative*, 32–3)

It is, of course, this same beautiful mystery woman whom
Brown is trying to expand and recreate in the figure of Lizzie:
the just as beautiful and briefly seen creature of purity and
pathos on board the "Patriot."

On the fourth morning, the Patriot landed at Grand Gulf,
a beautiful town on the left bank of the Mississippi.
Among the numerous passengers who came on board at
Rodney was another slave-trader, with nine human chattels which he was conveying to the Southern market. The
passengers, both ladies and gentlemen, were startled at
seeing among the new lot of slaves a woman so white as
not to be distinguishable from the other white women on
board. She had in her arms a child so white that no one
would suppose a drop of African blood flowed through
its blue veins.
   No one could behold that mother with her helpless
babe, without feeling that God would punish the oppressor. There she sat, with an expressive and intellectual
forehead, and a countenance full of dignity and heroism,
her dark golden locks rolled back from her almost snow-
white forehead and floating over her swelling bosom. The
tears that stood in her mild blue eyes showed that she was
brooding over sorrows and wrongs that filled her bleeding
heart. (*Clotelle*, 15)

Furthermore, the *Narrative* was not the only bit of Brown's writing which he drew upon for *Clotelle*, nor was he always so imaginatively creative as to expand these writings and at least give them a new touch of life. Instead, in several cases, he completely borrowed a whole situation, or scene, or plot line, just as he had borrowed verse and advertisements in *Salem Lecture*, had borrowed realistic anecdotes and Jeffersonian speeches in *Clotel*, and had transferred whole characters, situations and even jokes from *Clotel* to *The Escape*.

In the "Memoir of the Author" which introduces Brown's *The Black Man* of 1863, therefore, we find, in its entirety, the complete Chapter IV of *Clotelle*. There is, first of all, the story of the riverboat race of the "Patriot," which makes up the first half of *Clotelle*'s chapter: five paragraphs of word-for-word exactness, differing in the "Memoir" version only by the existence of a small, minor sixth paragraph which does not appear in the later *Clotelle*. And there is also, in total exactness, the gambling scene which completes *Clotelle*'s Chapter IV: the one in which we find a Mr. Jones and a Mr. Thompson playing cards for the ownership of a "fine-looking, bright-eyed mulatto boy, apparently sixteen years of age" (*The Black Man*, 21; *Clotelle*, 13). And not only is each story alike in each book, but their back-to-back linkage is also the same—a glaringly forced linkage at best, since the quiet gambling scene completely negates all sense of catastrophe and danger which was the basis of the riverboat explosion only moments before. In fact, so extensive is this kind of borrowing in Brown, that this same combination of boat ride and gambling scene is even in the earlier *Clotel*. Its inappropriateness is not quite so protruding there since it is obscured by the blanketing fog of ever-present polemic, but it is essentially the same material handled in essentially the same way.

An even more interesting example of this sort of borrowing brings us now back to Chapter XXII of *Three Years in Europe* of 1852, for in that chapter is the germ of the final—and central—part of the novel which we now know as *Clotelle*. "A Narrative of American Slavery" is its title, and the debt which *Clotelle* owes to it is immense. Basically it is the full story of the separation and reunion of Jerome and Clotelle, which fills the last third of the novel.

Instead of "Jerome" and "Clotelle," however, in "A Narrative" we are concerned with "George" and "Mary." George is a "white" Negro slave and the "son of a member of the American Congress"—the role which the female Clotel fills one year later in the first *Clotel*. Mary, on the other hand, is also a "white" slave, in marked contrast to the patriotic strains which come through the fact that in *Clotelle* Jerome is "of pure African origin" and "perfectly black." With this minor alteration of character, the story of George and Mary is almost exactly the story of Jerome and Clotelle.

As we begin "A Narrative," we find George in prison in Virginia, about to be hanged, which is exactly Jerome's case in Natchez. His imprisonment is due to his participation in the Nat Turner Insurrection, and not a personal affront to his master as is the case with Jerome. But this is only a minor point, since Turner's revolt finds its way into *Clotelle* as well, though under different circumstances. The plot line in "A Narrative" from this point on is unchanged from that which we find in the 1864 novel. George, a favorite of his mistress, is allowed a visitor. In comes his lover, Mary, who exchanges clothes with him so that he can walk out the front door and escape. George eventually makes his way to Canada, makes a futile attempt to contact Mary back in the South through a white friend, and finally goes to England where he makes a success of himself in the business world (a success which is made somewhat less notable in "A Narrative" since George never declares his Negritude, in marked contrast to the black Jerome "of pure African origin"). After a period of ten years or so, George then makes a trip to France; enters a burial ground somewhere outside of Dunkirk; sees an older man, a woman and a child there; is recognized by the woman: who

faints, is carried home, sends for George to come to her
father-in-law's house, and reveals to George her identity and
how her late French husband (a Mr. Devanant in both stories)
had bought and married her from a New Orleans slave market
because she resembled his dead sister (the same motive in
both stories also). Reunited, George and Mary quickly marry
and happily settle down in France.

Borrowing, then, is the source of most of Brown's content
in *Clotelle* even as it was in his early anti-slavery lectures and
such compilations as *The Anti-Slavery Harp.* The material
which he is reusing here is fictional, rather than "documentary," and it is his own as well; and both of these differences go far in showing us how much Brown has achieved as
an artist by 1864. And yet, the point is that this kind of content
does very much effect a novel-structure: for when you have
this kind of self-contained, disparate material, which you can
reuse and place anywhere in your plot line, you are naturally
led into a loose and sporadic sense of structure. And this,
indeed, is *Clotelle*'s structure.

The Reception and Importance of *Clotelle*

In 1853, the first edition of *Clotel; or, The President's
Daughter* appeared on the London book market from the
press of Partridge and Oakey. At its roots lay the rumor which
William Lloyd Garrison was spreading in his press to the effect
that Thomas Jefferson's alleged "slave-daughter" had lately
been sold for $1000 on the New Orleans market. Clotel in the
novel, consequently, assumed the character of this "president's
daughter." It is suggested by some critics that this is the reason
why the novel did not meet with the same reception which
awaited most of the slave literature at that time. Whatever the
reason, the fact is that *Clotel* attracted no special attention at
the time, and eleven years were to pass before an American
audience was to be given the chance to read it. The second,

American version of *Clotel*, therefore, did not appear here until 1864, when James Redpath of Boston published it as *Clotelle: A Tale of the Southern States*. Besides the differences which we have already noted, a further change in the second version was made by the substitution of an anonymous senator for Mr. Jefferson as the white father in question.

It is clear to us today that Redpath at the time thought very highly of the novel and of Brown as author. His note at the end of the novel states that *Clotelle* is directed by him, Redpath, "to the soldiers of the Union," not only to relieve the monotony of camp life in 1864, but to kindle "their great zeal in the cause of universal emancipation." And even more important than this eulogy, as an expression of the publisher's regard for the book, is the actual literary company which Redpath allowed this first novel of Brown's to keep. As the dime novel cover of the 1864 edition states, and as Redpath's own advertisements in *The Liberator* of the time declare, this book, as a member of "Redpath's Books for the Camp Fire," is the second in an expanding series of books which are "Just the books to read to the soldiers" and "Equally adapted to home fires." The other four members of this series at the time were Louisa May Alcott's *On Picket Duty,* Jonathan Swift's *Gulliver's Travels,* Victor Hugo's *The Battle of Waterloo*, and an original translation of another "Civil War" story: Honoré de Balzac's *The Vendetta*. "Other books are in active preparation," Redpath's statement inside the cover assures us, "All by authors of accomplished genius." This, obviously, is pretty heady stuff for a relatively unknown fugitive slave who is writing essentially his first novel.

How the press of the period received *Clotelle*, however, is another story. Indeed if Garrison's *Liberator* is any criterion, *Clotelle* seems largely to have been ignored at the time of its publication. The first advertisement for *Clotelle* and the Camp Fire Series in general was printed in *The Liberator* of March 18, 1864, and subsequent advertisements appeared on March 25, April 8, and April 22. There is no other mention in the paper of this first novel by an admittedly important disciple and friend of Garrison. We can, of course, point to the fact that there was a war going on and that the call for troops and the bolstering of the public morale were more important than printing reviews of short paperback novels. And yet, during this same period, *The Liberator* did run occasional columns devoted to "New Publications;" did weekly devote one-fourth of the last page of its four-page issue to a poetry column; and, from the period of October 23, 1863 until March 4, 1864, did run sporadically a serialized bit of fiction entitled *Plantation Pictures*, by a Mrs. Emily C. Pearson, "Author of 'Cousin Frank's Household.' " Thus it seems clear that if *The Liberator* had wished, it had every opportunity to review and comment upon *Clotelle*, especially since both novel and newspaper were published right there in the same city. For whatever reason, *The Liberator* never mentioned Brown's novel.

Relatedly, in the "Memoir of the Author" which precedes the anatomy of Brown's *The Rising Son; or, The Antecedents and Advancement of the Colored Race*, published in 1874, Alonzo D. Moore introduces the author as "William Wells Brown, now so widely-known, both at home and abroad," and as one "whose name has for many years been a household word in our land." And yet, it soon becomes increasingly clear that Moore's—and presumably America's—high regard for Brown does not stem from his writing of the first American Negro novel.

Instead, a great deal is made of Brown's "reputation as a public speaker," and several incidents are related at length from the texts of his speeches. Similarly, much is made of Brown's several writings, but *Clotelle* receives neither elaborate nor favorable treatment. *Three Years in Europe*, for example, is given extensive notice and citation by Moore, this acclaim being buoyed up even higher by Moore's citation of a great many "extracts from some of the English journals" which reviewed it. *The Eclectic Review, The British Banner, The Times, The Literary Gazette*, the Glasgow *Citizen*, the Glasgow

Examiner—all are quoted in praise of the book. Again, mention of *Sketches* is bolstered by the statement that it "met with a rapid sale" and by the citation of the New York *Tribune*'s comment that it was "well-written and intensely interesting." So too is the Boston *Journal* cited as characterizing Brown's lyceum reading of his first drama, *Doughface*, as "interesting in its composition, and admirably rendered." Further on, *The Black Man* is also treated at length, and is described by Moore as "a work which ran through ten editions in three years, and which was spoken of by the press in terms of the highest commendation." Moore then continues his discussion of *The Black Man* by quoting several favorable comments on it by Frederick Douglass, William Lloyd Garrison, Gerrit Smith, and others.

Thus after a full sixteen pages of biographic and literary eulogy up to this point, we are forcibly struck when we find that *Clotelle* is now dismissed with the brief, merely personal and anthology-like statement that

> *Clotelle*, written by Dr. Brown, a romance founded on fact, is one of the most thrilling stories that we remember to have read, and shows the great versatility of the cast of mind of our author.

Clearly this sort of terse and blandly general treatment does not suggest that the general reception of *Clotelle* by its audience was of very much interest to Moore. Hence, when we remember that Moore's role is that of a favorable reviewer; and when we recall the intelligent and scholarly diligence with which he went about praising the rest of Brown's works; we can only conclude that *Clotelle*'s reception by its American audience, between its publication in 1864 and *The Rising Son*'s publication in 1874, did not give Moore very much favorable material with which to work.

And yet, in the final analysis, "reception" and "importance" are not necessarily the same thing. As a novel, admittedly, *Clotelle* is rather fragmented and weak; and yet it *is* a novel.

A piece of anti-slavery declaration to be sure, but one which has been put into fictionalized, artistic form, from which most of *Clotel's* bombast and polemic have been carefully pruned. That Brown did not really have the background for a well-structured novel is unfortunate; but this situation should not blind us to the fact that he did attempt it and did succeed on a number of levels. Thus there is probably more care put into the structure, descriptions, and dialogue in *Clotelle* than there is in the message itself; and we should remember how much Brown has gone out of his way in 1864 to eliminate the bald polemic and documentation which so cluttered up his 1853 version. In short, the man cared about his subject and cared about his form—and this is all we really ask of an artist.

CHAPTER ELEVEN

William Wells Brown:
A Final Assessment

As we come now to our final understanding of William Wells Brown and his importance for us, we find ourselves concerned with two separate, but interrelated, realms of appreciation. Essentially Brown as an artist is our greatest interest, and this is where his major importance lies. At the same time, our appreciation of him as an individual man is also significant. For, as with all artists, there is a strong bond between the man and his art, and this is especially true with Brown, where the same attributes which made him a successful social crusader and man in general also underlay and motivated his success as a literary artist.

Undoubtedly the greatest attribute in Brown's life was his continual search for freedom and for the unique personality which that freedom would allow him to develop. On its most basic level, this was obviously manifested in his strong determination from early childhood to geographically escape Southern slavery, a determination which resulted in his successful flight North in 1834. Of equal importance, moreover, is the way he set about freeing his mind and feelings from the less tangible shackles which slavery so often imposed upon its victims, and this is where our greatest appreciations of him as a man lie. Thus even as he physically fled slavery and dedicated himself to various social and literary Abolitionist pursuits, he simultaneously gave his inner inclinations free rein and let himself develop pursuits and interests which sprung from him alone—that is, interests which were neither the product of his life in slavery nor a direct reaction to that institution.

His most dramatic steps along this upward path are seen most clearly during his years abroad and are most directly shown us in his autobiographical travelogue, *Three Years in Europe*. For in this period of his life and in the book especially, Brown let his complete self come to the surface and engage in the European world which he so eagerly visited and commented upon. This ability to freely travel and observe was what had so deeply appealed to Brown ever since his work on the St. Louis steamboats at age thirteen, and it was this period in England and the Continent which gave him the chance to develop the intellectual and emotional interests which so naturally accompanied his new-found physical freedom. The boat ride from Boston to Liverpool, a stroll through Paris streets, pastoral scenes throughout the English countryside—all are described faithfully and expressively with a joy and spirit which capture Brown's own delight at being able to experience them. Nor are these "intensely carefree" tourist accounts all that comprise the book.

Despite its foreign setting, on the one hand, the book does contain a large number of statements and references to slavery in this country, most of which were obviously suggested by various comparisons between what Brown saw abroad and the United States which he remembered having fled from. And while these observations are generally unexceptional, they are nevertheless understandably necessary in such a book by such an author. For slavery was the major evil in America of 1849, and, as such, it merited the constant opposition of all men of social conscience who were concerned with freedom and human dignity. Furthermore, it was obviously the major evil in Brown's own life—especially after 1850, when the newly passed Fugitive Slave Law meant that he could be hunted down in any part of the United States and returned forcibly to Southern slavery. For both altruistic and personal reasons, therefore, it was to Brown's great credit that he fought so long and untiringly against the "peculiar institution" in his writings, even in travelogues like *Three Years.*

At the same time, the point is that Brown did not allow himself to be confined to this single interest. Though the fight against slavery formed the core of his moral and professional life, he nevertheless allowed his full personality to expand and develop—as a unique, individual man, and not merely as a "fugitive slave." This, then, is the significance of his many "guidebook" comments on the places which he visited; for there is here a spontaneous enjoyment of experiences and scenes for and in themselves, essentially the same sensuous enjoyment which most tourists bring to their meeting with new, exotic scenes. Hence it is this "Brown, the liberated tourist" which marks a major relaxation and expansive growth from the earlier, "fugitive slave" orator and polemicist.

Within these "tourist" comments, moreover, there were two levels. The first was Brown's interest in general scenes and colorful experiences, which we have just discussed, and much of the book is given over to these accounts and descriptions. On a second, higher level, *Three Years* also allowed Brown to respond to the even deeper artistic and intellectual interests inside himself. This is the importance of his desire to visit museums like the Louvre, to meet such major literary artists as Victor Hugo, to comment and cut his critical teeth on literary-social writers like Thomas Carlyle. For this was the level on which the inner Brown longed to live and breathe, and his several years in Europe marked his first exploration of this deeper man. As such, the period was a significant testament to Brown's achievement of freedom as a man.

From this expanded man, making various "visits" to famous writers and their art, it is now but a brief step for us to see the same "seeking" mind in Brown the artist. Just as the boy and man in him were determined to be physically and intellectually free in the world around them, so did the artist in him seek the same freedom to expand and develop. In the same way that he moved about from locale to locale during his European period, therefore, in order to realize as many facets of himself as possible, so did he as a writer pioneeringly "visit" and seek himself in a vast variety of literary forms and genre. Indeed this accounts for the breadth of his literary approaches and his willingness to experiment beyond the narrowly confined genre usually reserved for the fugitive slave writer.

Besides being a successful and effective Abolitionist orator and slave narrator, then, Brown was the first Negro journalist-reporter in American letters, with his professional work for various London newspapers in the early 1850's. Likewise, he wrote the first travel book in our literature by a Negro author, as we have just seen; and, toward the end of his life, he made significant "first" historical studies of the Negro's role in the country's growth. Finally, on the even higher, artistic level, of course, he crowned these other achievements by writing the first Negro novel and first Negro drama in our literature—an overall record of innovation and creative power which is unsurpassed in the history of American letters.

Such a career as man and artist, then, is William Wells Brown's importance to us. It is a formidable one—especially since he achieved so much of it on his own, through his own determination and courage. And whether we see this determination in the possibly apocryphal story, which his daughter tells, about how he learned to read and write by always carrying a spelling book with him from his very first moments of freedom in Buffalo; or whether we see it in his unique sense of self-reliance, when he alone refused to dependently accept the fugitive slave "charity" which the English abolitionists supplied to the other fugitive slaves in London at the time; we can see very clearly Brown's fundamental inner direction and independent sense of integrity. Indeed, in a very profound sense, it was this courage and self-reliance which lay at the heart of both his life and his art, especially his creation of the first Negro novel. For not only was it the basis of his lifelong personal and artistic search for unique self-expression, a search which led him to experiment with various new genres to convey his feelings and his social message. But, even more explicitly, it was his decision in 1850 London to independently support himself through literature which led directly to his pioneer experimenting with *Clotel* in 1853. Hence the power which made him a strong, individual man was the same power which motivated him as an artist; nor should we be surprised. For, in the final analysis, the portrait of every significant artist is always the portrait of an equally significant man, and William Wells Brown was outstandingly both.

REDPATH'S

BOOKS for the CAMP FIRES

CLOTELLE.

JOHN ANDREW

BOSTON.
JAMES REDPATH,
221 WASHINGTON ST.

BOOKS FOR THE CAMP FIRES.

No. I. *ON PICKET DUTY,* and Other Tales. By L. M. ALCOTT. Ten cents. (Second edition.)

No. II. *CLOTELLE.* A Tale of the Southern States By W. W. BROWN. With five fine illustrations. Ten cents (Now ready.)

No. III. *THE VENDETTA.* From the French of Balzac. An original translation. To which is added, THE BLACKSMITH OF TENNESSEE. Two Stories of Civil Wars! Ten cents. (Nearly ready.)

No. IV. *GULLIVER'S TRAVELS.* A Voyage to Lilliput. Unabridged. Ten cents. (In preparation.)

No. V. *THE BATTLE OF WATERLOO.* By VICTOR HUGO. Unabridged. A New York edition of this wonderful picture of the great Battle which decided the fate of Napoleon, omitted the three graphic introductory chapters. Te cents.

☞ Other Books are in active preparation; all by authors o acknowledged genius.

AGENTS.

NEW YORK. — H. Dexter, Hamilton & Co.
PHILADELPHIA. — A. WINCH.
CHICAGO. — J. R. WALSH.
BOSTON. — J. J. Dyer & Co., C. Thacher, A. Williams & Co. Lee & Shepard.

Any Book of this Series sent by mail on receipt of price, by

JAMES REDPATH,

BOSTON.

CLOTELLE:

A TALE

OF

THE SOUTHERN STATES.

BY W. W. BROWN.

Boston:

JAMES REDPATH, Publisher.

221 WASHINGTON STREET.

NEW YORK: H. DEXTER, HAMILTON & CO.

CLOTELLE.

CHAPTER I.

THE SLAVE'S SOCIAL CIRCLE.

WITH the growing population in the Southern States, the increase of mulattoes has been very great. Society does not frown upon the man who sits with his half-white child upon his knee whilst the mother stands, a slave, behind his chair. In nearly all the cities and towns of the Slave States, the real negro, or clear black, does not amount to more than one in four of the slave population. This fact is of itself the best evidence of the degraded and immoral condition of the relation of master and slave. Throughout the Southern States, there is a class of slaves who, in most of the towns, are permitted to hire their time from their owners, and who are always expected to pay a high price. This class is the mulatto women, distinguished for their fascinating beauty. The handsomest of these usually pay the greatest amount for their time. Many of these women are the favorites of men of property and standing, who furnish them with the means of compensating their owners, and not a few are dressed in the most extravagant manner.

When we take into consideration the fact that no safeguard is thrown around virtue, and no inducement held out to slave-women to be pure and chaste, we will not be surprised when told that immorality and vice pervade the cities and towns of the South to an extent unknown in the Northern States. Indeed, many of the slave-women have no higher aspiration than that of becoming the finely-dressed mistress of some white man. At negro balls and parties, this class of women usually make the most splendid appearance, and are eagerly sought after in the dance, or to entertain in the drawing-room or at the table.

A few years ago, among the many slave-women in Richmond, Virginia, who hired their time of their masters, was Agnes, a mulatto owned by John Graves, Esq., and who might be heard boasting that she was the

daughter of an American Senator. Although nearly forty years of age
at the time of which we write, Agnes was still exceedingly handsome.
More than half white, with long black hair and deep blue eyes, no one
felt like disputing with her when she urged her claim to her relationship
with the Anglo-Saxon.

In her younger days, Agnes had been a housekeeper for a young slaveholder, and in sustaining this relation had become the mother of two
daughters. After being cast aside by this young man, the slave-woman
betook herself to the business of a laundress, and was considered to be
the most tasteful woman in Richmond at her vocation.

Isabella and Marion, the two daughters of Agnes, resided with their
mother, and gave her what aid they could in her business. The mother,
however, was very choice of her daughters, and would allow them to
perform no labor that would militate against their lady-like appearance.
Agnes early resolved to bring up her daughters as ladies, as she termed it.

As the girls grew older, the mother had to pay a stipulated price for
them per month. Her notoriety as a laundress of the first class enabled
her to put an extra charge upon the linen that passed through her
hands; and although she imposed little or no work upon her daughters,
she was enabled to live in comparative luxury and have her daughters
dressed to attract attention, especially at the negro balls and parties.

Although the term "negro ball" is applied to these gatherings, yet a
large portion of the men who attend them are whites. Negro balls and
parties in the Southern States, especially in the cities and towns, are
usually made up of quadroon women, a few negro men, and any number of white gentlemen. These are gatherings of the most democratic
character. Bankers, merchants, lawyers, doctors, and their clerks and
students, all take part in these social assemblies upon terms of perfect
equality. The father and son not unfrequently meet and dance *vis a vis*
at a negro ball.

It was at one of these parties that Henry Linwood, the son of a
wealthy and retired gentleman of Richmond, was first introduced to
Isabella, the oldest daughter of Agnes. The young man had just returned from Harvard College, where he had spent the previous five
years. Isabella was in her eighteenth year, and was admitted by all
who knew her to be the handsomest girl, colored or white, in the city.
On this occasion, she was attired in a sky-blue silk dress, with deep
black lace flounces, and bertha of the same. On her well-moulded
arms she wore massive gold bracelets, while her rich black hair was arranged at the back in broad basket plaits, ornamented with pearls, and
the front in the French style (*a la Imperatrice*), which suited her classic
face to perfection.

Marion was scarcely less richly dressed than her sister.

Henry Linwood paid great attention to Isabella, which was looked upon with gratification by her mother, and became a matter of general conversation with all present. Of course, the young man escorted the beautiful quadroon home that evening, and became the favorite visitor at the house of Agnes.

It was on a beautiful moonlight night in the month of August, when all who reside in tropical climates are eagerly gasping for a breath of fresh air, that Henry Linwood was in the garden which surrounded Agnes' cottage, with the young quadroon by his side. He drew from his pocket a newspaper wet from the press, and read the following advertisement: —

NOTICE. — Seventy-nine negroes will be offered for sale on Monday, September 10, at 12 o'clock, being the entire stock of the late John Graves. The negroes are in an excellent condition, and all warranted against the common vices. Among them are several mechanics, ablebodied field-hands, plough-boys, and women with children, some of them very prolific, affording a rare opportunity for any one who wishes to raise a strong and healthy lot of servants for their own use. Also several mulatto girls of rare personal qualities, — two of these very superior.

Among the above slaves advertised for sale were Agnes and her two daughters. Ere young Linwood left the quadroon that evening, he promised her that he would become her purchaser, and make her free and her own mistress.

Mr. Graves had long been considered not only an excellent and upright citizen of the first standing among the whites, but even the slaves regarded him as one of the kindest of masters. Having inherited his slaves with the rest of his property, he became possessed of them without any consultation or wish of his own. He would neither buy nor sell slaves, and was exceedingly careful, in letting them out, that they did not find oppressive and tyrannical masters. No slave speculator ever dared to cross the threshold of this planter of the Old Dominion. He was a constant attendant upon religious worship, and was noted for his general benevolence. The American Bible Society, the American Tract Society, and the cause of Foreign Missions, found in him a liberal friend. He was always anxious that his slaves should appear well on the Sabbath, and have an opportunity of hearing the word of God.

CHAPTER II.

THE NEGRO SALE.

As might have been expected, the day of sale brought an unusually large number together to compete for the property to be sold. Farmers, who make a business of raising slaves for the market, were there, and slave-traders, who make a business of buying human beings in the slave-raising States and taking them to the far South, were also in attendance. Men and women, too, who wished to purchase for their own use, had found their way to the slave sale.

In the midst of the throng was one who felt a deeper interest in the result of the sale than any other of the bystanders. This was young Linwood. True to his promise, he was there with a blank bank-check in his pocket, awaiting with impatience to enter the list as a bidder for the beautiful slave.

It was indeed a heart-rending scene to witness the lamentations of these slaves, all of whom had grown up together on the old homestead of Mr. Graves, and who had been treated with great kindness by that gentleman, during his life. Now they were to be separated, and form new relations and companions. Such is the precarious condition of the slave. Even when with a good master, there is no certainty of his happiness in the future.

The less valuable slaves were first placed upon the auction-block, one after another, and sold to the high st bidder. Husbands and wives were separated with a degree of indifference that is unknown in any other relation in life. Brothers and sisters were torn from each other, and mothers saw their children for the last time on earth.

It was late in the day, and when the greatest number of persons were thought to be present, when Agnes and her daughters were brought out to the place of sale. The mother was first put upon the auction-block, and sold to a noted negro trader named Jennings. Marion was next ordered to ascend the stand, which she did with a trembling step, and was sold for $1200.

All eyes were now turned on Isaballa, as she was led forward by the auctioneer. The appearance of the handsome quadroon caused a deep sensation among the crowd. There she stood, with a skin as fair as most white women, her features as beautifully regular as any of her sex of pure Anglo-Saxon blood, her long black hair done up in the neatest manner, her form tall and graceful, and her whole appearance indicating one superior to her condition.

The auctioneer commenced by saying that Miss Isabella was fit to deck the drawing-room of the finest mansion in Virginia.

"How much, gentlemen, for this real Albino! — fit fancy-girl for any one! She enjoys good health, and has a sweet temper. How much do you say?"

"Five hundred dollars."

"Only five hundred for such a girl as this? Gentlemen, she is worth a deal more than that sum. You certainly do not know the value of the article you are bidding on. Here, gentlemen, I hold in my hand a paper certifying that she has a good moral character."

" Seven hundred."

" Ah, gentlemen, that is something like. This paper also states that she is very intelligent."

" Eight hundred."

" She was first sprinkled, then immersed, and is now warranted to be a devoted Christian, and perfectly trustworthy."

" Nine hundred dollars."

" Nine hundred and fifty."

" One thousand."

" Eleven hundred."

Here the bidding came to a dead stand. The auctioneer stopped, looked around, and began in a rough manner to relate some anecdote connected with the sale of slaves, which he said had come under his own observation.

At this juncture the scene was indeed a most striking one. The laughing, joking, swearing, smoking, spitting, and talking, kept up a continual hum and confusion among the crowd, while the slave-girl stood with tearful eyes, looking alternately at her mother and sister and toward the young man whom she hoped would become her purchaser.

" The chastity of this girl," now continued the auctioneer, " is pure. She has never been from under her mother's care. She is virtuous, and as gentle as a dove."

The bids here took a fresh start, and went on until $1800 was reached. The auctioneer once more resorted to his jokes, and concluded by assuring the company that Isabella was not only pious, but that she could make an excellent prayer.

" Nineteen hundred dollars."

" Two thousand."

This was the last bid, and the quadroon girl was struck off, and became the property of Henry Linwood.

This was a Virginia slave-auction, at which the bones, sinews, blood, and nerves of a young girl of eighteen were sold for $500; her moral character for $200; her superior intellect for $100; the benefits supposed to accrue from her having been sprinkled and immersed, together with a warranty of her devoted Christianity, for $300; her ability to make a good prayer for $200; and her chastity for $700 more. This, too, in a city thronged with churches, whose tall spires look like so many signals pointing to heaven, but whose ministers preach that slavery is a God-ordained institution!

The slaves were speedily separated, and taken along by their respective masters. Jennings, the slave-speculator, who had purchased Agnes and her daughter Marion, with several of the other slaves, took them to the county prison, where he usually kept his human cattle after purchasing them, previous to starting for the New Orleans market.

Linwood had already provided a place for Isabella, to which she was taken. The most trying moment for her was when she took leave of her mother and sister. The " Good-by " of the slave is unlike that of any other class in the community. It is indeed a farewell forever. With tears streaming down their cheeks, they embraced and commended each other to God, who is no respecter of persons, and before whom master and slave must one day appear.

CHAPTER III.

THE SLAVE-SPECULATOR.

DICK JENNINGS the slave-speculator, was one of the few Northern men, who go to the South and throw aside their honest mode of obtaining a living and resort to trading in human beings. A more repulsive-looking person could scarcely be found in any community of bad looking men. Tall, lean and lank, with high cheek-bones, face much pitted with the small-pox, gray eyes with red eyebrows, and sandy whiskers, he indeed stood alone without mate or fellow in looks. Jennings prided himself upon what he called his goodness of heart, and was always speaking of his humanity. As many of the slaves whom he intended taking to the New Orleans market had been raised in Richmond, and had relations there, he determined to leave the city early in the morning, so as not to witness any of the scenes so comm ʰ on the departure of a slave-gang to the far South. In this, he was most ɛ ɔcessful; for not even Isabella, who had called at the prison several times to see her mother and sister, was aware of the time that they were to leave.

The slave-trader started at early dawn, and was beyond the confines of the city long before the citizens were out of their beds. As a slave regards a life on the sugar, cotton, or rice plantation as even worse than death, they are ever on the watch for an opportunity to escape. The trader, aware of this, secures his victims in chains before he sets out on ᷄is journey. On this occasion, Jennings had the men chained in pairs, while the women were allowed to go unfastened, but were closely watched.

After a march of eight days, the company arrived on the banks of the Ohio River, where they took a steamer for the place of their destination. ᷄nnings had already advertised in the New Orleans papers, that he would be there with a prime lot of able-bodied slaves, men and women, fit for field-service, with a few extra ones calculated for house-servants, — all between the ages of fifteen and twenty-five years; but like most men who make a business of speculating in human beings, he often bought many who were far advanced in years, and would try to pass them off for five or six years younger than they were. Few persons can arrive at anything approaching the real age of the negro, by mere observation, unless they are well acquainted with the race. Therefore, the slave-trader frequently carried out the deception with perfect impunity.

After the steamer had left the wharf and was fairly out on the bosom of the broad Mississippi, the speculator called his servant Pompey to him; and instructed him as to getting the negroes ready for market. Among the forty slaves that the trader had on this occasion, were some whose appearance indicated that they had seen some years and had gone through considerable service. Their gray hair and whiskers at once pronounced them to be above the ages set down in the trader's advertisement. Pompey had long been with Jennings, and understood his business well, and if he did not take delight in the discharge of his duty, he did it at least with a degree of alacrity, so that he might receive the approbation of his master.

Pomp, as he was usually called by the trader, was of real negro blood, and would often say, when alluding to himself, "Dis nigger am no counterfelt, he is de ginuine artikle. Dis chile is none of your haf-and-haf, dere is no bogus about him."

Pompey was of low stature, round face, and, like most of his race, had a set of teeth, which, for whiteness and beauty, could not be surpassed; his eyes were large, lips thick, and hair short and woolly. Pompey had been with Jennings so long, and had seen so much of buying and selling of his fellow-creatures, that he appeared perfectly indifferent to the heart-rending scenes which daily occurred in his presence. Such is the force of habit: —

> "Vice is a monster of such frightful mien,
> That to be hated, needs but to be seen;
> But seen too oft, familiar with its face,
> We first endure, then pity, then embrace."

It was on the second day of the steamer's voyage, that Pompey selected five of the oldest slaves, took them into a room by themselves, and commenced preparing them for the market.

"Now," said he, addressing himself to the company, "I is de chap dat is to get you ready for de Orleans market, so dat you will bring marser a good price. How old is you?" addressing himself to a man not less than forty.

"If I live to see next sweet-potato-digging time, I shall be either forty or forty-five, I don't know which."

"Dat may be," replied Pompey; "but now you is only thirty years old,—dat's what marser says you is to be."

"I know I is more den dat," responded the man.

"I can't help nuffin' about dat," returned Pompey; "but when you get into de market and any one ax you how old you is, and you tell um you is forty or forty-five, marser will tie you up and cut you all to pieces. But if you tell um dat you is only thirty, den he won't. Now remember dat you is thirty years old and no more."

"Well den, I guess I will only be thirty when dey ax me."

"What's your name?" said Pompey, addressing himself to another. "Jeems."

"Oh! Uncle Jim, is it?"

"Yes."

"Den you must have all them gray whiskers shaved off, and all dem gray hairs plucked out of your head." This was all said by Pompey in a manner which showed that he knew what he was about.

"How old is you?" asked Pompey of a tall, strong-looking man. "What's your name?"

"I am twenty-nine years old, and my name is Tobias, but they calls me Toby."

"Well, Toby, or Mr. Tobias, if dat will suit you better, you are now twenty-three years old; dat's all,—do you understand dat?"

"Yes," replied Toby.

Pompey now gave them all to understand how old they were to be when asked by persons who were likely to purchase, and then went and reported to his master that the old boys were all right.

"Be sure," said Jennings, "that the niggers don't forget what you have taught them, for our luck this time in the market depends upon their appearance. If any of them have so many gray hairs that you cannot pluck them out, take the blacking and brush, and go at them."

CHAPTER IV.

THE BOAT-RACE.

At eight o'clock, on the evening of the third day of the passage, the lights of another steamer were seen in the distance, and apparently coming up very fast. This was the signal for a general commotion on board the Patriot, and everything indicated that a steamboat-race was at hand. Nothing can exceed the excitement attendant upon the racing of steamers on the Mississippi.

By the time the boats had reached Memphis they were side by side, and each exerting itself to get in advance of the other. The night was clear, the moon shining brightly, and the boats so near to each other that the passengers were within speaking distance. On board the Patriot the firemen were using oil, lard, butter, and even bacon, with wood, for the purpose of raising the steam to its highest pitch. The blaze mingled with the black smoke that issued from the pipes of the other boat, which showed that she also was burning something more combustible than wood.

The firemen of both boats, who were slaves, were singing songs such as can only be heard on board a Southern steamer. The boats now came abreast of each other, and nearer and nearer, until they were ocked so that men could pass from one to the other. The wildest excitement prevailed among the men employed on the steamers, in which the passengers freely participated.

The Patriot now stopped to take in passengers, but still no steam was permitted to escape. On the starting of the boat again, cold water was forced into the boilers by the feed-pumps, and, as might have been expected, one of the boilers exploded with terrific force, carrying away the boiler-deck and tearing to pieces much of the machinery. One dense fog of steam filled every part of the vessel, while shrieks, groans, and cries were heard on every side. Men were running hither and thither looking for their wives, and women were flying about in the wildest confusion seeking for their husbands. Dismay appeared on every countenance.

The saloons and cabins soon looked more like hospitals than anything else; but by this time the Patriot had drifted to the shore, and the other steamer had come alongside to render assistance to the disabled boat. The killed and wounded (nineteen in number) were put on shore, and the Patriot, taken in tow by the Washington, was once more on her journey.

It was half-past twelve, and the passengers, instead of retiring to their berths, once more assembled at the gambling-tables. The practice of gambling on the western waters has long been a source of annoyance to the more moral persons who travel on our great rivers. Thousands of dollars often change owners during a passage from St. Louis or Louisville to New Orleans, on a Mississippi steamer. Many men are completely ruined on such occasions, and duels are often the consequence.

" Go call my boy, steward," said Mr. Jones, as he took his cards one by one from the table.

In a few minutes a fine-looking, bright-eyed mulatto boy, apparently about sixteen years of age, was standing by his master's side at the table.

"I am broke, all but my boy," said Jones, as he ran his fingers through his cards; "but he is worth a thousand dollars, and I will bet the half of him."

"I will call you," said Thompson, as he laid five hundred dollars at the feet of the boy, who was standing on the table, and at the same time throwing down his cards before his adversary.

"You have beaten me," said Jones; and a roar of laughter followed from the other gentleman as poor Joe stepped down from the table.

"Well, I suppose I owe you half the nigger," said Thompson, as he took hold of Joe and began examining his limbs.

"Yes," replied Jones, "he is half yours. Let me have five hundred dollars, and I will give you a bill of sale of the boy."

"Go back to your bed," said Thompson to his chattel, "and remember that you now belong to me."

The poor slave wiped the tears from his eyes, as, in obedience, he turned to leave the table.

"My father gave me that boy," said Jones, as he took the money "and I hope, Mr. Thompson, that you will allow me to redeem him."

"Most certainly, sir," replied Thompson. "Whenever you hand over the cool thousand the negro is yours."

Next morning, as the passengers were assembling in the cabin and on deck, and while the slaves were running about waiting on or looking for their masters, poor Joe was seen entering his new master's stateroom, boots in hand.

"Who do you belong to?" inquired a gentleman of an old negro, who passed along leading a fine Newfoundland dog which he had been feeding.

"When I went to sleep las' night," replied the slave, "I 'longed to Massa Carr; but he bin gamblin' all night, an' I don't know who I 'longs to dis mornin'."

Such is the uncertainty of a slave's life. He goes to bed at night the pampered servant of his young master, with whom he has played in childhood, and who would not see his slave abused under any consideration, and gets up in the morning the property of a man whom he has never before seen.

To behold five or six tables in the saloon of a steamer, with half a dozen men playing cards at each, with money, pistols, and bowie-knives spread in splendid confusion before then, is an ordinary thing on the Mississippi River.

CHAPTER V.

THE YOUNG MOTHER.

On the fourth morning, the Patriot landed at Grand Gulf, a beautiful town on the left bank of the Mississippi. Among the numerous passengers who came on board at Rodney was another slave-trader, with nine human chattels which he was conveying to the Southern market. The passengers, both ladies and gentlemen, were startled at seeing among the new lot of slaves a woman so white as not to be distinguishable from the other white women on board. She had in her arms a child so white that no one would suppose a drop of African blood flowed through its blue veins.

No one could behold that mother with her helpless babe, without feeling that God would punish the oppressor. There she sat, with an expressive and intellectual forehead, and a countenance full of dignity and heroism, her dark golden locks rolled back from her almost snow-white forehead and floating over her swelling bosom. The tears that stood in her mild blue eyes showed that she was brooding over sorrows and wrongs that filled her bleeding heart.

The hearts of the passers-by grew softer, while gazing upon that young mother as she pressed sweet kisses on the sad, smiling lips of the infant that lay in her lap. The small, dimpled hands of the innocent creature were slyly hid in the warm bosom on which the little one nestled. The blood of some proud Southerner, no doubt, flowed through the veins of that child.

When the boat arrived at Natches, a rather good-looking, genteel-appearing man came on board to purchase a servant. This individual introduced himself to Jennings as the Rev. James Wilson. The slave-trader conducted the preacher to the deck-cabin, where he kept his slaves, and the man of God, after having some questions answered, selected Agnes as the one best suited to his service.

It seemed as if poor Marion's heart would break when she found that she was to be separated from her mother. The preacher, however, appeared to be but little moved by their sorrow, and took his newly-purchased victim on shore. Agnes begged him to buy her daughter, but he refused, on the ground that he had no use for her.

During the remainder of the passage, Marion wept bitterly.

After a run of a few hours, the boat stopped at Baton Rouge, where an additional number of passengers were taken on board, among whom were a number of persons who had been attending the races at that place. Gambling and drinking were now the order of the day.

The next morning, at ten o'clock, the boat arrived at New Orleans, where the passengers went to their hotels and homes, and the negroes to the slave-pens.

Lizzie, the white slave-mother, of whom we have already spoken, created as much of a sensation by the fairness of her complexion and the alabaster whiteness of her child, when being conveyed on shore at New Orleans, as she had done when brought on board at Grand Gulf. Every one that saw her felt that slavery in the Southern States was not confined to the negro. Many had been taught to think that slavery was a benefit rather than an injury, and those who were not opposed to the institution before, now felt that if whites were to become its victims, it was time at least that some security should be thrown around the Anglo-Saxon to save him from this servile and degraded position.

CHAPTER VI.

THE SLAVE-MARKET.

NOT far from Canal Street, in the city of New Orleans, stands a large two-story, flat building, surrounded by a stone wall some twelve feet high, the top of which is covered with bits of glass, and so constructed as to prevent even the possibility of any one's passing over it without sustaining great injury. Many of the rooms in this building resemble the cells of a prison, and in a small apartment near the "office" are to be seen any number of iron collars, hobbles, handcuffs, thumbscrews, cowhides, chains, gags, and yokes.

A back-yard, enclosed by a high wall, looks something like the playground attached to one of our large New England schools, in which are rows of benches and swings. Attached to the back premises is a good-sized kitchen, where, at the time of which we write, two old negresses were at work, stewing, boiling, and baking, and occasionally wiping the perspiration from their furrowed and swarthy brows.

The slave-trader, Jennings, on his arrival at New Orleans, took up his quarters here with his gang of human cattle, and the morning after, at 10 o'clock, they were exhibited for sale. First of all came the beautiful Marion, whose pale countenance and dejected look told how many sad hours she had passed since parting with her mother at Natchez. There, too, was a poor woman who had been separated from her husband; and another woman, whose looks and manners were expressive of deep anguish, sat by her side. There was "Uncle Jeems," with his whiskers off, his face shaven clean, and the gray hairs plucked out, ready to be sold for ten years younger than he was. Toby was also there, with his face shaven and greased, ready for inspection.

The examination commenced, and was carried on in such a manner as to shock the feelings of any one not entirely devoid of the milk of human kindness.

"What are you wiping your eyes for?" inquired a fat, red-faced man, with a white hat set on one side of his head and a cigar in his mouth, of a woman who sat on one of the benches.

"Because I left my man behind."

"Oh, if I buy you, I will furnish you with a better man than you left. I've got lots of young bucks on my farm."

"I don't want and never will have another man," replied the woman.

"What's your name?" asked a man in a straw hat of a tall negro who stood with his arms folded across his breast, leaning against the wall.

"My name is Aaron, sar."

"How old are you?"

"Twenty-five."

"Where were you raised?"

"In ole Virginny, sar."

"How many men have owned you?"

"Four."

"Do you enjoy good health?"

"Yes, sar."

"How long did you live with your first owner?"

"Twenty years."

"Did you ever run away?"

"No, sar."

"Did you ever strike your master?"

"No, sar."

"Were you ever whipped much?"

"No, sar; I s'pose I didn't desarve it, sar."

"How long did you live with your second master?"

"Ten years, sar."

"Have you a good appetite?"

"Yes, sar."

"Can you eat your allowance?"

"Yes, sar, — when I can get it."

"Where were you employed in Virginia?"

"I worked de tobacker fiel'."

"In the tobacco field, eh?"

"Yes, sar."

"How old did you say you was?"

"Twenty-five, sar, nex' sweet-'tater-diggin' time."

"I am a cotton-planter, and if I buy you, you will have to work in

2

the cotton-field. My men pick one hundred and fifty pounds a day, and the women one hundred and forty pounds; and those who fail to perform their task receive five stripes for each pound that is wanting. Now, do you think you could keep up with the rest of the hands?"

"I don't know, sar, but I 'specs I'd have to."

"How long did you live with your third master?"

"Three years, sar."

"Why, that makes you thirty-three. I thought you told me you were only twenty-five?"

Aaron now looked first at the planter, then at the trader, and seemed perfectly bewildered. He had forgotten the lesson given him by Pompey relative to his age; and the planter's circuitous questions — doubtless to find out the slave's real age — had thrown the negro off his guard.

"I must see your back, so as to know how much you have been whipped, before I think of buying."

Pompey, who had been standing by during the examination, thought that his services were now required, and, stepping forth with a degree of officiousness, said to Aaron, —

"Don't you hear de gemman tell you he wants to 'zamin you. Cum, unharness yo'seff, ole boy, and don't be standin' dar."

Aaron was soon examined, and pronounced "sound;" yet the conflicting statement about his age was not satisfactory.

Fortunately for Marion, she was spared the pain of undergoing such an examination. Mr. Cardney, a teller in one of the banks, had just been married, and wanted a maid-servant for his wife, and, passing through the market in the early part of the day, was pleased with the young slave's appearance, and his dwelling the quadroon found a much better home than often falls to the lot of a slave sold in the New Orleans market.

CHAPTER VII.

THE SLAVE-HOLDING PARSON.

THE Rev. James Wilson was a native of the State of Connecticut, where he was educated for the ministry in the Methodist persuasion. His father was a strict follower of John Wesley, and spared no pains in his son's education, with the hope that he would one day be as renowned as the leader of his sect. James had scarcely finished his education at New Haven, when he was invited by an uncle, then on a visit to his father, to spend a few months at Natchez in Mississippi. Young Wilson accepted his uncle's invitation, and accompanied him to the South. Few young men, and especially clergymen, going fresh from college to the

South, but are looked upon as geniuses in a small way, and who are not invited to all the parties in the neighborhood. Mr. Wilson was not an exception to this rule. The society into which he was thrown, on his arrival at Natchez, was too brilliant for him not to be captivated by it, and, as might have been expected, he succeeded in captivating a plantation with seventy slaves if not the heart of the lady to whom it belonged.

Added to this, he became a popular preacher, and had a large congregation with a snug salary. Like other planters, Mr. Wilson confided the care of his farm to Ned Huckelby, an overseer of high reputation in his way.

The Poplar Farm, as it was called, was situated in a beautiful valley, nine miles from Natchez, and near the Mississippi River. The once unshorn face of nature had given way, and the farm now blossomed with a splendid harvest. The neat cottage stood in a grove, where Lombardy poplars lift their tops almost to prop the skies, where the willow, locust, and horse-chestnut trees spread forth their branches, and flowers never ceased to blossom.

This was the parson's country residence, where the family spent only two months during the year. His town residence was a fine villa, seated on the brow of a hill, at the edge of the city.

It was in the kitchen of this house that Agnes found her new home. Mr. Wilson was every inch a democrat, and early resolved that "his people," as he called his slaves, should be well-fed and not over-worked, and therefore laid down the law and gospel to the overseer as well as to the slaves. "It is my wish," said he to Mr. Carlingham, an old schoolfellow who was spending a few days with him, — "It is my wish that a new system be adopted on the plantations in this State. I believe that the sons of Ham should have the gospel, and I intend that mine shall have it. The gospel is calculated to make mankind better and none should be without it."

"What say you," said Carlingham, "about the right of man to his liberty?"

"Now, Carlingham, you have begun to harp again about men's rights. I really wish that you could see this matter as I do."

"I regret that I cannot see eye to eye with you," said Carlingham. "I am a disciple of Rousseau, and have for years made the rights of man my study, and I must confess to you that I see no difference between white and black, as it regards liberty."

"Now, my dear Carlingham, would you really have the negroes enjoy the same rights as ourselves?"

"I would most certainly. Look at our great Declaration of Independence! look even at the Constitution of our own Connecticut, and see what is said in these about liberty."

"I regard all this talk about rights as mere humbug. The Bible is older than the Declaration of Independence, and there I take my stand."

A long discussion followed, in which both gentlemen put forth their peculiar ideas with much warmth of feeling.

During this conversation, there was another person in the room, seated by the window, who, although at work, embroidering a fine collar, paid minute attention to what was said. This was Georgiana, the only daughter of the parson, who had but just returned from Connecticut, where she had finished her education. She had had the opportunity of contrasting the spirit of Christianity and liberty in New England with that of slavery in her native State, and had learned to feel deeply for the injured negro.

Georgiana was in her nineteenth year, and had been much benefited by her residence of five years at the North. Her form was tall and graceful, her features regular and well-defined, and her complexion was illuminated by the freshness of youth, beauty, and health.

The daughter differed from both the father and visitor upon the subject which they had been discussing; and as soon as an opportunity offered, she gave it as her opinion that the Bible was both the bulwark of Christianity and of liberty. With a smile she said,—

"Of course, papa will overlook my difference with him, for although I am a native of the South, I am by education and sympathy a Northerner."

Mr. Wilson laughed, appearing rather pleased than otherwise at the manner in which his daughter had expressed herself. From this Georgiana took courage and continued,—

"'Thou shalt love thy neighbor as thyself.' This single passage of Scripture should cause us to have respect for the rights of the slave. True Christian love is of an enlarged and disinterested nature. It loves all who love the Lord Jesus Christ in sincerity, without regard to color or condition."

"Georgiana, my dear, you are an abolitionist,—your talk is fanaticism!" said Mr. Wilson, in rather a sharp tone; but the subdued look of the girl and the presence of Carlingham caused him to soften his language.

Mr. Wilson having lost his wife by consumption, and Georgiana being his only child, he loved her too dearly to say more, even if he felt disposed. A silence followed this exhortation from the young Christian, but her remarks had done a noble work. The father's heart was touched, and the sceptic, for the first time, was viewing Christianity in its true light.

CHAPTER VIII.

A NIGHT IN THE PARSON'S KITCHEN.

BESIDES Agnes, whom Mr. Wilson had purchased from the slave-trader, Jennings, he kept a number of house-servants. The chief one of these was Sam, who must be regarded as second only to the parson himself. If a dinner-party was in contemplation, or any company was to be invited, after all the arrangements had been talked over by the minister and his daughter, Sam was sure to be consulted on the subject by "Miss Georgy," as Miss Wilson was called by all the servants. If furniture, crockery, or anything was to be purchased, Sam felt that he had been slighted if his opinion was not asked. As to the marketing, he did it all. He sat at the head of the servants' table in the kitchen, and was master of the ceremonies. A single look from him was enough to silence any conversation or noise among the servants in the kitchen or in any other part of the premises.

There is in the Southern States a great amount of prejudice in regard to color, even among the negroes themselves. The nearer the negro or mulatto approaches to the white, the more he seems to feel his superiority over those of a darker hue. This is no doubt the result of the prejudice that exists on the part of the whites against both the mulattoes and the blacks.

Sam was originally from Kentucky, and through the instrumentality of one of his young masters, whom he had to take to school, he had learned to read so as to be well understood, and, owing to that fact, was considered a prodigy, not only among his own master's slaves, but also among those of the town who knew him. Sam had a great wish to follow in the footsteps of his master and be a poet, and was therefore often heard singing doggerels of his own composition.

But there was one drawback to Sam, and that was his color. He was one of the blackest of his race. This he evidently regarded as a great misfortune; but he endeavored to make up for it in dress. Mr. Wilson kept his house-servants well dressed, and as for Sam, he was seldom seen except in a ruffled shirt. Indeed, the washerwoman feared him more than any one else in the house.

Agnes had been inaugurated chief of the kitchen department, and had a general supervision of the household affairs. Alfred, the coachman, Peter, and Hetty made up the remainder of the house-servants. Besides these, Mr. Wilson owned eight slaves who were masons. These worked in the city. Being mechanics, they were let out to greater advantage than to keep them on the farm.

Every Sunday evening, Mr. Wilson's servants, including the bricklayers, assembled in the kitchen, where the events of the week were fully discussed and commented upon. It was on a Sunday evening, in the month of June, that there was a party at Mr. Wilson's house, and, according to custom in the Southern States, the ladies had their maid-servants with them. Tea had been served in "the house," and the servants, including the strangers, had taken their seats at the table in the kitchen. Sam, being a "single gentleman," was unusually attentive to the "ladies" on this occasion. He seldom let a day pass without spending an hour or two in combing and brushing his "har." He had an idea that fresh butter was better for his hair than any other kind of grease, and therefore on churning days half a pound of butter had always to be taken out before it was salted. When he wished to appear to great advantage, he would grease his face to make it "shiny." Therefore, on the evening of the party, when all the servants were at the table, Sam cut a big figure. There he sat, with his wool well combed and buttered, face nicely greased, and his ruffles extending five or six inches from his bosom. The parson in his drawing-room did not make a more imposing appearance than did his servant on this occasion.

"I jis bin had my fortune tole last Sunday night," said Sam, while helping one of the girls.

"Indeed!" cried half a dozen voices.

"Yes," continued he; "Aunt Winny tole me I's to hab de prettiest yallah gal in de town, and dat I's to be free!"

All eyes were immediately turned toward Sally Johnson, who was seated near Sam.

"I 'specs I see somebody blush at dat remark," said Alfred.

"Pass dem pancakes an' 'lasses up dis way, Mr. Alf., and none ob your 'sinuwashuns here," rejoined Sam.

"Dat reminds me," said Agnes, "dat Dorcas Simpson is gwine to git married."

"Who to, I want to know?" inquired Peter.

"To one of Mr. Darby's field-hands," answered Agnes.

"I should tink dat gal wouldn't frow herself away in dat ar way," said Sally: "She's good lookin' 'nough to git a house-servant, and not hab to put up wid a field-nigger."

"Yes," said Sam, "dat's a werry unsensible remark ob yourn, Miss Sally. I admires your judgment werry much, I 'sures you. Dar's plenty ob susceptible an' well-dressed house-serbants dat a gal ob her looks can git widout takin' up wid dem common darkies."

The evening's entertainment concluded by Sam's relating a little of his own experience while with his first master, in old Kentucky. This master was a doctor, and had a large practice among his neighbors, doc-

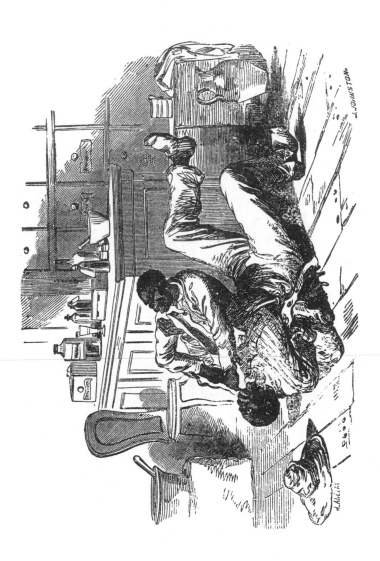

toring both masters and slaves. When Sam was about fifteen years old, his master set him to grinding up ointment and making pills. As the young student grew older and became more practised in his profession, his services were of more importance to the doctor. The physician having a good business, and a large number of his patients being slaves, —the most of whom had to call on the doctor when ill, — he put Sam to bleeding, pulling teeth, and administering medicine to the slaves. Sam soon acquired the name among the slaves of the " Black Doctor." With this appellation he was delighted; and no regular physician could have put on more airs than did the black doctor when his services were required. In bleeding, he must have more bandages, and would rub and smack the arm more than the doctor would have thought of.

Sam was once seen taking out a tooth for one of his patients, and nothing appeared more amusing. He got the poor fellow down on his back, and then getting astride of his chest, he applied the turnkeys and pulled away for dear life. Unfortunately, he had got hold of the wrong tooth, and the poor man screamed as loud as he could; but it was to no purpose, for Sam had him fast, and after a pretty severe tussle out came the sound grinder. The young doctor now saw his mistake, but consoled himself with the thought that as the wrong tooth was out of the way, there was more room to get at the right one.

Bleeding and a dose of calomel were always considered indispensable by the " old boss," and as a matter of course, Sam followed in his footsteps.

On one occasion the old doctor was ill himself, so as to be unable to attend to his patients. A slave, with pass in hand, called to receive medical advice, and the master told Sam to examine him and see what he wanted. This delighted him beyond measure, for although he had been acting his part in the way of giving out medicine as the master ordered it, he had never been called upon by the latter to examine a patient, and this seemed to convince him after all that he was no sham doctor. As might have been expected, he cut a rare figure in his first examination. Placing himself directly opposite his patient, and folding his arms across his breast, looking very knowingly, he began, —

" What's de matter wid you ? "

" I is sick."

" Where is you sick ? "

" Here," replied the man, putting his hand upon his stomach.

" Put out your tongue," continued the doctor.

The man ran out his tongue at full length.

" Let me feel your pulse;" at the same time taking his patient's hand in his, and placing his fingers upon his pulse, he said, —

" Ah! your case is a bad one; ef I don't do something for you, and dat pretty quick, you'll be a gone coon, and dat's sartin."

At this the man appeared frightened, and inquired what was the matter with him, in answer to which Sam said, —

" I done told dat your case is a bad one, and dat's enuff."

On Sam's returning to his master's bedside, the latter said, —

" Well, Sam, what do you think is the matter with him ? "

" His stomach is out ob order, sar," he replied.

" What do you think had better be done for him ? "

" I tink I'd better bleed him and gib him a dose ob calomel," returned Sam.

So, to the latter's gratification, the master let him have his own way.

On one occasion, when making pills and ointment, Sam made a great mistake. He got the preparations for both mixed together, so that he could not legitimately make either. But fearing that if he threw the stuff away, his master would flog him, and being afraid to inform his superior of the mistake, he resolved to make the whole batch of pill and ointment stuff into pills. He well knew that the powder over the pills would hide the inside, and the fact that most persons shut their eyes when taking such medicine led the young doctor to feel that all would be right in the end. Therefore Sam made his pills, boxed them up, put on the labels, and placed them in a conspicuous position on one of the shelves.

Sam felt a degree of anxiety about his pills, however. It was a strange mixture, and he was not certain whether it would kill or cure; but he was willing that it should be tried. At last the young doctor had his vanity gratified. Col. Tallen, one of Dr. Saxondale's patients, drove up one morning, and Sam as usual ran out to the gate to hold the colonel's horse.

" Call your master," said the colonel; " I will not get out."

The doctor was soon beside the carriage, and inquired about the health of his patient. After a little consultation, the doctor returned to his office, took down a box of Sam's new pills, and returned to the carriage.

" Take two of these every morning and night," said the doctor, " and if you don't feel relieved, double the dose."

" Good gracious," exclaimed Sam in an undertone, when he heard his master tell the colonel how to take the pills.

It was several days before Sam could learn the result of his new medicine. One afternoon, about a fortnight after the colonel's visit, Sam saw his master's patient riding up to the gate on horseback. The doctor happened to be in the yard, and met the colonel and said, —

" How are you now ? "

"I am entirely recovered," replied the patient. " ɪnose pills of yours put me on my feet the next day."

"I knew they would," rejoined the doctor.

Sam was near enough to hear the conversation, and was delighted beyond description. The negro immediately ran into the kitchen, amongst his companions, and commenced dancing.

"What de matter wid you?" inquired the cook.

"I is de greatest doctor in dis country," replied Sam. "Ef you ever get sick, call on me. No matter what ails you, I is de man dat can cure you in no time. If you do hab de backache, de rheumatics, de headache, de coller morbus, fits, er any ting else, Sam is de gentleman dat can put you on your feet wid his pills."

For a long time after, Sam did little else than boast of his skill as a doctor.

We have said that the "black doctor" was full of wit and good sense. Indeed, in that respect, he had scarcely an equal in the neighborhood. Although his master resided some little distance out of the city, Sam was always the first man in all the negro balls and parties in town. When his master could give him a pass, he went, and when he did not give him one, he would steal away after his master had retired, and run the risk of being taken up by the night-watch. Of course, the master never knew anything of the absence of the servant at night without permission. As the negroes at those parties tried to excel each other in the way of dress, Sam was often at a loss to make that appearance that his heart desired, but his ready wit ever helped him in this. When his master had retired to bed at night, it was the duty of Sam to put out the lights, and take out with him his master's clothes and boots, and leave them in the office until morning, and then black the boots, brush the clothes, and return them to his master's room.

Having resolved to attend a dress-ball one night, without his master's permission, and being perplexed for suitable garments, Sam determined to take his master's. So, dressing himself in the doctor's clothes, even to his boots and hat, off the negro started for the city. Being well acquainted with the usual walk of the patrols he found no difficulty in keeping out of their way. As might have been expected, Sam was the great gun with the ladies that night.

The next morning, Sam was back home long before his master's time for rising, and the clothes were put in their accustomed place. For a long time Sam had no difficulty in attiring himself for parties; but the old proverb that "It is a long lane that has no turning," was verified in the negro's case. One stormy night, when the rain was descending in torrents, the doctor heard a rap at his door. It was customary with him, when called up at night to visit a patient, to ring for Sam. But this time, the servant was nowhere to be found. The doctor struck a light and looked for clothes; they, too, were gone. It was twelve o'clock, and the doctor's clothes, hat, boots, and even his watch, were nowhere to be found. Here was a pretty dilemma for a doctor to be in. It was some time before the physician could fit himself out so as to make the visit. At last, however, he started with one of the farm-horses, for Sam had taken the doctor's best saddle-horse. The doctor felt sure that the negro had robbed him, and was on his way to Canada; but in this he was mistaken. Sam had gone to the city to attend a ball, and had decked himself out in his master's best suit. The physician returned before morning, and again retired to bed but with little hope of sleep, for his thoughts were with his servant and horse. At six o'clock, in walked Sam with his master's clothes, and the boots neatly blacked. The watch was placed on the shelf, and the hat in its place. Sam had not met any of the servants, and was therefore entirely ignorant of what had occurred during his absence.

"What have you been about, sir, and where was you last night when I was called?" said the doctor.

"I don't know, sir. I 'spose I was asleep," replied Sam.

But the doctor was not to be so easily satisfied, after having been put to so much trouble in hunting up another suit without the aid of Sam. After breakfast, Sam was taken into the barn, tied up, and severely flogged with the cat, which brought from him the truth concerning his absence the previous night. This forever put an end to his fine appearance at the negro parties. Had not the doctor been one of the most indulgent of masters, he would not have escaped with merely a severe whipping.

As a matter of course, Sam had to relate to his companions that evening in Mr. Wilson's kitchen all his adventures as a physician while with his old master.

CHAPTER IX.

THE MAN OF HONOR.

AUGUSTINE CARDINAY, the purchaser of Marion, was from the Green Mountains of Vermont, and his feelings were opposed to the holding of slaves; but his young wife persuaded him into the idea that it was no worse to own a slave than to hire one and pay the money to another. Hence it was that he had been induced to purchase Marion.

Adolphus Morton, a young physician from the same State, and who had just commenced the practice of his profession in New Orleans, was boarding with Cardinay when Marion was brought home. The young physician had been in New Orleans but a very few weeks, and had seen but little of slavery. In his own mountain-home, he had been taught that the slaves of the Southern States were negroes, and if not from the coast of Africa, the descendants of those who had been imported. He was unprepared to behold with composure a beautiful white girl of sixteen in the degraded position of a chattel slave.

The blood chilled in his young heart as he heard Cardinay tell how, by bantering with the trader, he had bought her two hundred dollars less than he first asked. His very looks showed that she had the deepest sympathies of his heart.

Marion had been brought up by her mother to look after the domestic concerns of her cottage in Virginia, and well knew how to perform the duties imposed upon her. Mrs. Cardinay was much pleased wjth her new servant, and often mentioned her good qualities in the presence of Mr. Morton.

After eight months acquaintance with Marion, Morton's sympathies ripened into love, which was most cordially reciprocated by the friendless and injured child of sorrow. There was but one course which the young man could honorably pursue, and that was to purchase Marion and make her his lawful wife; and this he did immediately, for he found Mr. and Mrs. Cardinay willing to second his liberal intentions.

The young man, after purchasing Marion from Cardinay, and marrying her, took lodgings in another part of the city. A private teacher was called in, and the young wife was taught some of those accomplishments so necessary for one taking a high position in good society.

Dr. Morton soon obtained a large and influential practice in his profession, and with it increased in wealth; but with all his wealth he never owned a slave. Probably the fact that he had raised his wife from that condition kept the hydra-headed system continually before him. To the credit of Marion be it said, she used every means to obtain the freedom of her mother, who had been sold to Parson Wilson, at Natchez. Her efforts, however, had come too late; for Agnes had died of a fever before the arrival of Dr. Morton's agent.

Marion found in Adolphus Morton a kind and affectionate husband; and his wish to purchase her mother, although unsuccessful, had doubly endeared him to her. Ere a year had elapsed from the time of their marriage, Mrs. Morton presented her husband with a lovely daughter, who seemed to knit their hearts still closer together. This child they named Jane; and before the expiration of the second year, they were blessed with another daughter, whom they named Adrika.

These children grew up to the ages of ten and eleven, and were then sent to the North to finish their education, and receive that refinement which young ladies cannot obtain in the Slave States.

CHAPTER X.

THE QUADROON'S HOME.

A FEW miles out of Richmond is a pleasant place, with here and there a beautiful cottage surrounded by trees so as scarcely to be seen. Among these was one far retired from the public roads, and almost hidden among the trees. This was the spot that Henry Linwood had selected for Isabella, the eldest daughter of Agnes. The young man hired the house, furnished it, and placed his mistress there, and for many months no one in his father's family knew where he spent his leisure hours.

When Henry was not with her, Isabella employed herself in looking after her little garden and the flowers that grew in front of her cottage. The passion-flower, peony, dahlia, laburnum, and other plants, so abundant in warm climates, under the tasteful hand of Isabella, lavished their beauty upon this retired spot, and miniature paradise.

Although Isabella had been assured by Henry that she should be free and that he would always consider her as his wife, she nevertheless felt that she ought to be married and acknowledged by him. But this was an impossibility under the State laws, even had the young man been disposed to do what was right in the matter. Related as he was, however, to one of the first families in Virginia, he would not have dared to marry a woman of so low an origin, even had the laws been favorable.

Here, in this secluded grove, unvisited by any other except her lover, Isabella lived for years. She had become the mother of a lovely daughter, which its father named Clotelle. The complexion of the child was still fairer than that of its mother. Indeed, she was not darker than other white children, and as she grew older she more and more resembled her father.

As time passed away, Henry became negligent of Isabella and his child, so much so, that days and even weeks passed without their seeing him, or knowing where he was. Becoming more acquainted with the world, and moving continually in the society of young women of his own station, the young man felt that Isabella was a burden to him, and having as some would say, " outgrown his love," he longed to free himself of the responsibility; yet every time he saw the child, he felt that he owed it his fatherly care.

Henry had now entered into political life, and been elected to a seat in the legislature of his native State; and in his intercourse with his friends had become acquainted with Gertrude Miller, the daughter of a wealthy gentleman living near Richmond. Both Henry and Gertrude were very good-looking, and a mutual attachment sprang up between them.

Instead of finding fault with the unfrequent visits of Henry, Isabella always met him with a smile, and tried to make both him and herself believe that business was the cause of his negligence. When he was with her, she devoted every moment of her time to him, and never failed to speak of the growth and increasing intelligence of Clotelle.

The child had grown so large as to be able to follow its father on his departure out to the road. But the impression made on Henry's feelings by the devoted woman and her child was momentary. His heart had grown hard, and his acts were guided by no fixed principle. Henry and Gertrude had been married nearly two years before Isabella knew anything of the event, and it was merely by accident that she became acquainted with the facts.

One beautiful afternoon, when Isabella and Clotelle were picking wild strawberries some two miles from their home, and near the road-side, they observed a one-horse chaise driving past. The mother turned her face from the carriage not wishing to be seen by strangers, little dreaming that the chaise contained Henry and his wife. The child, however, watched the chaise, and startled her mother by screaming out at the top of her voice, " Papa! papa!" and clapped her little hands for joy. The mother turned in haste to look at the strangers, and her eyes encountered those of Henry's pale and dejected countenance. Gertrude's eyes were on the child. The swiftness with which Henry drove by could not hide from his wife the striking resemblance of the child to himself. The young wife had heard the child exclaim " Papa! papa!" and she immediately saw by the quivering of his lips and the agitation depicted in his countenance, that all was not right.

" Who is that woman? and why did that child call you papa?" she inquired, with a trembling voice.

Henry was silent; he knew not what to say, and without another word passing between them, they drove home.

On reaching her room, Gertrude buried her face in her handkerchief and wept. She loved Henry, and when she had heard from the lips of her companions how their husbands had proved false, she felt that he was an exception, and fervently thanked God that she had been so blessed.

When Gertrude retired to her bed that night, the sad scene of the day followed her. The beauty of Isabella, with her flowing curls, and the look of the child, so much resembling the man whom she so dearly loved, could not be forgotten; and little Clotelle's exclamation of " Papa! papa!" rang in her ears during the whole night.

The return of Henry at twelve o'clock did not increase her happiness. Feeling his guilt, he had absented himself from the house since his return from the ride.

CHAPTER XI.

TO-DAY A MISTRESS, TO-MORROW A SLAVE.

THE night was dark, the rain- descended in torrents from the black and overhanging clouds, and the thunder, accompanied with vivid flashes of lightning, resounded fearfully, as Henry Linwood stepped from his chaise and entered Isabella's cottage.

More than a fortnight had elapsed since the accidental meeting, and Isabella was in doubt as to who the lady was that Henry was with in the carriage. Little, however, did she think that it was his wife. With a smile, Isabella met the young man as he entered her little dwelling. Clotelle had already gone to bed, but her father's voice aroused her from her sleep, and she was soon sitting on his knee.

The pale and agitated countenance of Henry betrayed his uneasiness, but Isabella's mild and laughing allusion to the incident of their meeting him on the day of his pleasure-drive, and her saying, "I presume, dear Henry, that the lady was one of your relatives," led him to believe that she was still in ignorance of his marriage. She was, in fact, ignorant who the lady was who accompanied the man she loved on that eventful day. He, aware of this, now acted more like himself, and passed the thing off as a joke. At heart, however, Isabella felt uneasy, and this uneasiness would at times show itself to the young man. At last, and with a great effort, she said, —

"Now, dear Henry, if I am in the way of your future happiness, say so, and I will release you from any promises that you have made me. I know there is no law by which I can hold you, and if there was, I would not resort to it. You are as dear to me as ever, and my thoughts shall always be devoted to you. It would be a great sacrifice for me to give you up to another, but if it be your desire, as great as the sacrifice is, I will make it. Send me and your child into a Free State if we are in your way."

Again and again Linwood assured her that no woman possessed his love but her. Oh, what falsehood and deceit man can put on when dealing with woman's love!

The unabated storm kept Henry from returning home until after the clock had struck two, and as he drew near his residence he saw his wife standing at the window. Giving his horse in charge of the servant who was waiting, he entered the house, and found his wife in tears. Although he had never satisfied Gertrude as to who the quadroon woman and child were, he had kept her comparatively easy by his close attention to her, and by telling her that she was mistaken in regard to the child's calling him "papa." His absence that night, however, without any apparent cause, had again aroused the jealousy of Gertrude; but Henry told her that he had been caught in the rain while out, which prevented his sooner returning, and she, anxious to believe him, received the story as satisfactory.

Somewhat heated with brandy, and wearied with much loss of sleep, Linwood fell into a sound slumber as soon as he retired. Not so with Gertrude. That faithfulness which has ever distinguished her sex, and the anxiety with which she watched all his movements, kept the wife awake while the husband slept. His sleep, though apparently sound, was nevertheless uneasy. Again and again she heard him pronounce the name of Isabella, and more than once she heard him say, "I am not married; I will never marry while you live." Then he would speak the name of Clotelle and say, "My dear child, how I love you!"

After a sleepless night, Gertrude arose from her couch, resolved that she would reveal the whole matter to her mother. Mrs. Miller was a woman of little or no feeling, proud, peevish, and passionate, thus making everybody miserable that came near her; and when she disliked any one, her hatred knew no bounds. This Gertrude knew; and had she not considered it her duty, she would have kept the secret locked in her own heart.

During the day, Mrs. Linwood visited her mother and told her all that had happened. The mother scolded the daughter for not having informed her sooner, and immediately determined to find out who the woman and child were that Gertrude had met on the day of her ride. Three days were spent by Mrs. Miller in this endeavor, but without success.

Four weeks had elapsed, and the storm of the old lady's temper had somewhat subsided, when, one evening, as she was approaching her daughter's residence, she saw Henry walking in the direction of where the quadroon was supposed to reside. Being satisfied that the young man had not seen her, the old woman at once resolved to follow him. Linwood's boots squeaked so loudly that Mrs. Miller had no difficulty in following him without being herself observed.

After a walk of about two miles, the young man turned into a narrow and unfrequented road, and soon entered the cottage occupied by Isabella. It was a fine starlight night, and the moon was just rising when they got to their journey's end. As usual, Isabella met Henry with a smile, and expressed her fears regarding his health.

Hours passed, and still old Mrs. Miller remained near the house, determined to know who lived there. When she undertook to ferret out anything, she bent her whole energies to it. As Michael Angelo, who subjected all things to his pursuit and the idea he had formed of it,
3

painted the crucifixion by the side of a writhing slave and would have broken up the true cross for pencils, so Mrs. Miller would have entered the sepulchre, if she could have done it, in search of an object she wished to find.

The full moon had risen, and was pouring its beams upon surrounding objects as Henry stepped from Isabella's door, and looking at his watch, said, —

"I must go, dear; it is now half-past ten."

Had little Clotelle been awake, she too would have been at the door. As Henry walked to the gate, Isabella followed with her left hand locked in his. Again he looked at his watch, and said, —

"I must go."

"It is more than a year since you staid all night," murmured Isabella, as he folded her convulsively in his arms, and pressed upon her beautiful lips a parting kiss.

He was nearly out of sight when, with bitter sobs, the quadroon retraced her steps to the door of the cottage. Clotelle had in the mean time awoke, and now inquired of her mother how long her father had been gone. At that instant, a knock was heard at the door, and supposing that it was Henry returning for something he had forgotten, as he frequently did, Isabella flew to let him in. To her amazement, however, a strange woman stood in the door.

"Who are you that comes here at this late hour?" demanded the half-frightened Isabella.

Without making any reply, Mrs. Miller pushed the quadroon aside, and entered the house.

"What do you want here?" again demanded Isabella.

"I am in search of you," thundered the maddened Mrs. Miller; but thinking that her object would be better served by seeming to be kind, she assumed a different tone of voice, and began talking in a pleasing manner.

In this way, she succeeded in finding out the connection existing between Linwood and Isabella, and after getting all she could out of the unsuspecting woman, she informed her that the man she so fondly loved had been married for more than two years. Seized with dizziness, the poor, heart-broken woman fainted and fell upon the floor. How long she remained there she could not tell; but when she returned to consciousness, the strange woman was gone, and her child was standing by her side. When she was so far recovered as to regain her feet, Isabella went to the door, and even into the yard, to see if the old woman was not somewhere about.

As she stood there, the full moon cast its bright rays over her whole person, giving her an angelic appearance and imparting to her flowing hair a still more golden hue. Suddenly-another change came over her features, and her full red lips trembled as with suppressed emotion. The muscles around her faultless mouth became convulsed, she gasped for breath, and exclaiming, " Is it possible that man can be so false! " again fainted.

Clotelle stood and bathed her mother's temples with cold water until she once more revived.

Although the laws of Virginia forbid the education of slaves, Agnes had nevertheless employed an old free negro to teach her two daughters to read and write. After being separated from her mother and sister, Isabella turned her attention to the subject of Christianity, and received that consolation from the Bible which is never denied to the children of God. This was now her last hope, for her heart was torn with grief and filled with all the bitterness of disappointment.

The night passed away, but without sleep to poor Isabella. At the dawn of day, she tried to make herself believe that the whole of the past night was a dream, and determined to be satisfied with the explanation which Henry should give on his next visit.

CHAPTER XII.

THE MOTHER-IN-LAW.

WHEN Henry returned home, he found his wife seated at the window, awaiting his approach. Secret grief was gnawing at her heart. Her sad, pale cheeks and swollen eyes showed too well that agony, far deeper than her speech portrayed, filled her heart. A dull and death-like silence prevailed on his entrance. His pale face and brow, dishevelled hair, and the feeling that he manifested on finding Gertrude still up, told Henry in plainer words than she could have used that his wife was aware that her love had never been held sacred by him. The window-blinds were still unclosed, and the full-orbed moon shed her soft refulgence over the unrivalled scene, and gave it a silvery lustre which sweetly harmonized with the silence of the night. The clock's iron tongue, in a neighboring belfry, proclaimed the hour of twelve, as the truant and unfaithful husband seated himself by the side of his devoted and loving wife, and inquired if she was not well.

" I am, dear Henry," replied Gertrude; " but I fear *you* are not. If well in body, I fear you are not at peace in mind."

" Why? " inquired he.

" Because," she replied, " you are so pale and have such a wild look in your eyes."

Again he protested his innocence, and vowed she was the only woman who had any claim upon his heart.　To behold one thus playing upon the feelings of two lovely women is enough to make us feel that evil must at last bring its own punishment.

Henry and Gertrude had scarcely risen from the breakfast-table next morning ere old Mrs. Miller made her appearance.　She immediately took her daughter aside, and informed her of her previous night's experience, telling her how she had followed Henry to Isabella's cottage, detailing the interview with the quadroon, and her late return home alone.　The old woman urged her daughter to demand that the quadroon and her child be at once sold to the negro speculators and taken out of the State, or that Gertrude herself should separate from Henry.

"Assert your rights, my dear. Let no one share a heart that justly belongs to you," said Mrs. Miller, with her eyes flashing fire. "Don't sleep this night, my child, until that wench has been removed from that cottage ; and as for the child, hand that over to me,—I saw at once that it was Henry's."

During these remarks, the old lady was walking up and down the room like a caged lioness.　She had learned from Isabella that she had been purchased by Henry, and the innocence of the injured quadroon caused her to acknowledge that he was the father of her child.　Few women could have taken such a matter in hand and carried it through with more determination and success than old Mrs. Miller.　Completely inured in all the crimes and atrocities connected with the institution of slavery, she was also aware that, to a greater or less extent, the slave women shared with their mistress the affections of their master.　This caused her to look with a suspicious eye on every good-looking negro woman that she saw.

While the old woman was thus lecturing her daughter upon her rights and duties, Henry, unaware of what was transpiring, had left the house and gone to his office.　As soon as the old woman found that he was gone, she said, —

"I will venture anything that he is on his way to see that wench again. I'll lay my life on it."

The entrance, however, of little Marcus, or Mark, as he was familiarly called, asking for Massa Linwood's blue bag, satisfied her that her son-in-law was at his office.　Before the old lady returned home, it was agreed that Gertrude should come to her mother's to tea that evening, and Henry with her, and that Mrs. Miller should there charge the young husband with inconstancy to her daughter, and demand the removal of Isabella.

With this understanding, the old woman retraced her steps to her own dwelling.

Had Mrs. Miller been of a different character and not surrounded by slavery, she could scarcely have been unhappy in such a home as hers. Just at the edge of the city, and sheltered by large poplar-trees was the old homestead in which she resided. There was a splendid orchard in the rear of the house, and the old weather-beaten sweep, with " the moss-covered bucket " at its end, swung majestically over the deep well. The garden was scarcely to be equalled. Its grounds were laid out in excellent taste, and rare exotics in the greenhouse made it still more lovely.

It was a sweet autumn evening, when the air breathed through the fragrant sheaves of grain, and the setting sun, with his golden kisses, burnished the rich clusters of purple grapes, that Henry and Gertrude were seen approaching the house on foot; it was nothing more than a pleasant walk. Oh, how Gertrude's heart beat as she seated herself, on their arrival!

The beautiful parlor, surrounded on all sides with luxury and taste, with the sun creeping through the damask curtains, added a charm to the scene. It was in this room that Gertrude had been introduced to Henry, and the pleasant hours that she had spent there with him rushed unbidden on her memory. It was here that, in former days, her beautiful countenance had made her appearance as fascinating and as lovely as that of Cleopatra's. Her sweet, musical voice might have been heard in every part of the house, occasionally thrilling you with an unexpected touch. How changed the scene! Her pale and wasted features could not be lighted up by any thoughts of the past, and she was sorrowful at heart.

As usual, the servants in the kitchen were in ecstasies at the announcement that " Miss Gerty," as they called their young mistress, was in the house, for they loved her sincerely. Gertrude had saved them from many a flogging, by interceding for them, when her mother was in one of her uncontrollable passions. Dinah, the cook, always expected Miss Gerty to visit the kitchen as soon as she came, and was not a little displeased, on this occasion, at what she considered her young mistress's neglect. Uncle Tony, too, looked regularly for Miss Gerty to visit the green house, and congratulate him on his superiority as a gardener.

When tea was over, Mrs. Miller dismissed the servants from the room, then told her son-in-law what she had witnessed the previous night, and demanded for her daughter that Isabella should be immediately sent out of the State, and to be sure that the thing would be done, she wanted him to give her the power to make such disposition of the woman and child as she should think best. Gertrude was Mrs. Miller's only child, and Henry felt little like displeasing a family upon whose friendship he so much depended, and, no doubt, long wishing to free himself from Isabella, he at once yielded to the demands of his mother-in-law. Mr. Miller was a mere cipher about his premises. If any one came on business connected with the farm, he would invariably say, "Wait till I see my wife," and the wife's opinion was sure to be law in every case. Bankrupt in character, and debauched in body and mind, with seven mulatto children who claimed him as their father, he was badly prepared to find fault with his son-in-law. It was settled that Mrs. Miller should use her own discretion in removing Isabella from her little cottage, and her future disposition. With this understanding Henry and Gertrude returned home. In the deep recesses of his heart the young man felt that he would like to see his child and its mother once more; but fearing the wrath of his mother-in-law, he did not dare to gratify his inclination. He had not the slightest idea of what would become of them; but he well knew that the old woman would have no mercy on them.

CHAPTER XIII.

A HARD-HEARTED WOMAN.

WITH no one but her dear little Clotelle, Isabella passed her weary hours without partaking of either food or drink, hoping that Henry would soon return, and that the strange meeting with the old woman would be cleared up.

While seated in her neat little bedroom with her fevered face buried in her handkerchief, the child ran in and told its mother that a carriage had stopped in front of the house. With a palpitating heart she arose from her seat and went to the door, hoping that it was Henry; but, to her great consternation, the old lady who had paid her such an unceremonious visit on the evening that she had last seen Henry, stepped out of the carriage, accompanied by the slave-trader, Jennings.

Isabella had seen the trader when he purchased her mother and sister, and immediately recognized him. What could these persons want there? thought she. Without any parleying or word of explanation, the two entered the house, leaving the carriage in charge of a servant.

Clotelle ran to her mother, and clung to her dress as if frightened by the strangers.

"She's a fine-looking wench," said the speculator, as he seated himself, unasked, in the rocking-chair; "yet I don't think she is worth the money you ask for her."

"What do you want here?" inquired Isabella, with a quivering voice.

"None of your insolence to me," bawled out the old woman, at the top of her voice; "if you do, I will give you what you deserve so much, my lady, — a good whipping."

In an agony of grief, pale, trembling, and ready to sink to the floor, Isabella was only sustained by the hope that she would be able to save her child. At last, regaining her self-possession, she ordered them both to leave the house. Feeling herself insulted, the old woman seized the tongs that stood by the fire-place, and raised them to strike the quadroon down; but the slave-trader immediately jumped between the women, exclaiming, —

"I won't buy her, Mrs. Miller, if you injure her."

Poor little Clotelle screamed as she saw the strange woman raise the tongs at her mother. With the exception of old Aunt Nancy, a free colored woman, whom Isabella sometimes employed to work for her, the child had never before seen a strange face in her mother's dwelling. Fearing that Isabella would offer some resistance, Mrs. Miller had ordered the overseer of her own farm to follow her; and, just as Jennings had stepped between the two women, Mull, the negro-driver, walked into the room.

"Seize that impudent hussy," said Mrs. Miller to the overseer, "and tie her up this minute, that I may teach her a lesson she won't forget in a hurry."

As she spoke, the old woman's eyes rolled, her lips quivered, and she looked like a very fury.

"I will have nothing to do with her, if you whip her, Mrs. Miller," said the slave-trader. "Niggers ain't worth half so much in the market with their backs newly scarred," continued he, as the overseer commenced his preparations for executing Mrs. Miller's orders.

Clotelle here took her father's walking-stick, which was lying on the back of the sofa where he had left it, and, raising it, said, —

"If you bad people touch my mother, I will strike you."

They looked at the child with astonishment; and her extreme youth, wonderful beauty, and uncommon courage, seemed for a moment to shake their purpose. The manner and language of this child were alike beyond her years, and under other circumstances would have gained for her the approbation of those present.

"Oh, Henry, Henry!" exclaimed Isabella, wringing her hands.

"You need not call on him, hussy; you will never see him again," said Mrs. Miller.

"What! is he dead?" inquired the heart-stricken woman.

It was then that she forgot her own situation, thinking only of the man she loved. Never having been called to endure any kind of abusive treatment, Isabella was not fitted to sustain herself against the brutality of Mrs. Miller, much less the combined ferociousness of the old woman and the overseer too. Suffice it to say, that instead of whipping Isabella, Mrs. Miller transferred her to the negro-speculator, who took her immediately to his slave-pen. The unfeeling old woman would not permit Isabella to take more than a single change of her clothing, remarking to Jennings, — ·

"I sold you the wench, you know, — not her clothes."

The injured, friendless, and unprotected Isabella fainted as she saw her child struggling to release herself from the arms of old Mrs. Miller, and as the wretch boxed the poor child's ears.

After leaving directions as to how Isabella's furniture and other effects should be disposed of, Mrs. Miller took Clotelle into her carriage and drove home. There was not even color enough about the child to make it appear that a single drop of African blood flowed through its blue veins.

Considerable sensation was created in the kitchen among the servants when the carriage drove up, and Clotelle entered the house.

"Jes' like Massa Henry fur all de worl'," said Dinah, as she caught a glimpse of the child through the window.

"Wondah whose brat dat ar' dat missis bringin' home wid her?" said Jane, as she put the ice in the pitchers for dinner. "I warrant it's some poor white nigger somebody bin givin' her."

The child was white. What should be done to make it look like other negroes, was the question which Mrs. Miller asked herself. The callous-hearted old woman bit her nether lip, as she viewed that child, standing before her, with her long, dark ringlets clustering over her alabaster brow and neck.

"Take this little nigger and cut her hair close to her head," said the mistress to Jane, as the latter answered the bell.

Clotelle screamed, as she felt the scissors grating over her head, and saw those curls that her mother thought so much of falling upon the floor.

A roar of laughter burst from the servants, as Jane led the child through the kitchen, with the hair cut so short that the naked scalp could be plainly seen.

"'Gins to look like nigger, now," said Dinah, with her mouth upon a grin.

The mistress smiled, as the shorn child reëntered the room; but there was something more needed. The child was white, and that was a great objection. However, she hit upon a plan to remedy this which seemed feasible. The day was excessively warm. Not a single cloud floated over the blue vault of heaven; not a breath of wind seemed moving, and the earth was parched by the broiling sun. Even the bees had stopped humming, and the butterflies had hid themselves under the broad leaves of the burdock. Without a morsel of dinner, the poor child was put in the garden, and set to weeding it, her arms, neck, and head completely bare. Unaccustomed to toil, Clotelle wept as she exerted herself in pulling up the weeds. Old Dinah, the cook, was as unfeeling as her mistress, and she was pleased to see the child made to work in the hot sun.

"Dat white nigger 'll soon be brack enuff if missis keeps her workin' out dar," she said, as she wiped the perspiration from her sooty brow.

Dinah was the mother of thirteen children, all of whom had been taken from her when young; and this, no doubt, did much to harden her feelings, and make her hate all white persons.

The burning sun poured its rays on the face of the friendless child until she sank down in the corner of the garden, and was actually broiled to sleep.

"Dat little nigger ain't workin' a bit, missus," said Dinah to Mrs. Miller, as the latter entered the kitchen.

"She's lying in the sun seasoning; she will work the better by and by," replied the mistress.

"Dese white niggers always tink dey seff good as white folks," said the cook.

"Yes; but we will teach them better, won't we, Dinah?" rejoined Mrs. Miller.

"Yes, missus," replied Dinah; "I don't like dese merlatter niggers, no how. Dey always want to set dey seff up for sumfin' big." With this remark the old cook gave one of her coarse laughs, and continued: "Missis understands human nature, don't she? Ah! ef she ain't a whole team and de ole gray mare to boot, den Dinah don't know nuffin'."

Of course, the mistress was out of the kitchen before these last remarks were made.

It was with the deepest humiliation that Henry learned from one of his own slaves the treatment which his child was receiving at the hands of his relentless mother-in-law.

The scorching sun had the desired effect; for in less than a fortnight, Clotelle could scarcely have been recognized as the same child. Often was she seen to weep, and heard to call on her mother.

Mrs. Miller, when at church on Sabbath, usually, on warm days, took Nancy, one of her servants, in her pew, and this girl had to fan her mistress during service. Unaccustomed to such a soft and pleasant seat, the servant would very soon become sleepy and begin to nod. Sometimes she would go fast asleep, which annoyed the mistress exceedingly. But Mrs. Miller had nimble fingers, and on them sharp nails, and, with an energetic pinch upon the bare arms of the poor girl, she would arouse the daughter of Africa from her pleasant dreams. But there was no one of Mrs. Miller's servants who received so much punishment as old Uncle Tony.

Fond of her greenhouse, and often in the garden, she was ever at the old gardener's heels. Uncle Tony was very religious, and, whenever his mistress flogged him, he invariably gave her a religious exhortation. Although unable to read, he, nevertheless, had on his tongue's end portions of Scripture which he could use at any moment. In one end of the greenhouse was Uncle Tony's sleeping room, and those who happened in that vicinity, between nine and ten at night, could hear the old man offering up his thanksgiving to God for his protection during the day. Uncle Tony, however, took great pride, when he thought that any of the whites were within hearing, to dwell, in his prayer, on his own goodness and the unfitness of others to die. Often was he heard to say, "O Lord, thou knowest that the white folks are not Christians, but the black people are God's own children." But if Tony thought that his old mistress was within the sound of his voice, he launched out into deeper water.

It was, therefore, on a sweet night, when the bright stars were looking out with a joyous sheen, that Mark and two of the other boys passed the greenhouse, and heard Uncle Tony in his devotions.

"Let's have a little fun," said the mischievous Marcus to his young companions. "I will make Uncle Tony believe that I am old mistress, and he'll give us an extra touch in his prayer." Mark immediately commenced talking in a strain of voice resembling, as well as he could, Mrs. Miller, and at once Tony was heard to say in a loud voice, "O Lord, thou knowest that the white people are not fit to die; but, as for old Tony, whenever the angel of the Lord comes, he's ready." At that moment, Mark tapped lightly on the door. "Who's dar?" thundered old Tony. Mark made no reply. The old man commenced and went through with the same remarks addressed to the Lord, when Mark again knocked at the door. "Who dat dar?" asked Uncle Tony, with a somewhat agitated countenance and trembling voice. Still Mark would not reply. Again Tony took up the thread of his discourse, and said, "O Lord, thou knowest as well as I do that dese white folks are not prepared to die, but here is old Tony, when de angel of de Lord comes, he's ready to go to heaven." Mark once more knocked on the door. "Who dat dar?" thundered Tony at the top of his voice.

"De angel of de Lord," replied Mark, in a somewhat suppressed and sepulchral voice.

"What de angel of de Lord want here?" inquired Tony, as if much frightened.

"He's come for poor old Tony, to take him out of the world," replied Mark, in the same strange voice.

"Dat nigger ain't here; he die troo wooks ago," responded Tony, in a still more agitated and frightened tone. Mark and his companions made the welkin ring with their shouts at the old man's answer. Uncle Tony hearing them, and finding that he had been imposed upon, opened his door, came out with stick in hand, and said, "Is dat you, Mr. Mark? you imp, if I can get to you I'll larn you how to come here wid your nonsense."

Mark and his companions left the garden, feeling satisfied that Uncle Tony was not as ready to go with " de angel of de Lord " as he would have others believe.

CHAPTER XIV.

THE PRISON.

WHILE poor little Clotelle was being kicked about by Mrs. Miller, on account of her relationship to her son-in-law, Isabella was passing lonely hours in the county jail, the place to which Jennings had removed her for safe-keeping, after purchasing her from Mrs. Miller. Incarcerated in one of the iron-barred rooms of that dismal place, those dark, glowing eyes, lofty brow, and graceful form wilted down like a plucked rose under a noonday sun, while deep in her heart's ambrosial cells was the most anguishing distress.

Vulgar curiosity is always in search of its victims, and Jennings' boast that he had such a ladylike and beautiful woman in his possession brought numbers to the prison who begged of the jailer the privilege of seeing the slave-trader's prize. Many who saw her were melted to tears at the pitiful sight, and were struck with admiration at her intelligence; and, when she spoke of her child, they must have been convinced that a mother's sorrow can be conceived by none but a mother's heart. The warbling of birds in the green bowers of bliss, which she occasionally heard, brought no tidings of gladness to her. Their joy fell cold upon her heart, and seemed like bitter mockery. They reminded her of her own cottage, where, with her beloved child, she had spent so many happy days.

The speculator had kept close watch over his valuable piece of property, for fear that it might damage itself. This, however, there was no danger of, for Isabella still hoped and believed that Henry would come to her rescue. She could not bring herself to believe that he would allow her to be sent away without at least seeing her, and the trader did all he could to keep this idea alive in her.

While Isabella, with a weary heart, was passing sleepless nights think-ing only of her daughter and Henry, the latter was seeking relief in that insidious enemy of the human race, the intoxicating cup. His wife did all in her power to make his life a pleasant and a happy one, for Gertrude was devotedly attached to him; but a weary heart gets no gladness out of sunshine. The secret remorse that rankled in his bosom caused him to see all the world blood-shot. He had not visited his mother-in-law since the evening he had given her liberty to use her own discretion as to how Isabella and her child should be disposed of. He feared even to go near the house, for he did not wish to see his child. Gertrude felt this every time he declined accompanying her to her mother's. Possessed of a tender and confiding heart, entirely unlike her mother, she sympathized deeply with her husband. She well knew that all young men in the South, to a greater or less extent, became enamored of the slave-women, and she fancied that his case was only one of the many, and if he had now forsaken all others for her she did not wish for him to be punished; but she dared not let her mother know that such were her feelings. Again and again had she noticed the great resemblance between Clotelle and Henry, and she wished the child in better hands than those of her cruel mother.

At last Gertrude determined to mention the matter to her husband. Consequently, the next morning, when they were seated on the back piazza, and the sun was pouring its splendid rays upon everything around, changing the red tints on the lofty hills in the distance into streaks of purest gold, and nature seeming by her smiles to favor the object, she said, —

" What, dear Henry, do you intend to do with Clotelle? "

A paleness that overspread his countenance, the tears that trickled down his cheeks, the deep emotion that was visible in his face, and the trembling of his voice, showed at once that she had touched a tender chord. Without a single word, he buried his face in his handkerchief, and burst into tears.

This made Gertrude still more unhappy, for she feared that he had misunderstood her; and she immediately expressed her regret that she had mentioned the subject. Becoming satisfied from this that his wife sympathized with him in his unhappy situation, Henry told her of the agony that filled his soul, and Gertrude agreed to intercede for him with her mother for the removal of the child to a boarding-school in one of the Free States.

In the afternoon, when Henry returned from his office, his wife met him with tearful eyes, and informed him that her mother was filled with rage at the mere mention of the removal of Clotelle from her premises.

In the mean time, the slave-trader, Jennings, had started for the South with his gang of human cattle, of whom Isabella was one. Most quad-roon women who are taken to the South are either sold to gentlemen for their own use or disposed of as house-servants or waiting-maids. For-tunately for Isabella, she was sold for the latter purpose. Jennings found a purchaser for her in the person of Mr. James French.

Mrs. French was a severe mistress. All who lived with her, though well-dressed, were scantily fed and over-worked. Isabella found her new situation far different from her Virginia cottage-life. She had frequently heard Vicksburg spoken of as a cruel place for slaves, and now she was in a position to test the truthfulness of the assertion.

A few weeks after her arrival, Mrs. French began to show to Isabella that she was anything but a pleasant and agreeable mistress. What social virtues are possible in a society of which injustice is a primary characteristic, — in a society which is divided into two classes, masters and slaves? Every married woman at the South looks upon her hus-band as unfaithful, and regards every negro woman as a rival.

Isabella had been with her new mistress but a short time when she was ordered to cut off her long and beautiful hair. The negro is natu-rally fond of dress and outward display. He who has short woolly hair combs and oils it to death; he who has long hair would sooner have his teeth drawn than to part with it. But, however painful it was to Isabella, she was soon seen with her hair cut short, and the sleeves of her dress altered to fit tight to her arms. Even with her hair short and with her ill-looking dress, Isabella was still handsome. Her life had been a secluded one, and though now twenty-eight years of age, her beauty had only assumed a quieter tone. The other servants only laughed at Isabella's misfortune in losing her beautiful hair.

"Miss 'Dell needn't strut so big; she got short nappy har 's well 's I," said Nell, with a broad grin that showed her teeth.

"She tink she white when she cum here, wid dat long har ob hers," replied Mill.

"Yes," continued Nell, "missus make her take down her wool, so she no put it up to-day."

The fairness of Isabella's complexion was regarded with envy by the servants as well as by the mistress herself. This is one of the hard fea-tures of slavery. To-day a woman is mistress of her own cottage; to-morrow she is sold to one who aims to make her life as intolerable as possible. And let it be remembered that the house-servant has the best situation a slave can occupy.

But the degradation and harsh treatment Isabella experienced in her new home was nothing compared to the grief she underwent at being separated from her dear child. Taken from her with scarcely a mo-ment's warning, she knew not what had become of her.

This deep and heartfelt grief of Isabella was soon perceived by her owners, and fearing that her refusal to take proper food would cause her death, they resolved to sell her. Mr. French found no difficulty in securing a purchaser for the quadroon woman, for such are usually the most marketable kind of property. Isabella was sold at private sale to a young man for a housekeeper; but even he had missed his aim.

Mr. Gordon, the new master, was a man of pleasure. He was the owner of a large sugar plantation, which he had left under the charge of an overseer, and was now giving himself up to the pleasures of a city life. At first Mr. Gordon sought to win Isabella's favor by flattery and presents, knowing that whatever he gave her he could take from her again. The poor innocent creature dreaded every moment lest the scene should change. At every interview with Gordon she stoutly maintained that she had left a husband in Virginia, and could never think of taking another. In this she considered that she was truthful, for she had ever regarded Henry as her husband. The gold watch and chain and other glittering presents which Gordon gave to her were all kept unused.

In the same house with Isabella was a man-servant who had from time to time hired himself from his master. His name was William. He could feel for Isabella, for he, like her, had been separated from near and dear relatives, and he often tried to console the poor woman. One day Isabella observed to him that her hair was growing out again.

"Yes," replied William; "you look a good deal like a man with your short hair."

"Oh," rejoined she, "I have often been told that I would make a better looking man than woman, and if I had the money I might avail myself of it to bid farewell to this place."

In a moment afterwards, Isabella feared that she had said too much, and laughingly observed, "I am always talking some nonsense; you must not heed me."

William was a tall, full-blooded African, whose countenance beamed with intelligence. Being a mechanic, he had by industry earned more money than he had paid to his owner for his time, and this he had laid aside, with the hope that he might some day get enough to purchase his freedom. He had in his chest about a hundred and fifty dollars. His was a heart that felt for others, and he had again and again wiped the tears from his eyes while listening to Isabella's story.

"If she can get free with a little money, why not give her what I have?" thought he, and then resolved to do it.

An hour after, he entered the quadroon's room, and, laying the money in her lap, said, —

"There, Miss Isabella, you said just now that if you had the means you would leave this place. There is money enough to take you to England, where you will be free. You are much fairer than many of the white women of the South, and can easily pass for a free white woman."

At first Isabella thought it was a plan by which the negro wished to try her fidelity to her owner; but she was soon convinced, by his earnest manner and the deep feeling he manifested, that he was entirely sincere.

"I will take the money," said she, " only on one condition, and that is that I effect your escape, as well as my own."

"How can that be done?" he inquired, eagerly.

"I will assume the disguise of a gentleman, and you that of a servant, and we will thus take passage in a steamer to Cincinnati, and from thence to Canada."

With full confidence in Isabella's judgment, William consented at once to the proposition. The clothes were purchased; everything was arranged, and the next night, while Mr. Gordon was on one of his sprees, Isabella, under the assumed name of Mr. Smith, with William in attendance as a servant, took passage for Cincinnati in the steamer Heroine.

With a pair of green glasses over her eyes, in addition to her other disguise, Isabella made quite a gentlemanly appearance. To avoid conversation, however, she kept closely to her state-room, under the plea of illness.

Meanwhile, William was playing his part well with the servants. He was loudly talking of his master's wealth, and nothing on the boat appeared so good as in his master's fine mansion.

"I don't like dese steamboats, no how," said he; "I hope when massa goes on anoder journey, he take de carriage and de hosses."

After a nine-days' passage, the Heroine landed at Cincinnati, and Mr. Smith and his servant walked on shore.

"William, you are now a free man, and can go on to Canada," said Isabella; "I shall go to Virginia, in search of my daughter."

This sudden announcement fell heavily upon William's ears, and with tears he besought her not to jeopardize her liberty in such a manner; but Isabella had made up her mind to rescue her child if possible.

Taking a boat for Wheeling, Isabella was soon on her way to her native State. Several months had elapsed since she left Richmond, and all her thoughts were centred on the fate of her dear Clotelle. It was with a palpitating heart that this injured woman entered the stage-coach at Wheeling and set out for Richmond.

CHAPTER XV.

THE ARREST.

It was late in the evening when the coach arrived at Richmond, and Isabella once more alighted in her native city. She had intended to seek lodgings somewhere in the outskirts of the town, but the lateness of the hour compelled her to stop at one of the principal hotels for the night. She had scarcely entered the inn before she recognized among the numerous black servants one to whom she was well known, and her only hope was that her disguise would keep her from being discovered. The imperturbable calm and entire forgetfulness of self which induced Isabella to visit a place from which she could scarcely hope to escape, to attempt the rescue of a beloved child, demonstrate that over-willingness of woman to carry out the promptings of the finer feelings of the heart. True to woman's nature, she had risked her own liberty for another's. She remained in the hotel during the night, and the next morning, under the plea of illness, took her breakfast alone.

That day the fugitive slave paid a visit to the suburbs of the town, and once more beheld the cottage in which she had spent so many happy hours. It was winter, and the clematis and passion-flower were not there; but there were the same walks her feet had so often pressed, and the same trees which had so often shaded her as she passed through the garden at the back of the house. Old remembrances rushed upon her memory and caused her to shed tears freely. Isabella was now in her native town, and near her daughter; but how could she communicate with her? how could she see her? To have made herself known would have been a suicidal act; betrayal would have followed, and she arrested. Three days passed away, and still she remained in the hotel at which she had first put up, and yet she got no tidings of her child.

Unfortunately for Isabella, a disturbance had just broken out among the slave population in the State of Virginia, and all strangers were treated with suspicion.

The insurrection to which we now refer was headed by a full-blooded negro, who had been born and brought up a slave. He had heard the crack of the driver's whip, and seen the warm blood streaming from the negro's body. He had witnessed the separation of parents from children, and was made aware, by too many proofs, that the slave could expect no justice from the hands of the slave-owner. The name of this man was Nat Turner. He was a preacher amongst the negroes, distinguished for his eloquence, respected by the whites, loved and venerated by the negroes. On the discovery of the plan for the outbreak, Turner fled to the swamps, followed by those who had joined in the insurrection.

Here the revolted negroes numbered some hundreds, and for a time bade defiance to their oppressors. The Dismal Swamps cover many thousand acres of wild land, and a dense forest, with wild animals and insects such as are unknown in any other part of Virginia. Here runaway negroes usually seek a hiding-place, and some have been known to reside here for years. The revolters were joined by one of these. He was a large, tall, full-blooded negro, with a stern and savage countenance; the marks on his face showed that he was from one of the barbarous tribes in Africa, and claimed that country as his native land. His only covering was a girdle around his loins, made of skins of wild beasts which he had killed. His only token of authority among those that he led was a pair of epaulettes, made of the tail of a fox, and tied to his shoulder by a cord. Brought from the coast of Africa, when only fifteen years of age, to the island of Cuba, he was smuggled from thence into Virginia. He had been two years in the swamps, and considered it his future home. He had met a negro woman, who was also a runaway, and, after the fashion of his native land, had gone through the process of oiling her, as the marriage ceremony. They had built a cave on a rising mound in the swamp, and this was their home. This man's name was Picquilo. His only weapon was a sword made from a scythe which he had stolen from a neighboring plantation. His dress, his character, his manners, and his mode of fighting were all in keeping with the early training he had received in the land of his birth. He moved about with the activity of a cat, and neither the thickness of the trees nor the depth of the water could stop him. His was a bold, turbulent spirit; and, from motives of revenge, he imbrued his hands in the blood of all the whites he could meet. Hunger, thirst, and loss of sleep, he seemed made to endure, as if by peculiarity of constitution. His air was fierce, his step oblique, his look sanguinary.

Such was the character of one of the negroes in the Southampton Insurrection. All negroes were arrested who were found beyond their master's threshold, and all white strangers were looked upon with suspicion.

Such was the position in which Isabella found affairs when she returned to Virginia in search of her child. Had not the slave-owners been watchful of strangers, owing to the outbreak, the fugitive could not have escaped the vigilance of the police; for advertisements announcing her escape, and offering a large reward for her arrest, had been received in the city previous to her arrival, and officers were therefore on the lookout for her.

It was on the third day after her arrival in Richmond, as the quadroon was seated in her room at the hotel, still in the disguise of a gentleman, that two of the city officers entered the apartment and informed

4

her that they were authorized to examine all strangers, to assure the authorities that they were not in league with the revolted negroes.

With trembling heart the fugitive handed the key of her trunk to the officers. To their surprise they found nothing but female apparel in the trunk, which raised their curiosity, and caused a further investigation that resulted in the arrest of Isabella as a fugitive slave. She was immediately conveyed to prison, there to await the orders of her master.

For many days, uncheered by the voice of kindness, alone, hopeless, desolate, she waited for the time to arrive when the chains should be placed on her limbs, and she returned to her inhuman and unfeeling owner.

The arrest of the fugitive was announced in all the newspapers, but created little or no sensation. The inhabitants were too much engaged in putting down the revolt among the slaves; and, although all the odds were against the insurgents, the whites found it no easy matter, with all their caution. Every day brought news of fresh outbreaks. Without scruple and without pity, the whites massacred all blacks found beyond the limits of their owners' plantations. The negroes, in return, set fire to houses, and put to death those who attempted to escape from the flames. Thus carnage was added to carnage, and the blood of the whites flowed to avenge the blood of the blacks.

These were the ravages of slavery. No graves were dug for the negroes, but their bodies became food for dogs and vultures; and their bones, partly calcined by the sun, remained scattered about, as if to mark the mournful fury of servitude and lust of power. When the slaves were subdued, except a few in the swamps, bloodhounds were employed to hunt out the remaining revolters.

CHAPTER XVI

DEATH IS FREEDOM.

ON receiving intelligence of the arrest of Isabella, Mr. Gordon authorized the sheriff to sell her to the highest bidder. She was, therefore, sold; the purchaser being the noted negro-trader, Hope H. Slater, who at once placed her in prison. Here the fugitive saw none but slaves like herself, brought in and taken out to be placed in ships, and sent away to some part of the country to which she herself would soon be compelled to go. She had seen or heard nothing of her daughter while in Richmond, and all hopes of seeing her had now fled.

At the dusk of the evening previous to the day when she was to be sent off, as the old prison was being closed for the night, Isabella suddenly darted past the keeper, and ran for her life. It was not a great distance from the prison to the long bridge which passes from the lower part of the city across the Potomac to the extensive forests and woodlands of the celebrated Arlington Heights, then occupied by that distinguished relative and descendant of the immortal Washington, Mr. Geo. W. Custis. Thither the poor fugitive directed her flight. So unexpected was her escape that she had gained several rods the start before the keeper had secured the other prisoners, and rallied his assistants to aid in the pursuit. It was at an hour, and in a part of the city where horses could not easily be obtained for the chase; no bloodhounds were at hand to run down the flying woman, and for once it seemed as if there was to be a fair trial of speed and endurance between the slave and the slave-catchers.

The keeper and his force raised the hue-and-cry on her path as they followed close behind; but so rapid was the flight along the wide avenue that the astonished citizens, as they poured forth from their dwellings to learn the cause of alarm, were only able to comprehend the nature of the case in time to fall in with the motley throng in pursuit, or raise an anxious prayer to heaven as they refused to join in the chase (as many a one did that night) that the panting fugitive might escape, and the merciless soul-dealer for once be disappointed of his prey. And now, with the speed of an arrow, having passed the avenue, with the distance between her and her pursuers constantly increasing, this poor, hunted female gained the "Long Bridge," as it is called, where interruption seemed improbable. Already her heart began to beat high with the hope of success. She had only to pass three-quarters of a mile across the bridge, when she could bury herself in a vast forest, just at the time when the curtain of night would close around her, and protect her from the pursuit of her enemies.

But God, by his providence, had otherwise determined. He had ordained that an appalling tragedy should be enacted that night within plain sight of the President's house, and the Capitol of the Union, which would be an evidence wherever it should be known of the unconquerable love of liberty which the human heart may inherit, as well as a fresh admonition to the slave-dealer of the cruelty and enormity of his crimes.

Just as the pursuers passed the high draw, soon after entering upon the bridge, they beheld three men slowly approaching from the Virginia side. They immediately called to them to arrest the fugitive, proclaiming her a runaway slave. True to their Virginia instincts, as she came near, they formed a line across the narrow bridge to intercept her. Seeing that escape was impossible in that quarter, she stopped suddenly, and turned upon her pursuers.

On came the profane and ribald crew faster than ever, already exult-
ing in her capture, and threatening punishment for her flight. For a
moment she looked wildly and anxiously around to see if there was no
hope of escape. On either hand, far down below, rolled the deep, foaming waters of the Potomac, and before and behind were the rapidly approaching steps and noisy voices of her pursuers. Seeing how vain
would be any further effort to escape, her resolution was instantly
taken. She clasped her hands convulsively together, raised her tearful
and imploring eyes toward heaven, and begged for the mercy and compassion there which was unjustly denied her on earth; then, exclaiming, " Henry, Clotelle, I die for thee!" with a single bound, vaulted
over the railing of the bridge, and sank forever beneath the angry
and foaming waters of the river!

Such was the life, and such the death, of a woman whose virtues and
goodness of heart would have done honor to one in a higher station of
life, and who, had she been born in any other land but that of slavery,
would have been respected and beloved. What would have been her
feelings if she could have known that the child for whose rescue she
had sacrificed herself would one day be free, honored, and loved in
another land?

CHAPTER XVII.

CLOTELLE.

THE curtain rises seven years after the death of Isabella. During
that interval, Henry, finding that nothing could induce his mother-in-
law to relinquish her hold on poor little Clotelle, and not liking to contend with one on whom a future fortune depended, gradually lost all
interest in the child, and left her to her fate.

Although Mrs. Miller treated Clotelle with a degree of harshness
scarcely equalled, when applied to one so tender in years, still the child
grew every day more beautiful, and her hair, though kept closely cut,
seemed to have improved in its soft, silk-like appearance. Now twelve
years of age, and more than usually well-developed, her harsh old mistress began to view her with a jealous eye.

Henry and Gertrude had just returned from Washington, where the
husband had been on his duties as a member of Congress, and where
he had remained during the preceding three years without returning
home. It was on a beautiful evening, just at twilight, while seated at
his parlor window, that Henry saw a young woman pass by and go into
the kitchen. Not aware of ever having seen the person before, he made

an errand into the cook's department to see who the girl was. He, however, met her in the hall, as she was about going out.

" Whom did you wish to see? " he inquired.

" Miss Gertrude," was the reply.

" What did you want to see her for? " he again asked.

" My mistress told me to give her and Master Henry her compliments, and ask them to come over and spend the evening."

" Who is your mistress? " he eagerly inquired.

" Mrs. Miller, sir," responded the girl.

" And what's your name? " asked Henry, with a trembling voice.

" Clotelle, sir," was the reply.

The astonished father stood completely amazed, looking at the now womanly form of her who, in his happier days, he had taken on his knee with so much fondness and alacrity. It was then that he saw his own and Isabella's features combined in the beautiful face that he was then beholding. It was then that he was carried back to the days when with a woman's devotion, poor Isabella hung about his neck and told him how lonely were the hours in his absence. He could stand it no longer. Tears rushed to his eyes, and turning upon his heel, he went back to his own room. It was then that Isabella was revenged; and she no doubt looked smilingly down from her home in the spirit-land on the scene below.

On Gertrude's return from her shopping tour, she found Henry in a melancholy mood, and soon learned its cause. As Gertrude had borne him no children, it was but natural, that he should now feel his love centering in Clotelle, and he now intimated to his wife his determination to remove his daughter from the hands of his mother-in-law.

When this news reached Mrs. Miller, through her daughter, she became furious with rage, and calling Clotelle into her room, stripped her shoulders bare and flogged her in the presence of Gertrude.

It was nearly a week after the poor girl had been so severely whipped and for no cause whatever, that her father learned of the circumstance through one of the servants. With a degree of boldness unusual for him, he immediately went to his mother-in-law and demanded his child. But it was too late, — she was gone. To what place she had been sent no one could tell, and Mrs. Miller refused to give any information whatever relative to the girl.

It was then that Linwood felt deepest the evil of the institution under which he was living; for he knew that his daughter would be exposed to all the vices prevalent in that part of the country where marriage is not recognized in connection with that class.

CHAPTER XVIII.

A SLAVE—HUNTING PARSON.

IT was a delightful evening after a cloudless day, with the setting sun reflecting his golden rays on the surrounding hills which were covered with a beautiful greensward, and the luxuriant verdure that forms the constant garb of the tropics, that the steamer Columbia ran into the dock at Natchez, and began unloading the cargo, taking in passengers and making ready to proceed on her voyage to New Orleans. The plank connecting the boat with the shore had scarcely been secured in its place, when a good-looking man about fifty years of age, with a white neck-tie, and a pair of gold-rimmed glasses on, was seen hurrying on board the vessel. Just at that moment could be seen a stout man with his face pitted with the small-pox, making his way up to the above-mentioned gentleman.

" How do you do, my dear sir? this is Mr. Wilson, I believe," said the short man, at the same time taking from his mouth a large chew of tobacco, and throwing it down on the ship's deck.

" You have the advantage of me, sir," replied the tall man.

" Why, don't you know me? My name is Jennings; I sold you a splendid negro woman some years ago."

" Yes, yes," answered the Natchez man. " I remember you now, for the woman died in a few months, and I never got the worth of my money out of her."

" I could not help that," returned the slave-trader; " she was as sound as a roach when I sold her to you."

" Oh, yes," replied the parson, " I know she was; but now I want a young girl, fit for house use, — one that will do to wait on a lady."

" I am your man," said Jennings, " just follow me," continued he, " and I will show you the fairest little critter you ever saw." And the two passed to the stern of the boat to where the trader had between fifty and sixty slaves, the greater portion being women.

" There," said Jennings, as a beautiful young woman shrunk back with modesty. " There, sir, is the very gal that was made for you. If she had been made to your order, she could not have suited you better."

" Indeed, sir, is not that young woman white? " inquired the parson.

" Oh, no, sir; she is no whiter than you see! "

" But is she a slave? " asked the preacher.

" Yes," said the trader, " I bought her in Richmond, and she comes from an excellent family. She was raised by Squire Miller, and her mistress was one of the most pious ladies in that city, I may say; she was the salt of the earth, as the ministers say."

"But she resembles in some respect Agnes, the woman I bought from you," said Mr. Wilson. As he said the name of Agnes, the young woman started as if she had been struck. Her pulse seemed to quicken, but her face alternately flushed and turned pale, and tears trembled upon her eyelids. It was a name she had heard her mother mention, and it brought to her memory those days, — those happy days, when she was so loved and caressed. This young woman was Clotelle, the granddaughter of Agnes. The preacher, on learning the fact, purchased her, and took her home, feeling that his daughter Georgiana would prize her very highly. Clotelle found in Georgiana more a sister than a mistress, who, unknown to her father, taught the slave-girl how to read, and did much toward improving and refining Clotelle's manners, for her own sake. Like her mother fond of flowers, the "Virginia Maid," as she was sometimes called, spent many of her leisure hours in the garden. Beside the flowers which sprang up from the fertility of soil unplanted and unattended, there was the heliotrope, sweet-pea, and cup-rose, transplanted from the island of Cuba. In her new home Clotelle found herself saluted on all sides by the fragrance of the magnolia. When she went with her young mistress to the Poplar Farm, as she sometimes did, nature's wild luxuriance greeted her, wherever she cast her eyes.

The rustling citron, lime, and orange, shady mango, with its fruits of gold, and the palmetto's umbrageous beauty, all welcomed the child of sorrow. When at the farm, Huckelby, the overseer, kept his eye on Clotelle if within sight of her, for he knew she was a slave, and no doubt hoped that she might some day fall into his hands. But she shrank from his looks as she would have done from the charm of the rattlesnake. The negro-driver always tried to insinuate himself into the good opinion of Georgiana and the company that she brought. Knowing that Miss Wilson at heart hated slavery, he was ever trying to show that the slaves under his charge were happy and contented. One day, when Georgiana and some of her Connecticut friends were there, the overseer called all the slaves up to the "great house," and set some of the young ones to dancing. After awhile whiskey was brought in and a dram given to each slave, in return for which they were expected to give a toast, or sing a short piece of his own composition; when it came to Jack's turn he said, —

"The big bee flies high, the little bee makes the honey: the black folks make the cotton, and the white folks gets the money."

Of course, the overseer was not at all elated with the sentiment contained in Jack's toast. Mr. Wilson had lately purchased a young man to assist about the house and to act as coachman. This slave, whose name was Jerome, was of pure African origin, was perfectly black, very fine-looking, tall, slim, and erect as any one could possibly be. His features were not bad, lips thin, nose prominent, hands and feet small. His brilliant black eyes lighted up his whole countenance. His hair which was nearly straight, hung in curls upon his lofty brow. George Combe or Fowler would have selected his head for a model. He was brave and daring, strong in person; fiery in spirit, yet kind and true in his affections, earnest in his doctrines. Clotelle had been at the parson's but a few weeks when it was observed that a mutual feeling had grown up between her and Jerome. As time rolled on, they became more and more attached to each other. After satisfying herself that these two really loved, Georgiana advised their marriage. But Jerome contemplated his escape at some future day, and therefore feared that if married it might militate against it. He hoped, also, to be able to get Clotelle away too, and it was this hope that kept him from trying to escape by himself. Dante did not more love his Beatrice, Swift his Stella, Waller his Saccharissa, Goldsmith his Jessamy bride, or Burns his Mary, than did Jerome his Clotelle. Unknown to her father, Miss Wilson could permit these two slaves to enjoy more privileges than any of the other servants. The young mistress taught Clotelle, and the latter imparted her instructions to her lover, until both could read so as to be well understood. Jerome felt his superiority, and always declared that no master should ever flog him. Aware of his high spirit and determination, Clotelle was in constant fear lest some difficulty might arise between her lover and his master.

One day Mr. Wilson, being somewhat out of temper and irritated at what he was pleased to call Jerome's insolence, ordered him to follow him to the barn to be flogged. The young slave obeyed his master, but those who saw him at the moment felt that he would not submit to be whipped.

" No, sir," replied Jerome, as his master told him to take off his coat: " I will serve you, Master Wilson, I will labor for you day and night, if you demand it, but I will not be whipped."

This was too much for a white man to stand from a negro, and the preacher seized his slave by the throat, intending to choke him. But for once he found his match. Jerome knocked him down, and then escaped through the back-yard to the street, and from thence to the woods.

Recovering somewhat from the effect of his fall, the parson regained his feet and started in pursuit of the fugitive. Finding, however, that the slave was beyond his reach, he at once resolved to put the dogs on his track. Tabor, the negro-catcher, was sent for, and in less than an hour, eight or ten men, including the parson, were in the woods with hounds, trying the trails. These dogs will attack a negro at their master's bidding; and cling to him as the bull-dog will cling to a beast. Many are the speculations as to whether the negro will be secured alive

or dead, when these dogs once get on his track. Whenever there is to be a negro hunt, there is no lack of participants. Many go to enjoy the fun which it is said they derive from these scenes.

The company had been in the woods but a short time ere they got on the track of two fugitives, one of whom was Jerome. The slaves immediately bent their steps toward the swamp, with the hope that the dogs, when put upon their scent would be unable to follow them through the water.

The slaves then took a straight course for the Baton Rouge and Bayou Sara road, about four miles distant. Nearer and nearer the whimpering pack pressed on; their delusion begins to dispel. All at once the truth flashes upon the minds of the fugitives like a glare of light,— 'tis Tabor with his dogs!

The scent becomes warmer and warmer, and what was at first an irregular cry now deepens into one ceaseless roar, as the relentless pack presses on after its human prey.

They at last reach the river, and in the negroes plunge, followed by the catch-dog. Jerome is caught and is once more in the hands of his master, while the other poor fellow finds a watery grave. They return, and the preacher sends his slave to jail.

CHAPTER XIX.

THE TRUE HEROINE.

In vain did Georgiana try to console Clotelle, when the latter heard, through one of the other slaves, that Mr. Wilson had started with the dogs in pursuit of Jerome. The poor girl well knew that he would be caught, and that severe punishment, if not death, would be the result of his capture. It was therefore with a heart filled with the deepest grief that the slave-girl heard the footsteps of her master on his return from the chase. The dogged and stern manner of the preacher forbade even his daughter inquiring as to the success of his pursuit. Georgiana secretly hoped that the fugitive had not been caught; she wished it for the sake of the slave, and more especially for her maid-servant, whom she regarded more as a companion than a menial. But the news of the capture of Jerome soon spread through the parson's household, and found its way to the ears of the weeping and heart-stricken Clotelle.

The reverend gentleman had not been home more than an hour ere some of his parishioners called to know if they should not take the negro from the prison and execute *Lynch law* upon him.

"No negro should be permitted to live after striking a white man; let us take him and hang him at once," remarked an elderly-looking man, whose gray hairs thinly covered the crown of his head.

" I think the deacon is right," said another of the company; " if our slaves are allowed to set the will of their masters at defiance, there will be no getting along with them, — an insurrection will be the next thing we hear of."

" No, no," said the preacher; " I am willing to let the law take its course, as it provides for the punishment of a slave with death if he strikes his master. We had better let the court decide the question. Moreover, as a Christian and God-fearing people, we ought to submit to the dictates of justice. Should we take this man's life by force, an Allwise Providence would hold us responsible for the act."

The company then quietly withdrew, showing that the preacher had some influence with his people.

" This," said Mr. Wilson, when left alone with his daughter, — " this, my dear Georgiana, is the result of your kindness to the negroes. You have spoiled every one about the house. I can't whip one of them, without being in danger of having my life taken."

" I am sure, papa," replied the young lady, — " I am sure I never did any thing intentionally to induce any of the servants to disobey your orders."

" No, my dear," said Mr. Wilson, " but you are too kind to them. Now, there is Clotelle,—that girl is completely spoiled. She walks about the house with as dignified an air as if she was mistress of the premises. By and by you will be sorry for this foolishness of yours."

" But," answered Georgiana, " Clotelle has a superior mind, and God intended her to hold a higher position in life than that of a servant."

" Yes, my dear, and it was your letting her know that she was intended for a better station in society that is spoiling her. Always keep a negro in ignorance of what you conceive to be his abilities," returned the parson.

It was late on the Saturday afternoon, following the capture of Jerome that, while Mr. Wilson was seated in his study preparing his sermon for the next day, Georgiana entered the room and asked in an excited tone if it were true that Jerome was to be hanged on the following Thursday.

The minister informed her that such was the decision of the court.

" Then," said she, " Clotelle will die of grief."

" What business has she to die of grief? " returned the father, his eyes at the moment flashing fire.

" She has neither eaten nor slept since he was captured," replied Georgiana; " and I am certain that she will not live through this."

" I cannot be disturbed now," said the parson; " I must get my

sermon ready for to-morrow. I expect to have some strangers to preach to, and must, therefore, prepare a sermon that will do me credit."

While the man of God spoke, he seemed to say to himself, —

> " With devotion's visage, and pious actions,
> We do sugar over the devil himself. "

Georgiana did all in her power to soothe the feelings of Clotelle, and to induce her to put her trust in God. Unknown to her father, she allowed the poor girl to go every evening to the jail to see Jerome, and during these visits, despite her own grief, Clotelle would try to comfort her lover with the hope that justice would be meted out to him in the spirit-land.

Thus the time passed on, and the day was fast approaching when the slave was to die. Having heard that some secret meeting had been held by the negroes, previous to the attempt of Mr. Wilson to flog his slave, it occurred to a magistrate that Jerome might know something of the intended revolt. He accordingly visited the prison to see if he could learn anything from him, but all to no purpose. Having given up all hopes of escape, Jerome had resolved to die like a brave man. When questioned as to whether he knew anything of a conspiracy among the slaves against their masters, he replied, —

" Do you suppose that I would tell you if I did?"

" But if you know anything," remarked the magistrate, " and will tell us, you may possibly have your life spared."

" Life," answered the doomed man, " is worth nought to a slave. What right has a slave to himself, his wife, or his children? We are kept in heathenish darkness, by laws especially enacted to make our instruction a criminal offence; and our bones, sinews, blood, and nerves are exposed in the market for sale.

" My liberty is of as much consequence to me as Mr. Wilson's is to him. I am as sensitive to feeling as he. If I mistake not, the day will come when the negro will learn that he can get his freedom by fighting for it; and should that time arrive, the whites will be sorry that they have hated us so shamefully. I am free to say that, could I live my life over again, I would use all the energies which God has given me to get up an insurrection."

Every one present seemed startled and amazed at the intelligence with which this descendant of Africa spoke.

" He's a very dangerous man," remarked one.

" Yes," said another, " he got some book-learning somewhere, and that has spoiled him."

An effort was then made to learn from Jerome where he had learned to read, but the black refused to give any information on the subject.

The sun was just going down behind the trees as Clotelle entered the prison to see Jerome for the last time. He was to die on the next day Her face was bent upon her hands, and the gushing tears were forcing their way through her fingers. With beating heart and trembling hands, evincing the deepest emotion, she threw her arms around her lover's neck and embraced him. But, prompted by her heart's unchanging love, she had in her own mind a plan by which she hoped to effect the escape of him to whom she had pledged her heart and hand. While the overcharged clouds which had hung over the city during the day broke, and the rain fell in torrents, amid the most terrific thunder and lightning, Clotelle revealed to Jerome her plan for his escape.

"Dress yourself in my clothes," said she, "and you can easily pass the jailer."

This Jerome at first declined doing. He did not wish to place a confiding girl in a position where, in all probability, she would have to suffer; but being assured by the young girl that her life would not be in danger, he resolved to make the attempt. Clotelle being very tall, it was not probable that the jailer would discover any difference in them.

At this moment, she took from her pocket a bunch of keys and unfastened the padlock, and freed him from the floor.

"Come, girl, it is time for you to go," said the jailer, as Jerome was holding the almost fainting girl by the hand.

Being already attired in Clotelle's clothes, the disguised man embraced the weeping girl, put his handkerchief to his face, and passed out of the jail, without the keeper's knowing that his prisoner was escaping in a disguise and under cover of the night.

CHAPTER XX.

THE HERO OF MANY ADVENTURES.

JEROME had scarcely passed the prison-gates, ere he reproached himself for having taken such a step. There seemed to him no hope of escape out of the State, and what was a few hours or days at most, of life to him, when, by obtaining it, another had been sacrificed. He was on the eve of returning, when he thought of the last words uttered by Clotelle. "Be brave and determined, and you will still be free." The words sounded like a charm in his ears and he went boldly forward.

Clotelle had provided a suit of men's clothes and had placed them where her lover could get them, if he should succeed in getting out.

Returning to Mr. Wilson's barn, the fugitive changed his apparel, and again retraced his steps into the street. To reach the Free States by travelling by night and lying by during the day, from a State so far south as Mississippi, no one would think for a moment of attempting to escape. To remain in the city would be a suicidal step. The deep sound of the escape of steam from a boat, which was at that moment ascending the river, broke upon the ears of the slave. " If that boat is going up the river," said he, " why not I conceal myself on board, and try to escape? " He went at once to the steamboat landing, where the boat was just coming in. " Bound for Louisville," said the captain, to one who was making inquiries. As the passengers were rushing on board, Jerome followed them, and proceeding to where some of the hands were stowing away bales of goods, he took hold and aided them.

" Jump down into the hold, there, and help the men," said the mate to the fugitive, supposing that, like many persons, he was working his way up the river. Once in the hull among the boxes, the slave concealed himself. Weary hours, and at last days, passed without either water or food with the hidden slave. More than once did he resolve to let his case be known; but the knowledge that he would be sent back to Natchez kept him from doing so. At last, with lips parched and fevered to a crisp, the poor man crawled out into the freight-room, and began wandering about. The hatches were on, and the room dark. There happened to be on board a wedding party, and a box, containing some of the bridal cake, with several bottles of port wine, was near Jerome. He found the box, opened it, and helped himself. In eight days, the boat tied up at the wharf at the place of her destination. It was late at night; the boat's crew, with the single exception of the man on watch, were on shore. The hatches were off, and the fugitive quietly made his way on deck and jumped on shore. The man saw the fugitive, but too late to seize him.

Still in a Slave State, Jerome was at a loss to know how he should proceed. He had with him a few dollars, enough to pay his way to Canada, if he could find a conveyance. The fugitive procured such food as he wanted from one of the many eating-houses, and then, following the direction of the North Star, he passed out of the city, and took the road leading to Covington. Keeping near the Ohio River, Jerome soon found an opportunity to cross over into the State of Indiana. But liberty was a mere name in the latter State, and the fugitive learned, from some colored persons that he met, that it was not safe to travel by daylight. While making his way one night, with nothing to cheer him but the prospect of freedom in the future, he was pounced upon by three men who were lying in wait for another fugitive, an advertisement of whom they had received through the mail. In vain did Jerome tell them that he was not a slave. True, they had not caught the man they expected; but, if they could make this slave tell from what place he had escaped, they knew that a good price would be paid them for the negro's arrest.

Tortured by the slave-catchers, to make him reveal the name of his master and the place from whence he had escaped, Jerome gave them a fictitious name in Virginia, and said that his master would give a large reward, and manifested a willingness to return to his "old boss." By this misrepresentation, the fugitive hoped to have another chance of getting away. Allured with the prospect of a large sum of the needful, the slave-catchers started back with their victim. Stopping on the second night at an inn, on the banks of the Ohio River, the kidnappers, in lieu of a suitable place in which to confine their prize during the night, chained him to the bed-post of their sleeping-chamber. The white men were late in retiring to rest, after an evening spent in drinking. At dead of night, when all was still, the slave arose from the floor, upon which he had been lying, looked around and saw that Morpheus had possession of his captors. For once, thought he, the brandy bottle has done a noble work. With palpitating heart and trembling limbs, he viewed his position. The door was fast, but the warm weather had compelled them to leave the window open. If he could but get his chains off, he might escape through the window to the piazza. The sleepers' clothes hung upon chairs by the bedside. The slave thought of the padlock-key, examined the pockets, and found it. The chains were soon off, and the negro stealthily making his way to the window. He stopped, and said to himself, "These men are villains; they are enemies to all who, like me, are trying to be free. Then why not I teach them a lesson?" He then dressed himself in the best suit, hung his own worn-out and tattered garments on the same chair, and silently passed through the window to the piazza, and let himself down by one of the pillars, and started once more for the North.

Daylight came upon the fugitive before he had selected a hiding-place for the day, and he was walking at a rapid rate, in hopes of soon reaching some woodland or forest. The sun had just begun to show itself, when the fugitive was astounded at seeing behind him, in the distance, two men upon horseback. Taking a road to the right, the slave saw before him a farmhouse, and so near was he to it that he observed two men in front of it looking at him. It was too late to turn back. The kidnappers were behind him — strange men before him. Those in the rear he knew to be enemies, while he had no idea of what principles were the farmers. The latter also saw the white men coming, and called to the fugitive to come that way. The broad-brimmed hats that the farmers wore told the slave that they were Quakers.

Jerome had seen some of these people passing up and down the river, when employed on a steamer between Natchez and New Orleans, and had heard that they disliked slavery. He, therefore, hastened toward the drab-coated men, who, on his approach, opened the barn-door, and told him to "run in."

When Jerome entered the barn, the two farmers closed the door, remaining outside themselves, to confront the slave-catchers, who now came up and demanded admission, feeling that they had their prey secure.

"Thee can't enter my premises," said one of the Friends, in rather a musical voice.

The negro-catchers urged their claim to the slave, and intimated that, unless they were allowed to secure him, they would force their way in. By this time, several other Quakers had gathered around the barn-door. Unfortunately for the kidnappers, and most fortunately for the fugitive, the Friends had just been holding a quarterly meeting in the neighborhood, and a number of them had not yet returned to their homes.

After some talk, the men in drab promised to admit the hunters, provided they procured an officer and a search-warrant from a justice of the peace. One of the slave-catchers was left to see that the fugitive did not get away, while the others went in pursuit of an officer. In the mean time, the owner of the barn sent for a hammer and nails, and began nailing up the barn-door.

After an hour in search of the man of the law, they returned with an officer and a warrant. The Quaker demanded to see the paper, and, after looking at it for some time, called to his son to go into the house for his glasses. It was a long time before Aunt Ruth found the leather case, and when she did, the glasses wanted wiping before they could be used. After comfortably adjusting them on his nose, he read the warrant over leisurely.

"Come, Mr. Dugdale, we can't wait all day," said the officer.

"Well, will thee read it for me?" returned the Quaker.

The officer complied, and the man in drab said, —

"Yes, thee may go in, now. I am inclined to throw no obstacles in the way of the execution of the law of the land."

On approaching the door, the men found some forty or fifty nails in it, in the way of their progress.

"Lend me your hammer and a chisel, if you please, Mr. Dugdale," said the officer.

"Please read that paper over again, will thee?" asked the Quaker.

The officer once more read the warrant.

"I see nothing there which says I must furnish thee with tools to open my door. If thee wants a hammer, thee must go elsewhere for it; I tell thee plainly, thee can't have mine."

The implements for opening the door are at length obtained, and, after another half-hour, the slave-catchers are in the barn. Three hours is a long time for a slave to be in the hands of Quakers. The hay is turned over, and the barn is visited in every part; but still the runaway is not found. Uncle Joseph has a glow upon his countenance; Ephraim shakes his head knowingly; little Elijah is a perfect know-nothing, and, if you look toward the house, you will see Aunt Ruth's smiling face, ready to announce that breakfast is ready.

" The nigger is not in this barn," said the officer.

" I know he is not," quietly answered the Quaker.

" What were you nailing up your door for, then, as if you were afraid we would enter?" inquired one of the kidnappers.

" I can do what I please with my own door, can't I," said the Quaker.

The secret was out; the fugitive had gone in at the front door and out at the back; and the reading of the warrant, nailing up of the door, and other preliminaries of the Quaker, was to give the fugitive time and opportunity to escape.

It was now late in the morning, and the slave-catchers were a long way from home, and the horses were jaded by the rapid manner in which they had travelled. The Friends, in high glee, returned to the house for breakfast; the man of the law, after taking his fee, went home, and the kidnappers turned back, muttering, " Better luck next time."

CHAPTER XXI.

SELF-SACRIFICE.

Now in her seventeenth year, Clotelle's personal appearance presented a great contrast to the time when she lived with old Mrs. Miller. Her tall and well-developed figure; her long, silky black hair, falling in curls down her swan-like neck; her bright, black eyes lighting up her olive-tinted face, and a set of teeth that a Tuscarora might envy, she was a picture of tropical-ripened beauty. At times, there was a heavenly smile upon her countenance, which would have warmed the heart of an anchorite. Such was the personal appearance of the girl who was now in prison by her own act to save the life of another. Would she be hanged in his stead, or would she receive a different kind of punishment? These questions Clotelle did not ask herself. Open, frank, free, and generous to a fault, she always thought of others, never of her own welfare.

The long stay of Clotelle caused some uneasiness to Miss Wilson; yet she dared not tell her father, for he had forbidden the slave-girl's going to the prison to see her lover. While the clock on the church near by was striking eleven, Georgiana called Sam, and sent him to the prison in search of Clotelle.

" The girl went away from here at eight o'clock," was the jailer's answer to the servant's inquiries.

The return of Sam without having found the girl saddened the heart of the young mistress. " Sure, then," said she, " the poor, heart-broken thing has made way with herself."

Still, she waited till morning before breaking the news of Clotelle's absence to her father.

The jailer discovered, the next morning, to his utter astonishment, that his prisoner was white instead of black, and his first impression was that the change of complexion had taken place during the night, through fear of death. But this conjecture was soon dissipated; for the dark, glowing eyes, the sable curls upon the lofty brow, and the mild, sweet voice that answered his questions, informed him that the prisoner before him was another being.

On learning, in the morning, that Clotelle was in jail dressed in male attire, Miss Wilson immediately sent clothes to her to make a change in her attire. News of the heroic and daring act of the slave-girl spread through the city with electric speed.

" I will sell every nigger on the place," said the parson, at the break-fast-table, — " I will sell them all, and get a new lot, and whip them every day."

Poor Georgiana wept for the safety of Clotelle, while she felt glad that Jerome had escaped. In vain did they try to extort from the girl the whereabouts of the man whose escape she had effected. She was not aware that he had fled on a steamer, and when questioned, she replied, —

" I don't know; and if I did I would not tell you. I care not what you do with me, if Jerome but escapes."

The smile with which she uttered these words finely illustrated the poet's meaning, when he says, —

> " A fearful gift upon thy heart is laid,
> Woman — the power to suffer and to love."

Her sweet simplicity seemed to dare them to lay their rough hands amid her trembling curls.

Three days did the heroic young woman remain in prison, to be gazed at by an unfeeling crowd, drawn there out of curiosity. The intelli-gence came to her at last that the court had decided to spare her life, on condition that she should be whipped, sold, and sent out of the State within twenty-four hours.

This order of the court she would have cared but little for, had she not been sincerely attached to her young mistress.

" Do try and sell her to some one who will use her well," said Georgiana to her father, as he was about taking his hat to leave the house.

" I shall not trouble myself to do any such thing," replied the hardhearted parson. " I leave the finding of a master for her with the slave-dealer."

Bathed in tears, Miss. Wilson paced her room in the absence of her father. For many months Georgiana had been in a decline, and any little trouble would lay her on a sick bed for days. She was, therefore, poorly able to bear the loss of this companion, whom she so dearly loved.

Mr. Wilson had informed his daughter that Clotelle was to be flogged; and when Felice came in and informed her mistress that the poor girl had just received fifty lashes on her bare person, the young lady fainted and fell on the floor. The servants placed their mistress on the sofa, and went in pursuit of their master. Little did the preacher think, on returning to his daughter, that he should soon be bereft of her; yet such was to be his lot. A blood-vessel had been ruptured, and the three physicians who were called in told the father that he must prepare to lose his child. That moral courage and calmness, which was her great characteristic, did not forsake Georgiana in her hour of death. She had ever been kind to the slaves under her charge, and they loved and respected her. At her request, the servants were all brought into her room, and took a last farewell of their mistress. Seldom, if ever, was there witnessed a more touching scene than this. There lay the young woman, pale and feeble, with death stamped upon her countenance, surrounded by the sons and daughters of Africa, some of whom had been separated from every earthly tie, and the most of whose persons had been torn and gashed by the negro-whip. Some were upon their knees at the bedside, others standing around, and all weeping.

Death is a leveler; and neither age, sex, wealth, nor condition, can avert when he is permitted to strike. The most beautiful flowers must soon fade and droop and die. So, also, with man; his days are as uncertain as the passing breeze. This hour he glows in the blush of health and vigor, but the next, he may be counted with the number no more known on earth. Oh, what a silence pervaded the house when this young flower was gone! In the midst of the buoyancy of youth, this cherished one had drooped and died. Deep were the sounds of grief and mourning heard in that stately dwelling when the stricken friends, whose office it had been to nurse and soothe the weary sufferer, beheld her pale and motionless in the sleep of death.

Who can imagine the feeling with which poor Clotelle received the

intelligence of her kind friend's death? The deep gashes of the cruel
whip had prostrated the lovely form of the quadroon, and she lay upon
her bed of straw in the dark cell. The speculator had bought her, but
had postponed her removal till she should recover. Her benefactress
was dead, and —

"Hope withering fled, and mercy sighed farewell."

"Is Jerome safe?" she would ask herself continually. If her lover
could have but known of the sufferings of that sweet flower, — that
polyanthus over which he had so often been in his dreams, — he would
then have learned that she was worthy of his love.

It was more than a fortnight before the slave-trader could take his
prize to more comfortable quarters. Like Alcibiades, who defaced the
images of the gods and expected to be pardoned on the ground of ec-
centricity, so men who abuse God's image hope to escape the vengeance
of his wrath under the plea that the law sanctions their atrocious deeds.

CHAPTER XXII.

LOVE AT FIRST SIGHT AND WHAT FOLLOWED.

IT was a beautiful Sunday in September, with a cloudless sky, and
the rays of the sun parching the already thirsty earth, that Clotelle
stood at an upper window in Slater's slave-pen in New Orleans, gasping
for a breath of fresh air. The bells of thirty churches were calling the
people to the different places of worship. Crowds were seen wending
their way to the houses of God; one followed by a negro boy carrying
his master's Bible; another followed by her maid-servant holding the
mistress' fan; a third supporting an umbrella over his master's head to
shield him from the burning sun. Baptists immersed, Presbyterians
sprinkled, Methodists shouted, and Episcopalians read their prayers,
while ministers of the various sects preached that Christ died for all.
The chiming of the bells seemed to mock the sighs and deep groans of
the forty human beings then incarcerated in the slave-pen. These im-
prisoned children of God were many of them Methodists, some Baptists, and others claiming to believe in the faith of the Presbyterians
and Episcopalians.

Oh, with what anxiety did these creatures await the close of that
Sabbath, and the dawn of another day, that should deliver them from
those dismal and close cells. Slowly the day passed away, and once
more the evening breeze found its way through the barred windows of
the prison that contained these injured sons and daughters of America.

The clock on the calaboose had just struck nine on Monday morning, when hundreds of persons were seen threading the gates and doors of the negro-pen. It was the same gang that had the day previous been stepping to the tune and keeping time with the musical church bells. Their Bibles were not with them, their prayer-books were left at home, and even their long and solemn faces had been laid aside for the week. They had come to the man-market to make their purchases. Methodists were in search of their brethren. Baptists were looking for those that had been immersed, while Presbyterians were willing to buy fellow-Christians, whether sprinkled or not. The crowd was soon gazing at and feasting their eyes upon the lovely features of Clotelle.

" She is handsomer," muttered one to himself, " than the lady that sat in the pew next to me yesterday."

" I would that my daughter was half so pretty," thinks a second.

Groups are seen talking in every part of the vast building, and the topic on 'Change, is the " beautiful quadroon." By and by, a tall young man with a foreign face, the curling mustache protruding from under a finely-chiseled nose, and having the air of a gentleman, passes by. His dark hazel eye is fastened on the maid, and he stops for a moment; the stranger walks away, but soon returns — he looks, he sees the young woman wipe away the silent tear that steals down her alabaster cheek; he feels ashamed that he should gaze so unmanly on the blushing face of the woman. As he turns upon his heel he takes out his white hankerchief and wipes his eyes. It may be that he has lost a sister, a mother, or some dear one to whom he was betrothed. Again he comes, and the quadroon hides her face. She has heard that foreigners make bad masters, and she shuns his piercing gaze. Again he goes away and then returns. He takes a last look and then walks hurriedly off.

The day wears away, but long before the time of closing the sale the tall young man once more enters the slave-pen. He looks in every direction for the beautiful slave, but she is not there — she has been sold! He goes to the trader and inquires, but he is too late, and he therefore returns to his hotel.

Having entered a military school in Paris when quite young, and soon after been sent with the French army to India, Antoine Devenant had never dabbled in matters of love. He viewed all women from the same stand-point — respected them for their virtues, and often spoke of the goodness of heart of the sex, but never dreamed of taking to himself a wife. The unequalled beauty of Clotelle had dazzled his eyes, and every look that she gave was a dagger that went to his heart. He felt a shortness of breath, his heart palpitated, his head grew dizzy, and his limbs trembled; but he knew not its cause. This was the first stage of "love at first sight."

He who bows to the shrine of beauty when beckoned by this mysterious agent seldom regrets it. Devenant reproached himself for not having made inquiries concerning the girl before he left the market in the morning. His stay in the city was to be short, and the yellow fever was raging, which caused him to feel like making a still earlier departure. The disease appeared in a form unusually severe and repulsive. It seized its victims from amongst the most healthy of the citizens. The disorder began in the brain by oppressive pain accompanied or followed by fever. Fiery veins streaked the eye, the face was inflamed and dyed of a dark dull red color; the ears from time to time rang painfully. Now mucous secretions surcharged the tongue and took away the power of speech; now the sick one spoke, but in speaking had foresight of death. When the violence of the disease approached the heart, the gums were blackened. The sleep broken, troubled by convulsions, or by frightful visions, was worse than the waking hours; and when the reason sank under a delirium which had its seat in the brain, repose utterly forsook the patient's couch. The progress of the fever within was marked by yellowish spots, which spread over the surface of the body. If then, a happy crisis came not, all hope was gone. Soon the breath infected the air with a fetid odor, the lips were glazed, despair painted itself in the eyes, and sobs, with long intervals of silence, formed the only language. From each side of the mouth, spread foam tinged with black and burnt blood. Blue streaks mingled with the yellow all over the frame. All remedies were useless. This was the yellow fever. The disorder spread alarm and confusion throughout the city. On an average more than four hundred died daily. In the midst of disorder and confusion, death heaped victims on victims. Friend followed friend in quick succession. The sick were avoided from the fear of contagion, and for the same reason the dead were left unburied. Nearly two thousand dead bodies lay uncovered in the burial-ground, with only here and there a little lime thrown over them, to prevent the air becoming infected. The negro, whose home is in a hot climate, was not proof against the disease. Many plantations had to suspend their work for want of slaves to take the places of those who had been taken off by the fever.

CHAPTER XXIII.

MEETING OF THE COUSINS.

THE clock in the hall had scarcely finished striking three when Mr. Taylor entered his own dwelling, a fine residence in Camp Street, New Orleans, followed by the slave-girl whom he had just purchased at the negro-pen. Clotelle looked around wildly as she passed through the hall into the presence of her new mistress. Mrs. Taylor was much pleased with her servant's appearance, and congratulated her husband on his judicious choice.

"But," said Mrs. Taylor, after Clotelle had gone into the kitchen, "how much she looks like Miss Jane Morton."

"Indeed," replied the husband, "I thought, the moment I saw her that she looked like the Mortons."

"I am sure I never saw two faces more alike in my life, than that girl's and Jane Morton's," continued Mrs. Taylor.

Dr. Morton, the purchaser of Maron, the youngest daughter of Agnes, and sister to Isabella, had resided in Camp Street, near the Taylors, for more than eight years, and the families were on very intimate terms, and visited each other frequently. Every one spoke of Clotelle's close resemblance to the Mortons, and especially to the eldest daughter. Indeed, two sisters could hardly have been more alike. The large, dark eyes, black, silk-like hair, tall, graceful figure, and mould of the face, were the same.

The morning following Clotelle's arrival in her new home, Mrs. Taylor was conversing in a low tone with her husband, and both with their eyes following Clotelle as she passed through the room.

"She is far above the station of a slave," remarked the lady. "I saw her, last night, when removing some books, open one and stand over it a moment as if she was reading; and she is as white as I am. I am almost sorry you bought her."

At this juncture the front door-bell rang, and Clotelle hurried through the room to answer it.

"Miss Morton," said the servant as she returned to the mistress' room.

"Ask her to walk in," responded the mistress.

"Now, my dear," said Mrs. Taylor to her husband, "just look and see if you do not notice a marked resemblance between the countenances of Jane and Clotelle."

Miss Morton entered the room just as Mrs. Taylor ceased speaking.

"Have you heard that the Jamisons are down with the fever?" inquired the young lady, after asking about the health of the Taylors.

"No, I had not; I was in hopes it would not get into our street," replied Mrs. Taylor.

All this while mr. and Mrs. Taylor were keenly scrutinizing their visitor and Clotelle and even the two young women seemed to be conscious that they were in some way the objects of more than usual attention.

Miss Morton had scarcely departed before Mrs. Taylor began questioning Clotelle concerning her early childhood, and became more than ever satisfied that the slave-girl was in some way connected with the Mortons.

Every hour brought fresh news of the ravages of the fever, and the Taylors commenced preparing to leave town. As Mr. Taylor could not go at once, it was determined that his wife should leave without him, accompanied by her new maid-servant. Just as Mrs. Taylor and Clotelle were stepping into the carriage, they were informed that Dr. Morton was down with the epidemic.

It was a beautiful day, with a fine breeze for the time of year, that Mrs. Taylor and her servant found themselves in the cabin of the splendid new steamer "Walk-in-the-Water," bound from New Orleans to Mobile. Every berth in the boat was occupied by persons fleeing from the fearful contagion that was carrying off its hundreds daily.

Late in the day, as Clotelle was standing at one of the windows of the ladies' saloon, she was astonished to see near her, and with eyes fixed intently upon her, the tall young stranger whom she had observed in the slave-market a few days before. She turned hastily away, but the heated cabin and the want of fresh air soon drove her again to the window. The young gentleman again appeared, and coming to the end of the saloon, spoke to the slave-girl in broken English. This confirmed her in her previous opinion that he was a foreigner, and she rejoiced that she had not fallen into his hands.

" I want to talk with you," said the stranger.

" What do you want with me?" she inquired.

" I am your friend," he answered. "I saw you in the slave-market last week, and regretted that I did not speak to you then. I returned in the evening, but you was gone."

Clotelle looked indignantly at the stranger, and was about leaving the window again when the quivering of his lips and the trembling of his voice struck her attention and caused her to remain.

" I intended to buy you and make you free and happy, but I was too late," continued he.

" Why do you wish to make me free?" inquired the girl.

" Because I once had an only and lovely sister, who died three years ago in France, and you are so much like her that had I not known of her death I should certainly have taken you for her."

" However much I may resemble your sister, you are aware that I am not she; why, then, take so much interest in one whom you have never seen before and may never see again?"

"The love," said he, "which I had for my sister is transferred to you."

Clotelle had all along suspected that the man was a knave, and this profession of love at once confirmed her in that belief. She therefore immediately turned away and left him.

Hours elapsed. Twilight was just "letting down her curtain and pinning it with a star," as the slave-girl seated herself on a sofa by the window, and began meditating upon her eventful history, meanwhile watching the white waves as they seemed to sport with each other in the wake of the noble vessel, with the rising moon reflecting its silver rays upon the splendid scene, when the foreigner once more appeared near the window. Although agitated for fear her mistress would see her talking to a stranger, and be angry, Clotelle still thought she saw something in the countenance of the young man that told her he was sincere, and she did not wish to hurt his feelings.

"Why persist in your wish to talk with me?" she said, as he again advanced and spoke to her.

"I wish to purchase you and make you happy," returned he.

"But I am not for sale now," she replied. "My present mistress will not sell me, and if you wished to do so ever so much you could not."

"Then," said he, "if I cannot buy you, when the steamer reaches Mobile, fly with me, and you shall be free."

"I cannot do it," said Clotelle; and she was just leaving the stranger when he took from his pocket a piece of paper and thrust it into her hand.

After returning to her room, she unfolded the paper, and found, to her utter astonishment that it contained a one hundred dollar note on the Bank of the United States. The first impulse of the girl was to return the paper and its contents immediately to the giver, but examining the paper more closely, she saw in faint pencil-marks, "Remember this is from one who loves you." Another thought was to give it to her mistress, and she returned to the saloon for that purpose; but on finding Mrs. Taylor engaged in conversation with some ladies, she did not deem it proper to interrupt her.

Again, therefore, Clotelle seated herself by the window, and again the stranger presented himself. She immediately took the paper from her pocket, and handed it to him; but he declined taking it, saying, —

"No, keep it; it may be of some service to you when I am far away."

"Would that I could understand you," said the slave.

"Believe that I am sincere, and then you will understand me," returned the young man. " Would you rather be a slave than be free? " inquired he, with tears that glistened in the rays of the moon.

" No," said she, " I want my freedom, but I must live a virtuous life."

"Then, if you would be free and happy, go with me. We shall be in Mobile in two hours, and when the passengers are going on shore, you take my arm. Have your face covered with a veil, and you will not be observed. We will take passage immediately for France; you can pass as my sister, and I pledge you my honor that I will marry you as soon as we arrive in France."

This solemn promise, coupled with what had previously been said, gave Clotelle confidence in the man, and she instantly determined to go with him. " But then," thought she, "what if I should be detected? I would be forever ruined, for I would be sold, and in all probability have to end my days on a cotton, rice, or sugar plantation." However, the thought of freedom in the future outweighed this danger, and her resolve was taken.

Dressing herself in some of her best clothes, and placing her veiled bonnet where she could get it without the knowledge of her mistress, Clotelle awaited with a heart filled with the deepest emotions and anxiety the moment when she was to take a step which seemed so rash, and which would either make or ruin her forever.

The ships which leave Mobile for Europe lie about thirty miles down the bay, and passengers are taken down from the city in small vessels. The " Walk-in-the-Water " had just made her lines fast, and the passengers were hurrying on shore, when a tall gentleman with a lady at his side descended the stage-plank, and stepped on the wharf. This was Antoine Devenant and Clotelle.

CHAPTER XXIV

THE LAW AND ITS VICTIM.

THE death of Dr. Morton, on the third day of his illness, came like a shock upon his wife and daughters. The corpse had scarcely been committed to its mother earth before new and unforeseen difficulties appeared to them. By the laws of the Slave States, the children follow the condition of their mother. If the mother is free, the children are free; if a slave, the children are slaves. Being unacquainted with the Southern code, and no one presuming that Marion had any negro blood in her veins, Dr. Morton had not given the subject a single thought. The woman whom he loved and regarded as his wife was, after all, nothing more than a slave by the laws of the State. What would have been his feelings had he known that at his death his wife and children would be considered as his property? Yet such was the case. Like most men of means at that time, Dr. Morton was deeply engaged in speculation, and though generally considered wealthy, was very much involved in his business affairs.

After the disease with which Dr. Morton had so suddenly died had to some extent subsided, Mr. James Morton, a brother of the deceased, went to New Orleans to settle up the estate. On his arrival there, he was pleased with and felt proud of his nieces, and invited them to return with him to Vermont, little dreaming that his brother had married a slave, and that his widow and daughters would be claimed as such. The girls themselves had never heard that their mother had been a slave, and therefore knew nothing of the danger hanging over their heads.

An inventory of the property of the deceased was made out by Mr. Morton, and placed in the hands of the creditors. These preliminaries being arranged, the ladies, with their relative, concluded to leave the city and reside for a few days on the banks of Lake Ponchartrain, where they could enjoy a fresh air that the city did not afford. As they were about taking the cars, however, an officer arrested the whole party — the ladies as slaves, and the gentleman upon the charge of attempting to conceal the property of his deceased brother. Mr. Morton was overwhelmed with horror at the idea of his nieces being claimed as slaves, and asked for time, that he might save them from such a fate. He even offered to mortgage his little farm in Vermont for the amount which young slave-women of their ages would fetch. But the creditors pleaded that they were an "extra article," and would sell for more than common slaves, and must therefore be sold at auction.

The uncle was therefore compelled to give them up to the officers of the law, and they were separated from him. Jane, the oldest of the girls, as we have before mentioned, was very handsome, bearing a close resemblance to her cousin Clotelle. Alreka, though not as handsome as her sister, was nevertheless a beautiful girl, and both had all the accomplishments that wealth and station could procure.

Though only in her fifteenth year, Alreka had become strongly attached to Volney Lapie, a young Frenchman, a student in her father's office. This attachment was reciprocated, although the poverty of the young man and the extreme youth of the girl had caused their feelings to be kept from the young lady's parents.

The day of sale came, and Mr. Morton attended, with the hope that either the magnanimity of the creditors or his own little farm in Vermont might save his nieces from the fate that awaited them. His hope, however, was in vain. The feelings of all present seemed to be lost in the general wish to become the possessor of the young ladies, who stood trembling, blushing, and weeping as the numerous throng gazed at them, or as the intended purchaser examined the graceful proportions of their fair and beautiful frames. Neither the presence of the uncle nor young Lapie could at all lessen the gross language of the officers, or stay the rude hands of those who wished to examine the property thus offered for sale. After a fierce contest between the bidders, the girls were sold, one for two thousand three hundred, and the other for two thousand three hundred and fifty dollars. Had these girls been bought for servants only, they would in all probability have brought not more than nine hundred or a thousand dollars each. Here were two beautiful young girls, accustomed to the fondest indulgence, surrounded by all the refinements of life, and with the timidity and gentleness which such a life would naturally produce, bartered away like cattle in the markets of Smithfield or New York.

The mother, who was also to have been sold, happily followed her husband to the grave, and was spared the pangs of a broken heart.

The purchaser of the young ladies left the market in triumph, and the uncle, with a heavy heart, started for his New England home, with no earthly prospect of ever beholding his nieces again.

The seizure of the young ladies as slaves was the result of the administrator's having found among Dr. Morton's papers the bill-of-sale of Marion which he had taken when he purchased her. He had doubtless intended to liberate her when he married her, but had neglected from time to time to have the proper papers made out. Sad was the result of this negligence.

CHAPTER XXV.

THE FLIGHT.

On once gaining the wharf, Devenant and Clotelle found no difficulty in securing an immediate passage to France. The fine packet-ship Utica lay down the bay, and only awaited the return of the lighter that night to complete her cargo and list of passengers, ere she departed. The young Frenchman therefore took his prize on board, and started for the ship.

Daylight was just making its appearance the next morning when the Utica weighed anchor and turned her prow toward the sea. In the course of three hours, the vessel, with outspread sails, was rapidly flying from land. Everything appeared to be auspicious. The skies were beautifully clear, and the sea calm, with a sun that dazzled the whole scene. But clouds soon began to chase each other through the heavens and the sea became rough. It was then that Clotelle felt that there was hope of escaping. She had hitherto kept in the cabin, but now she expressed a wish to come on deck. The hanging clouds were narrowing the horizon to a span, and gloomily mingling with the rising surges. The old and grave-looking seamen shook their weather-wise heads as if foretelling a storm..

As Clotelle came on deck, she strained her eyes in vain to catch a farewell view of her native land. With a smile on her countenance, but with her eyes filled with tears, she said,—

"Farewell, farewell to the land of my birth, and welcome, welcome, ye dark blue waves. I care not where I go, so it is

> ' Where a tyrant never trod,
> 　　Where a slave was never known,
> 　But where nature worships God,
> 　　If in the wilderness alone.' "

Devenant stood by her side, seeming proud of his future wife, with his face in a glow at his success, while over his noble brow clustering locks of glossy black hair were hanging in careless ringlets. His finely-cut, classic features wore the aspect of one possessed with a large and noble heart.

Once more the beautiful Clotelle whispered in the ear of her lover,—

> "Away, away, o'er land and sea,
> 　America is now no home for me."

The winds increased with nightfall, and impenetrable gloom surrounded the ship. The prospect was too uncheering, even to persons in love. The attention which Devenant paid to Clotelle, although she had been registered on the ship's passenger list as his sister, caused more than one to look upon his as an agreeable travelling companion. His tall, slender figure and fine countenance bespoke for him at first sight one's confidence. That he was sincerely and deeply enamored of Clotelle all could see.

The weather became still more squally. The wind rushed through the white, foaming waves, and the ship groaned with its own wild and ungovernable labors, while nothing could be seen but the wild waste of waters. The scene was indeed one of fearful sublimity.

Day came and went without any abatement of the storm. Despair was now on every countenance. Occasionally a vivid flash of lightning would break forth and illuminate the black and boiling surges that surrounded the vessel, which was now scudding before the blast under bare poles.

After five days of most intensely stormy weather, the sea settled down into a dead calm, and the passengers flocked on deck. During the last three days of the storm, Clotelle had been so unwell as to be unable to raise her head. Her pale face and quivering lips and languid appearance made her look as if every pulsation had ceased. Her magnificent large and soft eyes, fringed with lashes as dark as night, gave her an angelic appearance. The unreserved attention of Devenant, even when sea-sick himself, did much to increase the little love that the at first distrustful girl had placed in him. The heart must always have some object on which to centre its affections, and Clotelle having lost all hope of ever again seeing Jerome, it was but natural that she should now transfer her love to one who was so greatly befriending her. At first she respected Devenant for the love he manifested for her, and for his apparent willingness to make any sacrifice for her welfare. True, this was an adventure upon which she had risked her all, and should her heart be foiled in this search for hidden treasures, her affections would be shipwrecked forever. She felt under great obligations to the man who had thus effected her escape, and that noble act alone would entitle him to her love.

Each day became more pleasant as the noble ship sped onward amid the rippled spray. The whistling of the breeze through the rigging was music to the ear, and brought gladness to the heart of every one on board. At last, the long suspense was broken by the appearance of land, at which all hearts leaped for joy. It was a beautiful morning in October. The sun had just risen, and sky and earth were still bathed in his soft, rosy glow, when the Utica hauled into the dock at Bordeaux. The splendid streets, beautiful bridges, glittering equipages, and smiling countenances of the people, gave everything a happy appearance, after a voyage of twenty-nine days on the deep, deep sea.

After getting their baggage cleared from the custom-house and going to a hotel, Devenant made immediate arrangements for the marriage. Clotelle, on arriving at the church where the ceremony was to take place, was completely overwhelmed at the spectacle. She had never beheld a scene so gorgeous as this. The magnificent dresses of the priests and choristers, the deep and solemn voices, the elevated crucifix, the burning tapers, the splendidly decorated altar, the sweet-smelling incense, made the occasion truly an imposing one. At the conclusion of the ceremony, the loud and solemn peals of the organ's swelling anthem were lost to all in the contemplation of the interesting scene.

The happy couple set out at once for Dunkirk, the residence of the bridegroom's parents. But their stay there was short, for they had scarcely commenced visiting the numerous friends of the husband ere orders came for him to proceed to India to join that portion of the French army then stationed there.

In due course of time theỹ left for India, passing through Paris and Lyons, taking ship at Marseilles. In the metropolis of France, they spent a week, where the husband took delight in introducing his wife to his brother officers in the French army, and where the newly-married couple were introduced to Louis Philippe, then King of France. In all of these positions, Clotelle sustained herself in a most ladylike manner.

At Lyons, they visited the vast factories and other public works, and all was pleasure with them. The voyage from Marseilles to Calcutta was very pleasant, as the weather was exceedingly fine. On arriving in India, Captain Devenant and lady were received with honors — the former for his heroic bravery in more than one battle, and the latter for her fascinating beauty and pleasing manners, and the fact that she was connected with one who was a general favorite with all who had his acquaintance. This was indeed a great change for Clotelle. Six months had not elapsed since her exposure in the slave-market of New Orleans. This life is a stage, and we are indeed all actors.

CHAPTER XXVI.

THE HERO OF A NIGHT.

MOUNTED on a fast horse, with the Quaker's son for a guide, Jerome pressed forward while Uncle Joseph was detaining the slave-catchers at the barn-door, through which the fugitive had just escaped. When out of present danger, fearing that suspicion might be aroused if he continued on the road in open day, Jerome buried himself in a thick, dark forest until nightfall. With a yearning heart, he saw the splendor of the setting sun lingering on the hills, as if loath to fade away and be lost in the more sombre hues of twilight, which, rising from the east, was slowly stealing over the expanse of heaven, bearing silence and repose, which should cover his flight from a neighborhood to him so full of dangers.

Wearily and alone, with nothing but the hope of safety before him to cheer him on his way, the poor fugitive urged his tired and trembling limbs forward for several nights. The new suit of clothes with which he had provided himself when he made his escape from his captors, and the twenty dollars which the young Quaker had slipped into his hand, when bidding him " Fare thee well," would enable him to appear genteelly as soon as he dared to travel by daylight, and would thus facilitate his progress toward freedom.

It was late in the evening when the fugitive slave arrived at a small town on the banks of Lake Erie, where he was to remain over night. How strange were his feelings! While his heart throbbed for that freedom and safety which Canada alone could furnish to the whip-scarred slave, on the American continent, his thoughts were with Clotelle. Was she still in prison, and if so, what would be her punishment for aiding him to escape from prison? Would he ever behold her again? These were the thoughts that followed him to his pillow, haunted him in his dreams, and awakened him from his slumbers.

The alarm of fire aroused the inmates of the hotel in which Jerome had sought shelter for the night from the deep sleep into which they had fallen. The whole village was buried in slumber, and the building was half consumed before the frightened inhabitants had reached the scene of the conflagration. The wind was high, and the burning embers were wafted like so many rockets through the sky. The whole town was lighted up, and the cries of women and children in the streets made the scene a terrific one. Jerome heard the alarm, and hastily dressing himself, he went forth and hastened toward the burning building.

" There, — there in that room in the second story, is my child! " exclaimed a woman, wringing her hands, and imploring some one to go to the rescue of her little one.

The broad sheets of fire were flying in the direction of the chamber in which the child was sleeping, and all hope of its being saved seemed gone. Occasionally the wind would lift the pall of smoke, and show that the work of destruction was not yet complete. At last a long ladder was brought, and one end placed under the window of the room. A moment more and a bystander mounted the ladder and ascended in haste to the window. The smoke met him as he raised the sash, and he cried out, " All is lost! " and returned to the ground without entering the room.

Another sweep of the wind showed that the destroying element had not yet made its final visit to that part of the doomed building. The mother, seeing that all hope of again meeting her child in this world was gone, wrung her hands and seemed inconsolable with grief.

At this juncture, a man was seen to mount the ladder, and ascend with great rapidity. All eyes were instantly turned to the figure of this unknown individual as it disappeared in the cloud of smoke escaping from the window. Those who a moment before had been removing furniture, as well as the idlers who had congregated at the ringing of the bells, assembled at the foot of the ladder, and awaited with breathless silence the reappearance of the stranger, who, regardless of his own safety, had thus risked his life to save another's. Three cheers broke the stillness that had fallen on the company, as the brave man was seen coming through the window and slowly descending to the ground, holding under one arm the inanimate form of the child. Another cheer, and then another, made the welkin ring, as the stranger, with hair burned and eyebrows closely singed, fainted at the foot of the ladder. But the child was saved.

The stranger was Jerome. As soon as he revived, he shrunk from every eye, as if he feared they would take from him the freedom which he had gone through so much to obtain.

The next day, the fugitive took a vessel, and the following morning found himself standing on the free soil of Canada. As his foot pressed the shore, he threw himself upon his face, kissed the earth, and exclaimed, " O God! I thank thee that I am a free man."

CHAPTER XXVII.

TRUE FREEDOM.

THE history of the African race is God's illuminated clock, set in the dark steeple of time. The negro has been made the hewer of wood and the drawer of water for nearly all other nations. The people of the United States, however, will have an account to settle with God, owing to their treatment of the negro, which will far surpass the rest of mankind.

Jerome, on reaching Canada, felt for the first time that personal freedom which God intended that all who bore his image should enjoy. That same forgetfulness of self which had always characterized him now caused him to think of others. The thoughts of dear ones in slavery were continually in his mind, and above all others, Clotelle occupied his thoughts. Now that he was free, he could better appreciate her condition as a slave. Although Jerome met, on his arrival in Canada, numbers who had escaped from the Southern States, he nevertheless shrank from all society, particularly that of females. The soft, silver-gray tints on the leaves of the trees, with their snow-spotted trunks, and a biting air, warned the new-born freeman that he was in another climate. Jerome sought work, and soon found it; and arranged with his employer that the latter should go to Natchez in search of Clotelle. The good Scotchman, for whom the fugitive was laboring, freely offered to go down and purchase the girl, if she could be bought, and let Jerome pay him in work. With such a prospect of future happiness in view, this injured descendant of outraged and bleeding Africa went daily to his toil with an energy hitherto unknown to him. But oh, how vain are the hopes of man!

CHAPTER XXVIII.

FAREWELL TO AMERICA.

THREE months had elapsed, from the time the fugitive commenced work for Mr. Streeter, when that gentleman returned from his Southern research, and informed Jerome that Parson Wilson had sold Clotelle, and that she had been sent to the New Orleans slave-market.

This intelligence fell with crushing weight upon the heart of Jerome, and he now felt that the last chain which bound him to his native land was severed. He therefore determined to leave America forever. His nearest and dearest friends had often been flogged in his very presence, and he had seen his mother sold to the negro-trader. An only sister had been torn from him by the soul-driver; he had himself been sold and resold, and been compelled to submit to the most degrading and humiliating insults; and now that the woman upon whom his heart doted, and without whom life was a burden, had been taken away forever, he felt it a duty to hate all mankind.

If there is one thing more than another calculated to make one hate and detest American slavery, it is to witness the meetings between fugitives and their friends in Canada. Jerome had beheld some of these scenes. The wife who, after years of separation, had escaped from her prison-house and followed her husband had told her story to him. He had seen the newly-arrived wife rush into the arms of the husband, whose dark face she had not looked upon for long, weary years. Some told of how a sister had been ill-used by the overseer; others of a husband's being whipped to death for having attempted to protect his wife. He had sat in the little log-hut, by the fireside, and heard tales that caused his heart to bleed; and his bosom swelled with just indignation when he thought that there was no remedy for such atrocious acts. It was with such feelings that he informed his employer that he should leave him at the expiration of a month.

In vain did Mr. Streeter try to persuade Jerome to remain with him; and late in the month of February, the latter found himself on board a small vessel loaded with pine-lumber, descending the St. Lawrence, bound for Liverpool. The bark, though an old one, was, nevertheless, considered seaworthy, and the fugitive was working his way out. As the vessel left the river and gained the open sea, the black man appeared to rejoice at the prospect of leaving a country in which his right to manhood had been denied him, and his happiness destroyed.

The wind was proudly swelling the white sails, and the little craft plunging into the foaming waves, with the land fast receding in the distance, when Jerome mounted a pile of lumber to take a last farewell of his native land. With tears glistening in his eyes, and with quivering lips, he turned his gaze toward the shores that were fast fading in the dim distance, and said, —

"Though forced from my native land by the tyrants of the South, I hope I shall some day be able to return. With all her faults, I love my country still."

CHAPTER XXIX.

A STRANGER IN A STRANGE LAND.

THE rain was falling on the dirty pavements of Liverpool as Jerome left the vessel after her arrival. Passing the custom-house, he took a cab, and proceeded to Brown's Hotel, Clayton Square.

Finding no employment in Liverpool, Jerome determined to go into the interior and seek for work. He, therefore, called for his bill, and made ready for his departure. Although but four days at the Albion, he found the hotel charges larger than he expected; but a stranger generally counts on being "fleeced" in travelling through the Old World, and especially in Great Britain. After paying his bill, he was about leaving the room, when one of the servants presented himself with a low bow, and said, —

"Something for the waiter, sir?"

"I thought I had paid my bill," replied the man, somewhat surprised at this polite dun.

"I am the waiter, sir, and gets only what strangers see fit to give me."

Taking from his pocket his nearly empty purse, Jerome handed the man a half-crown; but he had hardly restored it to his pocket, before his eye fell on another man in the waiting costume.

"What do you want?" he asked.

"Whatever your honor sees fit to give me, sir. I am the tother waiter."

The purse was again taken from the pocket, and another half-crown handed out. Stepping out into the hall, he saw standing there a good-looking woman, in a white apron, who made a very pretty courtesy.

"What's your business?" he inquired.

"I am the chambermaid, sir, and looks after the gentlemen's beds."

Out came the purse again, and was relieved of another half-crown; whereupon another girl, with a fascinating smile, took the place of the one who had just received her fee.

"What do you want?" demanded the now half-angry Jerome.

"Please, sir, I am the tother chambermaid."

Finding it easier to give shillings than half-crowns, Jerome handed the woman a shilling, and again restored his purse to his pocket, glad that another woman was not to be seen.

Scarcely had he commenced congratulating himself, however, before three men made their appearance, one after another.

"What have *you* done for me?" he asked of the first.

"I am the boots, sir."

The purse came out once more, and a shilling was deposited in the servant's hand.

"What do I owe you?" he inquired of the second.

"I took your honor's letter to the post, yesterday, sir."

Another shilling left the purse.

"In the name of the Lord, what am I indebted to you for?" demanded Jerome, now entirely out of patience, turning to the last of the trio.

"I told yer vership vot time it vas, this morning."

"Well!" exclaimed the indignant man, "ask here what o'clock it is, and you have got to pay for it."

He paid this last demand with a sixpence, regretting that he had not commenced with sixpences instead of half-crowns.

Having cleared off all demands in the house, he started for the railway station; but had scarcely reached the street, before he was accosted by an old man with a broom in his hand, who, with an exceedingly low bow, said,

"I is here, yer lordship."

"I did not send for you; what is your business?" demanded Jerome.

"I is the man what opened your lordship's cab-door, when your lordship came to the house on Monday last, and I know your honor won't allow a poor man to starve."

Putting a sixpence in the old man's hand, Jerome once more started for the depot. Having obtained letters of introduction to persons in Manchester, he found no difficulty in getting a situation in a large manufacturing house there. Although the salary was small, yet the situation was a much better one than he had hoped to obtain. His compensation as out-door clerk enabled him to employ a man to teach him at night, and, by continued study and attention to business, he was soon promoted.

After three years in his new home, Jerome was placed in a still higher position, where his salary amounted to fifteen hundred dollars a year. The drinking, smoking, and other expensive habits, which the clerks usually indulged in, he carefully avoided.

Being fond of poetry, he turned his attention to literature. Johnson's "Lives of the Poets," the writings of Dryden, Addison, Pope, Clarendon, and other authors of celebrity, he read with attention. The knowledge which he thus picked up during his leisure hours gave him a great advantage over the other clerks, and caused his employers to respect him far more than any other in their establishment. So eager was he to improve the time that he determined to see how much he could read during the unemployed time of night and morning, and his success was beyond his expectations.

CHAPTER XXX.

NEW FRIENDS.

BROKEN down in health, after ten years of close confinement in his situation, Jerome resolved to give it up, and thereby release himself from an employment which seemed calculated to send him to a premature grave.

It was on a beautiful morning in summer that he started for Scotland, having made up his mind to travel for his health. After visiting Edinburgh and Glasgow, he concluded to spend a few days in the old town of Perth, with a friend whose acquaintance he had made in Manchester. During the second day of his stay in Perth, while crossing the main street, Jerome saw a pony-chaise coming toward him with great speed. A lady, who appeared to be the only occupant of the vehicle, was using her utmost strength to stop the frightened horses. The footman, in his fright, had leaped from behind the carriage, and was following with the crowd. With that self-forgetfulness which was one of his chief characteristics, Jerome threw himself before the horses to stop them; and, seizing the high-spirited animals by the bit, as they dashed by him, he was dragged several rods before their speed was checked, which was not accomplished until one of the horses had fallen to the ground, with the heroic man struggling beneath him.

All present were satisfied that this daring act alone had saved the lady's life, for the chaise must inevitably have been dashed in pieces, had the horses not been thus suddenly checked in their mad career.

On the morning following this perilous adventure, Col. G—— called at Jerome's temporary residence, and, after expressing his admiration for his noble daring, and thanking him for having saved his daughter's life, invited him to visit him at his country residence. This invitation was promptly accepted in the spirit in which it was given ; and three days after, Jerome found himself at the princely residence of the father of the lady for whose safety he had risked his own life. The house was surrounded by fine trees, and a sweet little stream ran murmuring at the foot, while beds óf flowers on every hand shed their odors on the summer air. It was, indeed, a pleasant place to spend the warm weather, and the colonel and his family gave Jerome a most cordial welcome. Miss G. showed especial attention to the stranger. He had not intended remaining longer than the following day: but the family insisted on his taking part in a fox-hunt that was to come off on the morning of the third day. Wishing to witness a scene as interesting as the chase usually proves to be, he decided to remain.

Fifteen persons, five of whom were ladies, were on the ground at the appointed hour. Miss G. was, of course, one of the party. In vain Jerome endeavored to excuse himself from joining in the chase. His plea of ill-health was only met by smiles from the young ladies, and the reply that a ride would effect a cure.

Dressed in a scarlet coat and high boots, with the low, round cap worn in the chase, Jerome mounted a high-spirited horse, whip in hand, and made himself one of the party. In America, riding is a necessity; in England, it is a pleasure. Young men and women attend riding-school in our fatherland, and consider that they are studying a science. Jerome was no rider. He had not been on horseback for more than ten years, and as soon as he mounted, every one saw that he was a novice, and a smile was on the countenance of each member of the company.

The blowing of the horn, and assembling of the hounds, and finally the release of the fox from his close prison, were the signals for the chase to commence. The first half-mile the little animal took his course over a beautiful field where there was neither hedge nor ditch. Thus far the chase was enjoyed by all, even by the American rider, who was better fitted to witness the scene than to take part in it.

We left Jerome in our last reluctantly engaged in the chase; and though the first mile or so of the pursuit, which was over smooth meadow-land, had had an exhilarating effect upon his mind, and tended somewhat to relieve him of the embarrassment consequent upon his position, he nevertheless still felt that he was far from being in his proper element. Besides, the fox had now made for a dense forest which lay before, and he saw difficulties in that direction which to him appeared insurmountable.

Away went the huntsmen, over stone walls, high fences, and deep ditches. Jerome saw the ladies even leading the gentlemen, but this could not inspire him. They cleared the fences, four and five feet high with perfect ease, showing they were quite at home in the saddle. But alas for the poor American! As his fine steed came up to the first fence, and was about to make the leap, Jerome pulled at the bridle, and cried at the top of his voice, " Whoa! whoa! whoa!" the horse at the same time capering about, and appearing determined to keep up with the other animals.

Away dashed the huntsmen, following the hounds, and all were soon lost to the view of their colored companion. Jerome rode up and down the field looking for a gate or bars, that he might get through without risking his neck. Finding, however, that all hope of again catching up with the party was out of the question, he determined to return to the house, under a plea of sudden illness, and back he accordingly went.

"I hope no accident has happened to your honor," said the groom, as he met our hero at the gate.

"A slight dizziness," was the answer.

One of the servants, without being ordered, went at once for the family physician. Ashamed to own that his return was owing to his inability to ride, Jerome resolved to feign sickness. The doctor came, felt his pulse, examined his tongue, and pronounced him a sick man. He immediately ordered a tepid bath, and sent for a couple of leeches.

Seeing things taking such a serious turn, the American began to regret the part he was playing; for there was no fun in being rubbed and leeched when one was in perfect health. He had gone too far to recede, however, and so submitted quietly to the directions of the doctor; and, after following the injunctions given by that learned Esculapius, was put to bed.

Shortly after, the sound of the horns and the yelp of the hounds announced that the poor fox had taken the back track, and was repassing near the house. Even the pleasure of witnessing the beautiful sight from the window was denied to our hero; for the physician had ordered that he must be kept in perfect quiet.

The chase was at last over, and the huntsmen all in, sympathizing with their lost companion. After nine days of sweating, blistering, and leeching, Jerome left his bed convalescent, but much reduced in flesh and strength. This was his first and last attempt to follow the fox and hounds.

During his fortnight's stay at Colonel G.'s, Jerome spent most of his time in the magnificent library. Claude did not watch with more interest every color of the skies, the trees, the grass, and the water, to learn from nature, than did this son of a despised race search books to obtain that knowledge which his early life as a slave had denied him.

CHAPTER XXXI.

THE MYSTERIOUS MEETING.

AFTER more than a fortnight spent in the highlands of Scotland, Jerome passed hastily through London on his way to the continent.

It was toward sunset, on a warm day in October, shortly after his arrival in France, that, after strolling some distance from the Hotel de Leon, in the old and picturesque town of Dunkirk, he entered a burial-ground — such places being always favorite walks with him — and wandered around among the silent dead. All nature around was hushed in silence, and seemed to partake of the general melancholy that hung over the quiet resting-place of the departed. Even the birds seemed imbued with the spirit of the place, for they were silent, either flying noiselessly over the graves, or jumping about in the tall grass. After tracing the various inscriptions that told the characters and conditions of the deceased, and viewing the mounds beneath which the dust of mortality slumbered, he arrived at a secluded spot near where an aged weeping willow bowed its thick foliage to the ground, as though anxious to hide from the scrutinizing gaze of curiosity the grave beneath it. Jerome seated himself on a marble tombstone, and commenced reading from a book which he had carried under his arm. It was now twilight, and he had read but a few minutes when he observed a lady, attired in deep black, and leading a boy, apparently some five or six years old, coming up one of the beautiful, winding paths. As the lady's veil was drawn closely over her face, he felt somewhat at liberty to eye her more closely. While thus engaged, the lady gave a slight scream, and seemed suddenly to have fallen into a fainting condition. Jerome sprang from his seat, and caught her in time to save her from falling to the ground.

At this moment an elderly gentleman, also dressed in black, was seen approaching with a hurried step, which seemed to indicate that he was in some way connected with the lady. The old man came up, and in rather a confused manner inquired what had happened, and Jerome explained matters as well as he was able to do so. After taking up the vinaigrette, which had fallen from her hand, and holding the bottle a short time to her face, the lady began to revive. During all this time, the veil had still partly covered the face of the fair one, so that Jerome had scarcely seen it. When she had so far recovered as to be able to look around her, she raised herself slightly, and again screamed and swooned. The old man now feeling satisfied that Jerome's dark complexion was the immediate cause of the catastrophe, said in a somewhat petulant tone, —

" I will be glad, sir, if you will leave us alone."

The little boy at this juncture set up a loud cry, and amid the general confusion, Jerome left the ground and returned to his hotel.

While seated at the window of his room looking out upon the crowded street, with every now and then the strange scene in the grave-yard vividly before him, Jerome suddenly thought of the book he had been reading, and, remembering that he had left it on the tombstone, where he dropped it when called to the lady's assistance, he determined to return for it at once.

After a walk of some twenty minutes, he found himself again in the burial-ground and on the spot where he had been an hour before. The pensive moon was already up, and its soft light was sleeping on the little pond at the back of the grounds, while the stars seemed smiling at their own sparkling rays gleaming up from the beautiful sheet of water.

Jerome searched in vain for his book; it was nowhere to be found. Nothing, save the bouquet that the lady had dropped, and which lay half-buried in the grass, from having been trodden upon, indicated that any one had been there that evening. The stillness of death reigned over the place; even the little birds, that had before been twittering and flying about, had retired for the night.

Taking up the bunch of flowers, Jerome returned to his hotel. "What can this mean?" he would ask himself; "and why should they take my book?" These questions he put to himself again and again during his walk. His sleep was broken more than once that night, and he welcomed the early dawn as it made its appearance.

CHAPTER XXXII.

THE HAPPY MEETING.

AFTER passing a sleepless night, and hearing the clock strike six, Jerome took from his table a book, and thus endeavored to pass away the hours before breakfast-time. While thus engaged, a servant entered and handed him a note. Hastily tearing it open, Jerome read as follows: —

"SIR, — I owe you an apology for the abrupt manner in which I addressed you last evening, and the inconvenience to which you were subjected by some of my household. If you will honor us with your presence to-day at four o'clock, I shall be most happy to give you due satisfaction. My servant will be waiting with the carriage at half-past three.

I am, sir, yours, &c.,   J. DEVENANT.

JEROME FLETCHER, Esq.

Who this gentleman was, and how he had found out his name and the hotel at which he was stopping, were alike mysteries to Jerome. And this note seemed to his puzzled brain like a challenge. "Satisfaction?" He had not asked for satisfaction. However, he resolved to accept the invitation, and, if need be, meet the worst. At any rate, this most mysterious and complicated affair would be explained.

The clock on a neighboring church had scarcely finished striking three when a servant announced to Jerome that a carriage had called for him. In a few minutes, he was seated in a sumptuous barouche, drawn by a pair of beautiful iron-grays, and rolling over a splendid gravel road entirely shaded by trees, which appeared to have been the accumulated growth of many centuries. The carriage soon stopped at a low villa, which was completely embowered in trees.

Jerome alighted, and was shown into a superb room, with the walls finely decorated with splendid tapestry, and the ceilings exquisitely frescoed. The walls were hung with fine specimens from the hands of the great Italian masters, and one by a German artist, representing a beautiful monkish legend connected with the "Holy Catharine," an illustrious lady of Alexandria. High-backed chairs stood around the room, rich curtains of crimson damask hung in folds on either side of the window, and a beautiful, rich, Turkey carpet covered the floor. In the centre of the room stood a table covered with books, in the midst of which was a vase of fresh flowers, loading the atmosphere with their odors. A faint light, together with the quiet of the hour, gave beauty beyond description to the whole scene. A half-open door showed a fine marble floor to an adjoining room, with pictures, statues, and antiquated sofas, and flower-pots filled with rare plants of every kind and description.

Jerome had scarcely run his eyes over the beauties of the room when the elderly gentleman whom he had met on the previous evening made his appearance, followed by the little boy, and introduced himself as Mr. Devenant. A moment more and a lady, a beautiful brunette, dressed in black, with long black curls hanging over her shoulders, entered the room. Her dark, bright eyes flashed as she caught the first sight of Jerome. The gentleman immediately arose on the entrance of the lady, and Mr. Devenant was in the act of introducing the stranger when he observed that Jerome had sunk back upon the sofa, in a faint voice exclaiming, —

"It is she!"

After this, all was dark and dreary. How long he remained in this condition, it was for others to tell. The lady knelt by his side and wept; and when he came to, he found himself stretched upon the sofa with his boots off and his head resting upon a pillow. By his side sat the old man, with the smelling-bottle in one hand and a glass of water in the other, while the little boy stood at the foot of the sofa. As soon as Jerome had so far recovered as to be able to speak, he said,—

"Where am I, and what does all this mean?"

"Wait awhile," replied the old man, "and I will tell you all."

After the lapse of some ten minutes, Jerome arose from the sofa, adjusted his apparel, and said,—

"I am now ready to hear anything you have to say."

"You were born in America?" said the old man.

"I was," he replied.

"And you knew a girl named Clotelle," continued the old man.

"Yes, and I loved her as I can love none other."

"The lady whom you met so mysteriously last evening was she," said Mr. Devenant.

Jerome was silent, but the fountain of mingled grief and joy stole out from beneath his eyelashes, and glistened like pearls upon his ebony cheeks.

At this juncture, the lady again entered the room. With an enthusiasm that can be better imagined than described, Jerome sprang from the sofa, and they rushed into each other's arms, to the great surprise of the old gentleman and little Antoine, and to the amusement of the servants who had crept up, one by one and were hid behind the doors or loitering in the hall. When they had given vent to their feelings and sufficiently recovered their presence of mind, they resumed their seats.

"How did you find out my name and address?" inquired Jerome.

"After you had left the grave-yard," replied Clotelle, "our little boy said, 'Oh, mamma! if there ain't a book!' I opened the book, and saw your name written in it, and also found a card of the Hotel de Leon. Papa wished to leave the book, and said it was only a fancy of mine that I had ever seen you before; but I was perfectly convinced that you were my own dear Jerome."

As she uttered the last words, tears—the sweet bright tears that love alone can bring forth—bedewed her cheeks.

"Are you married?" now inquired Clotelle, with a palpitating heart and trembling voice.

"No, I am not, and never have been," was Jerome's reply.

"Then, thank God!" she exclaimed, in broken accents.

It was then that hope gleamed up amid the crushed and broken flowers of her heart, and a bright flash darted forth like a sunbeam.

"Are you single now?" asked Jerome.

"Yes, I am," was the answer.

"Then you will be mine after all?" said he with a smile.

Her dark, rich hair had partly come down, and hung still more loosely over her shoulders than when she first appeared; and her eyes, now full of animation and vivacity, and her sweet, harmonious, and well-modulated voice, together with her modesty, self-possession, and engaging manners, made Clotelle appear lovely beyond description. Although past the age when men ought to think of matrimony, yet the scene before Mr. Devenant brought vividly to his mind the time when he was young and had a loving bosom companion living, and tears were wiped from the old man's eyes. A new world seemed to unfold itself before the eyes of the happy lovers, and they were completely absorbed in contemplating the future. Furnished by nature with a disposition to study, and a memory so retentive that all who knew her were surprised at the ease with which she acquired her education and general information, Clotelle might now be termed a most accomplished lady. After her marriage with young Devenant, they proceeded to India, where the husband's regiment was stationed. Soon after their arrival, however, a battle was fought with the natives, in which several officers fell, among whom was Captain Devenant. The father of the young captain being there at the time, took his daughter-in-law and brought her back to France, where they took up their abode at the old homestead.

Old Mr. Devenant was possessed of a large fortune, all of which he intended for his daughter-in-law and her only child.

Although Clotelle had married young Devenant, she had not forgotten her first love, and her father-in-law now willingly gave his consent to her marriage with Jerome. Jerome felt that to possess the woman of his love, even at that late hour, was compensation enough for the years that he had been separated from her, and Clotelle wanted no better evidence of his love for her than the fact of his having remained so long unmarried. It was indeed a rare instance of devotion and constancy in a man, and the young widow gratefully appreciated it.

It was late in the evening when Jerome led his intended bride to the window, and the magnificent moonlight illuminated the countenance of the lovely Clotelle, while inward sunshine, emanating from a mind at ease, and her own virtuous thoughts, gave brightness to her eyes and made her appear a very angel. This was the first evening that Jerome had been in her company since the night when, to effect his escape from prison, she disguised herself in male attire. How different the scene now. Free instead of slaves, wealthy instead of poor, and on the eve of an event that seemed likely to result in a life of happiness to both.

7

CHAPTER XXXIII.

THE HAPPY DAY.

IT was a bright day in the latter part of October that Jerome and Clotelle set out for the church, where the marriage ceremony was to be performed. The clear, bracing air added buoyancy to every movement, and the sun poured its brilliant rays through the deeply-stained windows, as the happy couple entered the sanctuary, followed by old Mr. Devenant, whose form, bowed down with age, attracted almost as much attention from the assembly as did the couple more particularly interested.

As the ceremonies were finished and the priest pronounced the benediction on the newly-married pair, Clotelle whispered in the ear of Jerome, —

"'No power in death shall tear our names apart,
    As none in life could rend thee from my heart.'"

A smile beamed on every face as the wedding-party left the church and entered their carriage. What a happy day, after ten years' separation, when, both hearts having been blighted for a time, they are brought together by the hand of a beneficent and kind Providence, and united in holy wedlock.

Everything being arranged for a wedding tour extending up the Rhine, the party set out the same day for Antwerp. There are many rivers of greater length and width than the Rhine. Our Mississippi would swallow up half a dozen Rhines. The Hudson is grander, the Tiber, the Po, and the Mincio more classic; the Thames and Seine bear upon their waters greater amounts of wealth and commerce; the Nile and the Euphrates have a greater antiquity; but for a combination of interesting historical incidents and natural scenery, the Rhine surpasses them all. Nature has so ordained it that those who travel in the valley of the Rhine shall see the river, for there never will be a railroad upon its banks. So mountainous is the land that it would have to be one series of tunnels. Every three or four miles from the time you enter this glorious river, hills, dales, castles, and crags present themselves as the steamer glides onward.

Their first resting-place for any length of time was at Coblentz, at the mouth of the "Blue Moselle," the most interesting place on the river. From Coblentz they went to Brussels, where they had the greatest attention paid them. Besides being provided with letters of introduction, Jerome's complexion secured for him more deference than is usually awarded to travellers.

Having letters of introduction to M. Deceptiax, the great lace manufacturer, that gentleman received them with distinguished honors, and gave them a splendid *soiree*, at which the *elite* of the city were assembled. The sumptuously-furnished mansion was lavishly decorated for the occasion, and every preparation made that could add to the novelty or interest of the event.

Jerome, with his beautiful bride, next visited Cologne, the largest and wealthiest city on the banks of the Rhine. The Cathedral of Cologne is the most splendid structure of the kind in Europe, and Jerome and Clotelle viewed with interest the beautiful arches and columns of this stupendous building, which strikes with awe the beholder, as he gazes at its unequalled splendor, surrounded, as it is, by villas, cottages, and palace-like mansions, with the enchanting Rhine winding through the vine-covered hills.

After strolling over miles and miles of classic ground, and visiting castles, whose legends and tradions have given them an enduring fame, our delighted travellers started for Geneva, bidding the picturesque banks of the Rhine a regretful farewell. Being much interested in literature, and aware that Geneva was noted for having been the city of refuge to the victims of religious and political persecution, Jerome arranged to stay here for some days. He was provided with a letter of introduction to M. de Stee, who had been a fellow-soldier of Mr. Devenant in the East India wars, and they were invited to make his house their home during their sojourn. On the side of a noble mountain, whose base is kissed by the waves of Lake Geneva, and whose slopes are decked with verdure to the utmost peak of its rocky crown, is situated the delightful country residence of this wealthy, retired French officer. A winding road, with frequent climbs and brakes, leads from the valley to this enchanting spot, the air and scenery of which cannot be surpassed in the world.

CHAPTER XXXIV.

CLOTELLE MEETS HER FATHER.

THE clouds that had skirted the sky during the day broke at last, and the rain fell in torrents, as Jerome and Clotelle retired for the night, in the little town of Ferney, on the borders of Lake Leman. The peals of thunder, and flashes of vivid lightening, which seemed to leap from mountain to mountain and from crag to crag, reverberating among the surrounding hills, foretold a heavy storm.

"I would we were back at Geneva," said Clotelle, as she heard groans issuing from an adjoining room. The sounds, at first faint, grew louder and louder, plainly indicating that some person was suffering extreme pain.

"I did not like this hotel, much, when we came in," said Jerome, relighting the lamp, which had been accidentally extinguished.

"Nor I," returned Clotelle.

The shrieks increased, and an occasional "She's dead!" "I killed her!" "No, she is not dead!" and such-like expressions, would be heard from the person, who seemed to be deranged.

The thunder grew louder, and the flashes of lightening more vivid, while the noise from the sick-room seemed to increase.

As Jerome opened the door, to learn, if possible, the cause of the cries and groans, he could distinguish the words, "She's dead! yes, she's dead! but I did not kill her. She was my child! my own daughter. I loved her, and yet I did not protect her."

"Whoever he is," said Jerome, "he's crack-brained; some robber, probably, from the mountains."

The storm continued to rage, and the loud peals of thunder and sharp flashes of lightening, together with the shrieks and moans of the maniac in the adjoining room, made the night a fearful one. The long hours wore slowly away, but neither Jerome nor his wife could sleep, and they arose at an early hour in the morning, ordered breakfast, and resolved to return to Geneva.

"I am sorry, sir, that you were so much disturbed by the sick man last night," said the landlord, as he handed Jerome his bill. "I should be glad if he would get able to go away, or die, for he's a deal of trouble to me. Several persons have left my house on his account."

"Where is he from?" inquired Jerome.

"He's from the United States, and has been here a week to-day, and has been crazy ever since."

"Has he no friends with him?" asked the guest.

"No, he is alone," was the reply.

Jerome related to his wife what he had learned from the landlord, respecting the sick man, and the intelligence impressed her so strongly, that she requested him to make further inquiries concerning the stranger.

He therefore consulted the book in which guests usually register their names, and, to his great surprise, found that the American's name was Henry Linwood, and that he was from Richmond, Va.

It was with feelings of trepidation that Clotelle heard these particulars from the lips of her husband.

"We must see this poor man, whoever he is," said she, as Jerome finished the sentence.

The landlord was glad to hear that his guests felt some interest in the sick man, and promised that the invalid's room should be got ready for their reception.

The clock in the hall was just striking ten, as Jerome passed through and entered the sick man's chamber. Stretched upon a mattress, with both hands tightly bound to the bedstead, the friendless stranger was indeed a pitiful sight. His dark, dishevelled hair prematurely gray, his long, unshaven beard, and the wildness of the eyes which glanced upon them as they opened the door and entered, caused the faint hope which had so suddenly risen in Clotelle's heart, to sink, and she felt that this man could claim no kindred with her. Certainly, he bore no resemblance to the man whom she had called her father, and who had fondly dandled her on his knee in those happy days of childhood.

"Help!" cried the poor man, as Jerome and his wife walked into the room. His eyes glared, and shriek after shriek broke forth from his parched and fevered lips.

"No, I did not kill my daughter!—I did not! she is not dead! Yes, she is dead! but I did not kill her — poor girl! Look! that is she! No, it cannot be! she cannot come here! it cannot be my poor Clotelle."

At the sound of her own name, coming from the maniac's lips, Clotelle gasped for breath, and her husband saw that she had grown deadly pale. It seemed evident to him that the man was either guilty of some terrible act, or imagined himself to be. His eyeballs rolled in their sockets, and his features showed that he was undergoing "the tortures of that inward hell," which seemed to set his whole brain on fire.

After recovering her self-possession and strength, Clotelle approached the bedside, and laid her soft hand upon the stranger's hot and fevered brow.

One long, loud shriek rang out on the air, and a piercing cry, "It is she!—Yes, it is she! I see, I see! Ah! no, it is not my daughter! She would not come to me if she could!" broke forth from him.

"I am your daughter," said Clotelle, as she pressed her handkerchief to her face, and sobbed aloud.

Like balls of fire, the poor man's eyes rolled and glared upon the company, while large drops of perspiration ran down his pale and emaciated face. Strange as the scene appeared, all present saw that it was indeed a meeting between a father and his long-lost daughter. Jerome now ordered all present to leave the room, except the nurse, and every effort was at once made to quiet the sufferer. When calm, a joyous smile would illuminate the sick man's face, and a strange light beam in his eyes, as he seemed to realize that she who stood before him was indeed his child.

For two long days and nights did Clotelle watch at the bedside of her father before he could speak to her intelligently. Sometimes, in his insane fits, he would rave in the most frightful manner, and then, in a few moments, would be as easily governed as a child. At last, however, after a long and apparently refreshing sleep, he awoke suddenly to a full consciousness that it was indeed his daughter who was watching so patiently by his side.

The presence of his long absent child had a soothing effect upon Mr. Linwood, and he now recovered rapidly from the sad and almost hopeless condition in which she had found him. When able to converse, without danger of a relapse, he told Clotelle of his fruitless efforts to obtain a clew to her whereabouts after old Mrs. Miller had sold her to the slave-trader. In answer to his daughter's inquiries about his family affairs up to the time that he left America, he said, —

" I blamed my wife for your being sold and sent away, for I thought she and her mother were acting in collusion; But I afterwards found that I had blamed her wrongfully. Poor woman! she knew that I loved your mother, and feeling herself forsaken, she grew melancholy and died in a decline three years ago."

Here both father and daughter wept at the thought of other days. When they had recovered their composure, Mr. Linwood went on again :

" Old Mrs. Miller," said he, " after the death of Gertrude, aware that she had contributed much toward her unhappiness, took to the free use of intoxicating drinks, and became the most brutal creature that ever lived. She whipped her slaves without the slightest provocation, and seemed to take delight in inventing new tortures with which to punish them. One night last winter, after having flogged one of her slaves nearly to death, she returned to her room, and by some means the bedding took fire, and the house was in flames before any one was awakened. There was no one in the building at the time but the old woman and the slaves, and although the latter might have saved their mistress, they made no attempt to do so. Thus, after a frightful career of many years, this hard-hearted woman died a most miserable death, unlamented by a single person."

Clotelle wiped the tears from her eyes, as her father finished this story, for, although Mrs. Miller had been her greatest enemy, she regretted to learn that her end had been such a sad one.

" My peace of mind destroyed," resumed the father, " and broke down in health, my physician advised me to travel, with the hope o. recruiting myself, and I sailed from New York two months ago."

Being brought up in America, and having all the prejudice against color which characterizes his white fellow-countrymen, Mr. Linwood very much regretted that his daughter, although herself tinctured with African blood, should have married a black man, and he did not fail to express to her his dislike of her husband's complexion.

" I married him," said Clotelle, "because I loved him. Why should the white man be esteemed as better than the black? I find no difference in men on account of their complexion. One of the cardinal principles of Christianity and freedom is the equality and brotherhood of man."

Every day Mr. Linwood became more and more familiar with Jerome, and eventually they were on the most intimate terms.

Fifteen days from the time that Clotelle was introduced into her father's room, they left Ferney for Geneva. Many were the excursions Clotelle made under the shadows of Mont Blanc, and with her husband and father for companions; she was now in the enjoyment of pleasures hitherto unknown.

CHAPTER XXXV.

THE FATHER'S RESOLVE.

AWARE that her father was still a slave-owner, Clotelle determined to use all her persuasive power to induce him to set them free, and in this effort she found a substantial supporter in her husband.

" I have always treated my slaves well," said Mr. Linwood to Jerome, as the latter expressed his abhorrence of the system; " and my neighbors, too, are generally good men; for slavery in Virginia is not like slavery in the other States," continued the proud son of the Old Dominion.

" Their right to be free, Mr. Linwood," said Jerome, "is taken from them, and they have no security for their comfort, but the humanity and generosity of men, who have been trained to regard them not as brethren, but as mere property. Humanity and generosity are, at best, but poor guaranties for the protection of those who cannot assert their rights, and over whom law throws no protection."

It was with pleasure that Clotelle obtained from her father a promise that he would liberate all his slaves on his return to Richmond. In a beautiful little villa, situated in a pleasant spot, fringed with hoary rocks and thick dark woods, within sight of the deep blue waters of Lake Leman, Mr. Linwood, his daughter, and her husband, took up their residence for a short time. For more than three weeks, this little party spent their time in visiting the birth-place of Rousseau, and the former abodes of Byron, Gibbon, Voltaire, De Stael, Shelley, and other literary characters.

We can scarcely contemplate a visit to a more historic and interesting place than Geneva and its vicinity. Here, Calvin, that great luminary in the Church, lived and ruled for years; here, Voltaire, the mighty genius, who laid the foundation of the French Revolution, and who boasted, " When I shake my wig, I powder the whole republic," governed in the higher walks of life.

Fame is generally the recompense, not of the living, but of the dead, — not always do they reap and gather in the harvest who sow the seed; the flame of its altar is too often kindled from the ashes of the great. A distinguished critic has beautifully said, " The sound which the stream of high thought, carried down to future ages, makes, as it flows — deep, distant, murmuring ever more, like the waters of the mighty ocean." No reputation can be called great that will not endure this test. The distinguished men who had lived in Geneva transfused their spirit, by their writings, into the spirit of other lovers of literature and everything that treated of great authors. Jerome and Clotelle lingered long in and about the haunts of Geneva and Lake Leman.

An autumn sun sent down her bright rays, and bathed every object in her glorious light, as Clotelle, accompanied by her husband and father set out one fine morning on her return home to France. Throughout the whole route, Mr. Linwood saw by the deference paid to Jerome, whose black complexion excited astonishment in those who met him, that there was no hatred to the man in Europe, on account of his color; that what is called prejudice against color is the offspring of the institution of slavery; and he felt ashamed of his own countrymen, when he thought of the complexion as distinctions, made in the United States, and resolved to dedicate the remainder of his life to the eradication of this unrepublican and unchristian feeling from the land of his birth, on his return home.

After a stay of four weeks at Dunkirk, the home of the Fletchers, Mr. Linwood set out for America, with the full determination of freeing his slaves, and settling them in one of the Northern States, and then to return to France to end his days in the society of his beloved daughter.

THE END.

NOTE. — The author of the foregoing tale was formerly a Kentucky slave. If it serves to relieve the monotony of camp-life to the soldiers of the Union, and therefore of Liberty, and at the same time kindles their zeal in the cause of universal emancipation, the object both of its author and publisher will be gained.　　　　　　　　　　　　　J. R.

BOSTON: PRESS OF GEO. C. RAND & AVERY.

Bibliography of Pertinent Secondary Source Material

On Brown's Life and Writing

Brawley, Benjamin, *Early Negro American Writers.* Chapel Hill: The University of North Carolina Press, 1935.

Brown, Josephine, *Biography of an American Bondman, by His Daughter.* Boston: R. F. Wallcut, 1856.

Farrison, W. Edward, "William Wells Brown, Social Reformer." *Journal of Negro Education,* 18: 29–39, Winter 1949.

Loggins, Vernon, *The Negro Author: His Development in America.* New York: Columbia University Press, 1931.

On the Negro Literature of the Period

General

Brawley, Benjamin, *Early Negro American Writers. op. cit.*

Loggins, Vernon, *The Negro Author. op. cit.*

Orations

Woodson, Carter G., *Negro Orators and Their Orations.* Washington, D.C.: The Associated Publishers, 1925.

Slave Narratives

Bibb, Henry, *Narrative of the Life and Adventures of Henry Bibb, an American Slave, Written by Himself. With an Introduction by Lucia C. Matlack.* New York: The Author, 1849.

Clarke, Lewis, *Narrative of the Sufferings of Lewis Clarke, during a Captivity of More than Twenty-Five Years among the Algerines of Kentucky. Dictated by Himself.* Boston: D. H. Ela, 1845.

Douglass, Frederick, *Narrative of the Life of Frederick Douglass, an American Slave. Written by Himself.* Boston: Anti-Slavery Office, 1845.

Bibliography of Brown's Major Works
in Order of Publication

1847—*A Lecture Delivered before the Female Anti-Slavery Society of Salem, at Lyceum Hall, Nov. 14, 1847.* . . . Report by Henry M. Parkhurst, Phonographic Reporter. Boston: Massachusetts Anti-Slavery Society.

1847—*Narrative of William W. Brown, a Fugitive Slave.* Boston: The Anti-Slavery Office.

1848—"The American Slave Trade," pp. 231–237. *The Liberty Bell*, By Friends of Freedom. Boston: National Anti-Slavery Bazaar.

1848—*The Anti-Slavery Harp: a Collection of Songs for Anti-Slavery Meetings.* Boston: B. Marsh.

1849—*A Description of William Wells Brown's Original Panoramic Views of the Scenes in the Life of an American Slave, from His Birth in Slavery to His Death, or His Escape to His First Home of Freedom on British Soil.* London: Charles Gilpin.

1852—*Three Years in Europe: or, Places I Have Seen and People I Have Met.* . . . With a Memoir of the Author, by William Farmer. London: C. Gilpin.

1853—*Clotel; or, The President's Daughter. A Narrative of Slave Life in the United States.* London: Partridge and Oakey.

1854—"Visit of a Fugitive Slave to the Grave of Wilberforce," pp. 70–76. *Autographs for Freedom,* Julia Griffiths. Auburn: Alden, Beardsley and Co.

1855—*The American Fugitive in Europe. Sketches of Places and People Abroad*; with a Memoir by the Author. Boston: J. P. Jewett and Company.

1855—*St. Domingo: Its Revolutions and Its Patriots. A Lecture, Delivered before the Metropolitan Athenaeum, London, May 16, and at St. Thomas' Church, Philadelphia, December 20, 1854.* Boston: Bela Marsh.

185?—*Doughface*, possible first Negro drama about which almost nothing is known.

1858—*The Escape; or, A Leap for Freedom. A Drama in Five Acts*. Boston: R. F. Wallcut.

186?—*Miralda, or, The Beautiful Quadroon*, possible serialization of *Clotel* in an unknown New York newspaper.

1863—*The Black Man: His Antecedents, His Genius, and His Achievements*. Boston: R. F. Wallcut.

1864—*Clotelle: A Tale of the Southern States*. Boston: James Redpath and Company.

1867—*Clotelle; or, The Colored Heroine. A Tale of the Southern States*. Boston: Lee and Shepard.

1867—*The Negro in the American Rebellion, His Heroism and His Fidelity*. Boston: Lee and Shepard.

1874—*The Rising Son; or, The Antecedents and Advancement of the Colored Race*. Boston: A. G. Brown and Co.

1880—*My Southern Home: or, The South and Its People*. Boston: A. G. Brown and Co.